Tastes and Traditions

New Haven's Jewish Community Cooks

Jewish Community Center New Haven
350 Amity Road
Woodbridge, CT 06525

Tastes and *Traditions*

Disclaimer: This cookbook is a collection of favorite recipes which are not necessarily original recipes

Donor Credit: The entire publication cost of this cookbook has been generously underwritten by the following families:

Ruthann & David Beckerman
Jean & Steven Bortner
Eileen & Andrew Eder
Susie & Joel Kahan
Robin & Ken Kramer
Barbara & John Lichtman

These families have enabled the entire proceeds from the sale of *'Tastes and Traditions'* to go directly to scholarship, financial assistance and endowment funds for the Jewish Community Center of Greater New Haven.

The Jewish Community Center of Greater New Haven was established more than ninety years ago, with the purpose of implementing programs and services to enhance the quality of life in the Greater New Haven community. This book reflects the "heart and soul" of many of our Jewish New Haven homes. It is a modern updated slant on cooking and nutrition, linking recipes from generation to generation and reflecting our culture and traditions. Good food tends to bring people together. Our hope is that this book provides financial benefits to our community and other communities, and enables many people to enjoy food, fun, and friends.

ISBN 978-0-9791025-0-9
LCCN (Library of Congress Control Number) 2007904333
Copyright © 2008

WIMMER
COOKBOOKS

A CONSOLIDATED GRAPHICS COMPANY

800.548.2537   wimmerco.com

Welcome to *Tastes and Traditions*, a project of the Greater New Haven Jewish Community.

Laurie Colwin, a Jewish novelist, once wrote, "No one who cooks, cooks alone. Even at her most solitary, a cook in the kitchen is surrounded by generations of cooks past, the advice and menus of cooks present, the wisdom of cookbook writers."

Much like the community that inhabits Laurie's kitchen, our Jewish Community Center is supported by generations whose advice, example and wise counsel have built the JCC into a community institution. It is with that sense of community and continuity that this book is presented.

I would be remiss if I did not thank two extraordinary people who created this cookbook from a recipe of hard work, leadership and devotion to the JCC: Robin Kramer and Barbara Lichtman.

Thank you to all the members of the Cookbook Committee and especially to all the cooks who shared their family recipes. I hope the generations of cooks past keep you company in your kitchen as you try the delicious recipes in these pages. Enjoy!

Scott Cohen
EXECUTIVE DIRECTOR
JEWISH COMMUNITY CENTER OF GREATER NEW HAVEN

This book is dedicated to
Our parents who taught us the importance of "giving back",
And our children and spouses
Without whose patience, love, and support
This work would not have been possible.

Robin Kramer & Barbara Lichtman

PREFACE

We present *Tastes and Traditions* to add to your collection of cookbooks. In the Jewish world, food and entertaining are at the heart of all customs and traditions. We welcome you to enjoy the fruits of our labor. Many community friends and volunteers worked tirelessly to create a timeless array of recipes and stories for your pleasure. We wrote, edited, tasted and tested recipes from basic to exotic, and from traditional to contemporary. Many recipes will seem comforting and familiar, and others new and adventurous. We tried to please all palates.

All recipes are labeled *pareve*, meat, or dairy, as this is a kosher cookbook. Today, food substitutions are easier, and recipes are more adaptable. (Examples are soy milk for cow's milk, margarine for butter, and non-dairy cheeses for toppings and garnishes.)

Tastes and Traditions offered us a wonderful opportunity to bring friends of the Jewish Community of Greater New Haven together. Almost 1,000 recipes were submitted and reviewed by our loyal committee chairs. Sydney Perry, our Federation executive director, wrote the *kashrut* and holiday commentary. Our copy editors, Elaine Koufman and Judith Sklarz, spent many hours composing sidebars and special comments. Susie Kahan, Barbara Orell, John Lichtman and Ken Kramer reviewed and revised with grace. We thank you all for your dedication, energy and ideas.

We would like to thank our artists, Eileen Eder for her original, magnificent cover; Jean Bortner, for her talented and artful photography; Harvey Greenberg, Emily Kramer, Susan Skope, Colby Sirowich, and Benjy Kahan for their 'extra help'; and the Jewish Community Center staff, in particular, Scott Cohen, Ellen Eisenberg, Ginger McHugh, and Shelley Gans for their dedication and support.

We hope you use *Tastes and Traditions* as an inspiration to spend time in the kitchen, and enjoy exciting meals with family and friends.

Regards to you all,
Barbara and Robin

LETTER FROM THE EDITORIAL EDITORS

One of the most challenging parts of this project was deciding on a title. Independently of one another, and after listening to many people express their suggestions, we decided on *"Tastes and Traditions"*. We understood the tradition of *kashrut*, which sets Jewish cuisine apart from others, and began to understand the other major influences. Claudia Roden said it best in *The Book of Jewish Food*, "Every cuisine tells a story. Jewish food tells the story of an uprooted people, migrating people and their vanished worlds. It lives in people's minds and has been kept alive because of what it evokes and represents ... "

In America, we represent such a diverse culture. Having come from different places at different times, we tend to adapt the local cuisine to be our own, within the boundaries set by *kashrut*. The collection of memories and recipes by community members reflects the experience of Ashkenazi Jews from Central and Eastern Europe (it is cold and dark there), and the Sephardic Jews, who came from areas around the Mediterranean region of Europe and Africa (it is warm and sunny there). We think they combine our contemporary "tastes" in food with Jewish cooking "tradition". Blessed is the memory of those we have loved who came to this country so we would never be hungry. Eat well and enjoy!

B'Shalom,
Elaine G. Koufman and Judith Sklarz

Cookbook Committee

Co-Chairpersons ~ Robin Kramer Barbara Lichtman

Holiday & Kashruth Editor ~ Sydney Perry

Editorial Editors ~ Judith Sklarz Elaine Koufman

Recipe Editors ~ Barbara Green Orell Susie Kahan

Section Chairpersons

Beverages & Appetizers ~ Melissa Lawson Barbara Berg

Brunch & Breads ~ MaryBeth Zuckerberg Nancy Silverstein

Soups & Salads ~ Dale Felice Alison Isenstein Shelly Pinkert

Main Courses ~ Laurie Feldman Susan Skope
Ana White Robin Zygelman

Vegetables & Potatoes / Kugels, Pasta, Rice & Grains ~
Irene Greenberg Sylvia Horowitz Carole Slusky

Passover & Holidays ~ Stacey Perkins
Jill Schaeffer Karen Zeid

Desserts ~ Debra Epstein Elizabeth Reznik

Art & Design ~ Eileen Eder Jean Bortner

Kickoff Event(s) ~ Iny Karp Ruthann Beckerman

RECIPE CONTRIBUTORS & TESTERS

Neil Abel
Susan Abramson
Karen Adams
Esther Alexander
Sara Allinson
Randi Alpert
Linda Alpuche
Cheryl Alter
Wendy Andresen
Anat Arbib
Sara Ann Auerbach
Danieli Baliani
Stacey Battat
Ruthann Beckerman
Jo Ben-Atar
Andrea Benjamin
Barbara Berg
Kari Berg
Sherrie Bitterman
Sarah Blum
Susie Blumenfeld
Rhoda Blumenthal
Kimberly Bogert
Bob Brass
Brenda Brenner
Phyllis Brodoff
Rosalind Brodoff
Tina Brogidir
Mindy Brownstein
Barry Buxbaum
Bev Cedarbaum
Julie Chevan
Roslyn Chosak
Mazi Cipriani
Marilyn Cohen
Marsha Cohen
Miriam Cohen
Nancy Cohen

Shirley Cowan
Evelyn Dermer
Elaine Ditman
Betty Ann Donegan
Marjorie Drucker
Eileen Eder
Carol Evans
Joyce Feen
Laurie Feldman
Dale Felice
Shirley Fiedler
Norma Firtel
Betsy Fiske
Christine Fontana
Maureen Forte
Lori Forto
Claire Frankel
Deborah Fried
Ruth Frohman
Ina Furst Fischer
Shelley Gans
Mimi Glenn
Suzanne Gold
Jayne Goldstein
Michael Gordon
Linda Gottlieb
Danielle Granoff
Irene Greenberg
Marjorie Greenblatt
Lisa Greenwald
Velma Grodd
Fran Grodzinsky
Enid Groves
Gaby Guevara
Nancy Halleck
Yuval Hamenachen
Janet Hershman
Judith Hess

Bonnie Hoffman-Murdock
Donald Holstron
Sharon Horowitz
Sylvia Horowitz
Vicki Horowitz
Alison Isenstein
Devorah Kabakoff
Susie Kahan
Patricia Kalba
Shelley Kaminsky
Deborah Kamlot
Diane E. Kaplan
Iny Karp
Katz's Deli
Sue Kirschner
Elaine Klein
Jackie Knoll
Sernghee Ko
Robin Komisar
Elaine Koufman
Helga Kramer
Robin Kramer
Selma Krinick
Avery S. Kruger
Ruth Lambert
Sue Langerman
Sylvia Lavietes
Melissa Lawson
Marcia Ledewitz
Gerilyn Lehman
Helaine Lender
Joyce Lender
Audrey Levine
Jodi Levine
Linda Levine
Susan Levinson
Barbara Liberman
Dolores Libman

RECIPE CONTRIBUTORS & TESTERS

Barbara Lichtman
Miriam Lillian
Rhoda Linett
Roberta Litvinoff
Cathy Lombardo
Jess London
Deena Mack
Jess Mackenzie
Catherine Mansourian
Bettie Marks
Lisa Martin
Kelly McGuinness
Ginger McHugh
Phyllis Medvedow
Rhoda Meyers
Susan Millen
Dorothy Miller
Jan Miller
Susan Miller
Sandy Milles
Beverly Mohrer
Stanley Moniz
Irma Nesson
Ann Nishball
Annette Norton
Beryl Novitch
Jane Okunieu
Nancy Olins
Deneen Pearl
Stacey Perkins
Sydney Perry
Linda Philips
Noreen Pokras
Jodi Pollack

Marcia Reiter
Francine Richter
Lucille B. Ritvo
Ted Rogol
Pat Rogovin
Judy Rolnick
Deborah Rosen
Sue Rosen
Lynda Rosenfeld
Rose Rudich
Susan Sachar
Paula Samuel
Aniko Sarkany
Sue Schatz
Enid Scheps
Jean Schpero
Allan B. Schwartz
Arden S. Schwartz
Maxine Schwartz
Simmie Scott
Lauren Seplowitz
Mimi Setlow
Marsha Shapiro
Carol Shelnitz
Judith Siegel
Lilian Silverman
Evelyn Silvers
Nancy Silverstein
Florence Sinow
Judith Sklarz
Susan Skope
Carole Slusky
Albert Small
Darlene Smith

Elaine Sneiderman
Marilyn Sommers
Susan L. Spivak
Judy Sprotzer
Phyllis Strumpf
Ellen Swirsky
Edie Tanenbaum
Irene Teller
Sharon Teller
Stella Teller
Jane Tendler
Robyn Teplitzky
Stacey Trachten
Jeannie Ufland
Hyla Vine
Macky Wallace
Eunice Watstein
Beverly Weinberg
Marjorie Weiner
Ellen Weinstein
Martha Weisbart
Ana White
Marcia Witten
Jill Wurcel
Paul Yashanko
Naomi Young
Karen Zeid
Doris Zelinsky
Marcy Zoock
Marybeth Zuckerberg
Linda Zwerdling
Robin Zygelman

To the best of our knowledge, we have listed everyone who contributed to this cookbook. We apologize for any inadvertent omissions.

TABLE OF CONTENTS

KASHRUT

$\mathcal{K}$ eeping kosher is one of the fundamental cornerstones of Jewish life. The Torah says that Jews are not to eat camel, coney, rabbit, horse and pig, the eagle, the vulture, and "all the creatures in the seas … that do not have fins and scales." (Lev.11) The Torah says: "Do not cook a kid in its mother's milk" (Deut. 14:21)

Simple?? Clear?? Well, not entirely.

Although the Bible tells us which meats, fowl, and fish are not kosher, and not to mix meat and milk, the Rabbinic tradition over millennia has developed the rules of *kashrut* which we observe today.

Kosher means fit or proper and is generally used to describe foods that are prepared in accordance with the Jewish dietary laws. The rules and regulations, the two sets of dishes and utensils, the meticulous attention both to the ingredients in the products we use and to their certification, checking for blood spots in eggs, washing lettuces carefully and inspecting them to ensure that we do not ingest dirt and chemicals, are all part of the essential principle of sanctifying the ordinary.*

Although to be sure, there are hygienic and health benefits to *kashrut* — no trichinosis, or contamination from spoiled shellfish — the food that we eat, every day, three times a day, on *Shabbat* and the holidays, is a constant reminder of how we elevate the physical necessities of life into sacred awareness, in accordance with Jewish practice and Divine ordinance.

Taste and Tradition. Jews have always placed an emphasis on the pleasures of abundant food and good company. Happily, today with more and more kosher products on the market (buffalo, venison, duck breast, Thai, Japanese and Indian culinary delicacies, non-dairy substitutes which are palatable, *pareve* chocolate chips, tofutti ice cream, *pareve* sour cream, soy milk, margarine, better kosher cheeses, and award-winning kosher wines), the kosher kitchen can move beyond our traditional recipes to the most contemporary of meals. We no longer have to sacrifice flavor for practice, or forgo the latest food trends. The kosher table is every bit as varied, attractive, and appetizing as anything that appears in <u>Gourmet</u>, <u>Bon Appetit</u> or <u>Food and Wine</u>; and we can prepare it in consonance with age-old practices and adherence to our Jewish heritage.

PAREVE FOOD PREPARATION

Many of the recipes in this cookbook were originally tested as dairy dishes. However, in Kosher meal planning, it is often necessary to substitute *pareve* ingredients for either dairy (milk), or meat ingredients.

You can usually substitute *pareve* margarine or solid white shortening for butter in a recipe. Or, if you prefer, you can substitute oil for the butter or a combination of oil plus margarine or shortening.

Common ingredients used for dairy substitutions are *pareve* chocolate chips and non-dairy creamer instead of milk or cream.

We can have "taste" and "tradition", thanks to the outstanding addition of this cookbook to our bookshelves and to the many who worked so hard to make it possible.

Now, explore, experiment, and enjoy!

* Please consult with your own Rabbi if you have any questions about kashrut or kosher products. And remember that some people do not mix fish and meat, so check if the Worcestershire sauce you use contains anchovies, and double-check that the soy products you may use with fleischigs do not say "made with dairy equipment".

SHABBAT

*T*here is no holiday holier than *Shabbat*, no holiday which more clearly defines what it means to be Jewish, and no better time to harmonize tradition and taste. This wonderful holiday comes fifty-two times a year!

The seventh day of the week, when we cease our work and spend 25 hours with family in prayer, play, and relaxation, is the occasion for not one, not two, but for three special meals. The Friday night table, dressed with our best linens and china, flowers, *Shabbat* candles, two *challahs*, and a wine goblet, becomes a substitute for the Temple; the table is an altar at which we sing songs, bless our children, contemplate what was best in the week past, and say *kiddush*. So, too, the lunch meal with its different aromas beckons when we return from the synagogue. And what of the third meal? Just before daylight wanes, and we separate from the sacred to the more profane with the *Havdalah* ceremony, many participate in a third meal, usually lighter fare, but always with bread so one can say *ha-motzi* and the blessings after eating, which we call *Birkat Hamazon*.

Tradition, to be sure: prepare *gefilte fish* with pungent horseradish, golden chicken soup with *matzoh* balls, roast chicken, kugel, and cholent which has been cooking in the oven at a low heat overnight. Try herring at the *kiddush* at *shul*; enjoy sponge cake and *kichel* at *oneg Shabbat*. But *Shabbat* also offers an opportunity to try new recipes and to treat your family to more adventurous culinary options. Savor a salmon or tuna tartar; experiment with a roasted vegetable soup; taste a Moroccan couscous, a Spanish vegetable paella, a French beef bourguignon or a Hungarian chicken paprikash. Make your own sorbet with puréed fruit, or a luscious deep chocolate torte.

Rosh Hashanah – The New Year

$\mathcal{T}$he Jewish year revolves around holidays which bind us to our traditions, our history, our people and our families. The symbolism and inherent qualities of food are part of how we transmit the lofty ideal of Judaism into table-centered rituals of enhanced meaning. This includes time at Sukkot when we eat meals in specially constructed booths, at Chanukah with foods cooked in oil, and at Purim when we feast in triumphant jubilation at our salvation, eating *hamantashen* and sharing goodies with our friends. We see this at Passover with all the symbolic foods on our seder plates, at Shavuot when milk products are traditionally eaten, and on *Shabbat* with its two loaves of *challah*.

The celebration of Rosh Hashanah, when we search our souls and consider our deeds of the past year and repent, is also marked at our tables with traditions that symbolize our hopes for a sweet, prosperous, peaceful New Year.

We use a round *challah*, expressing our desire for a perfect New Year. Our tables are laden with delicacies which represent optimism for a sweet future — honey, dates, apples, and raisins. Many Jews will avoid certain foods on their festive table — no lemon, no horseradish or pickles. Some refrain from eating nuts because the numerical value of the Hebrew word *egoz* is equivalent to "sin". Others place dishes with carrots on the table because the equivalent of *meren* — the Yiddish word for carrot and also meaning "to increase" — illustrates a yearning for a prosperous year. The custom of stuffed foods, such as *kreplach* or stuffed veggies, also represents plenty of abundance.

When we say the *shehechiyanu* prayer, thanking G-d for allowing us to reach this season, we often say a blessing over an apple or a new fruit of the harvest season. Dipping with honey, we intone "May it be Thy will to renew unto us a good and sweet year." On the second night, another new fruit is used. Some families use a ruby colored pomegranate with the blessing, "In the coming year may we be rich and replete with acts inspired by religion and piety as this pomegranate is rich and replete with seeds". Taking care not to stain the tablecloth with the juice which spurts from the plentiful seeds, they begin their meal, mindful of Judaism's 613 commandments.

Whether you place a fish head on your menu, chicken soup with *kreplach*, chicken in pomegranate sauce, honeyed carrots or carrot *kugel*, baklava or apple strudel, may you and yours enjoy only happiness in the years to come.

YOM KIPPUR

*T*he days from Rosh Hashanah to Yom Kippur are called the Ten Days of Penance, when through our good deeds, fervent prayer, and charity, we do *teshuva*, or repentance. When Yom Kippur arrives, we enter into a 25 hour period of fasting — no food or drink. The meal before the fast, *seudah mafseket,* is usually one in which we abstain from heavily seasoned or salted foods, which tend to increase our thirst. The relatively bland meal before sunset — often chicken, rice, carrots, fresh fruit and honey cake, is eaten at home on white table cloths. White is symbolic, of course, of purity ("May your sins be as white as snow") and our synagogues, too, are draped in white garments. The mantles which adorn the Torahs are white, the Rabbi and Cantor wear white robes, and many people will also dress in white in keeping with the solemnity of the day.

Yet at the close of the Yom Kippur service, at the *neila* prayer, we are assured of forgiveness and we return to our homes to rejoice and partake of the break-fast meal. This meal recalls the feast of the High Priest in the Temple, celebrated after Yom Kippur, in gratitude for having been permitted to emerge from the Holy of Holies. Our break-fasts are joyous occasions to assemble with close friends and family. Some people break their fast with something sweet; others eat a hard-boiled egg, the symbol of hope and life.

Although many Jews indulge in a glorified brunch - bagels, lox, cream cheese spreads, sweet kugels and coffee cakes – the menu of the break-fast is really up to the imagination of the host and hostess. Everything tastes good after 25 hours of fasting, so remember that simplicity may be the best course to take here.

SUKKOT

*A*s soon as the High Holidays approach, we begin planning our menus for Sukkot. We love the crisp fall air and the glorious riot of color on the leaves. But most of all, we love the building and decorating of the *sukkah* and the delight of offering hospitality and savory delights to our guests for eight days.

We decorate our *sukkah* with the seven fruits of the land of Israel; dates, figs, pomegranates, barley, wheat, olives and grapes. And many of the dishes we prepare use these ingredients to complete the theme — from pomegranate martinis to begin the meal, to baked apples stuffed with dates and apricots, or sticky, gooey baklava with honey for dessert.

Sukkot is called the "festival of our happiness" — and why not? — surrounded by family and friends in our fragile, outdoor shelters, and the beauties of the fall harvest, good conversation, food and wine, we have much to celebrate. Sukkot is indeed a time to rejoice.

CHANUKAH

*C*hanukah, which means rededication, commemorates the restoration and consecration of the ancient Temple in Jerusalem in 165 BCE, following the Maccabean rebellion against the Greek Syrian tyrant Antiochus. The struggle of the tiny guerilla band of men, led by Judah, against the mighty army of the oppressor who sought to forbid the practice of Judaism, is the quintessential story of the triumph of religious freedom and the Jewish commitment to maintain its distinctive identity and customs in the face of a dominant culture.

But wait. What about the miracle of the oil? Once the desecrated Temple was cleansed and purified, the priests searched for pure oil to light the Temple's six-branched menorah. They found only one small cruse of oil — which was enough oil to last only for one day. The Book of Maccabees recounts that this oil lasted for eight days, miraculously giving enough time to prepare new oil.

The eight-branched Chanukah *menorah*, with a *shammas*, or helper candle, to illuminate the candles from right to left, is placed in our window for eight nights to announce the miracle of our resistance and our survival. With the *menorah* aglow, each evening is filled with light and song, with dreidel games and small gifts for the children.

Is it any wonder that this is every child's favorite Jewish holiday?

And ours too, because it is the one time we can freely indulge our cravings for fried foods. It's a *mitzvah*!!!! It's tradition. So fry your potato *latkes*, or sweet potato *latkes*, or zucchini or cauliflower fritters. Serve *milchig latkes* with sour cream one night, and brisket with *latkes* and applesauce another. Enjoy fried chicken, vegetable samosas, tempura, fried mozzarella, and *sufganiyot*, the delicious Israeli donuts.

No wonder that Chanukah is also many an adult's favorite holiday as well!

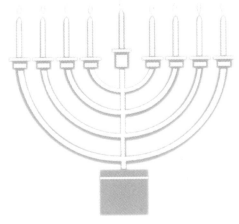

PURIM

*T*he Purim celebration is one of joy and merriment, of feasting and drinking, of masks and costumes. Gifts to the poor, and colorful baskets of fruits, pastries, candies, and nuts, are delivered to friends, relatives, neighbors, and newcomers to the community; no one is left out of the festivities.

Purim places more emphasis on physical delights and culinary indulgence than any other Jewish holiday. When the Hebrew month of Adar approaches, says our tradition, joy increases, troubles are forgotten and celebration begins. We masquerade, use our *groggers* to drown out the name of our nemesis, Haman, invite guests to a feast, and put on a Purim *shpiel*, or play. Purim is the one time that Jews are enjoined to drink to excess as we mark the topsy-turvy tale of the beautiful Queen Esther and her uncle Mordechai who provided leadership and cunning in foiling the nefarious plot of wicked Haman (the minister to the Persian king Ahasuerus), who wished to exterminate the Jews.

Here is the perfect opportunity to make all those delicious cookies and sweetmeats, to bake *hamantashen* filled with traditional poppy and prune or the more contemporary chocolate kisses or peanut butter. And remember, if it's Purim, Passover is only one month away. So, use up all your flour in your *shalach mones* goody baskets.

PASSOVER

*P*assover, the festival of our freedom, is a week-long holiday which celebrates the Exodus of the ancient Israelites from their slavery in Egypt and the signs and wonders wrought for the Jewish people as Moses led them towards the Promised Land.

Around our family tables, we recount the Pesach story at a feast called the *seder*, held on each of the first two nights of the holiday. The reading of the *Haggadah* is accompanied by rituals, symbols, traditions and songs which have endured in Jewish homes for many generations.

Tradition, tradition, tradition. But also a wonderful opportunity for innovation and creativity. We taste the bitterness of horseradish and remember slavery; we dip parsley in salt water and recall the tears we shed; we eat the *charoset* and recall the bricks and mortar we were forced to make for building Pharaoh's storehouses. Passover engages all of our senses and offers the quintessential pedagogic lesson. We point to the *seder* plate and see the *matzoh*, the roasted egg, and the shank bone; we hear the songs and melodies from our childhood; we taste the Hillel sandwich; we lean to the left, resting like free people and relishing our liberty.

"How is this night different from all other nights?", chants the youngest child. In the Jewish household, Passover is truly different from all other holidays: it requires much more preparation! In remembrance of the Israelites' hasty flight from Egypt, when there was no time to let bread rise before baking, our homes are thoroughly cleaned of every crumb of leavened bread, and of all food which is not deemed *pesadikhe* (fit for Passover). In many homes, special dishes and utensils are used only for Pesach to avoid contact with any *chametz* or yeast products. The entire home takes on a special atmosphere in recognition of the vicarious experience of reliving the Exodus, as if we ourselves were taking part in the actual journey.

Passover can test our stamina with the cleaning, shopping and preparation; it can challenge our ingenuity in planning meals. Ashkenazi Jews do not use pasta, rice, or legumes, but springtime and the advent of fresh produce can perk up the traditional foods we associate with this holiday. We may serve a golden chicken soup with *matzoh* balls just like *Bubbe* used to make, but there's also potato leek soup for the vegetarians; the *gefilte fish* our grandmothers made from carp and whitefish has been replaced by the jars of jellied fish that some of our mothers purchased, but we can also consider roasted Chilean sea bass or poached salmon as a variation on the theme. Make a turkey or a brisket, but don't hesitate to experiment with more contemporary side dishes. Who doesn't make a sponge cake with 12 egg yolks? But chocolate nut tortes and lemon mousse also make a delicious ending to the meal. Don't forget that the sweet Passover wine which was once enjoyed by our grandparents has been replaced by excellent new kosher wines. We still drink four cups, but what a difference! And when all is done, the *afikomen* is claimed by the children, we sing "Next Year in Jerusalem", and we say *dayenu* until next year.

SHAVUOT

*F*orty-nine days after Passover, at the end of a seven week period, we mark Shavuot. Jews in ancient Israel used to make a pilgrimage to the Temple with the offerings of their first harvest. To this day, we still decorate our homes and synagogues with baskets of fruits and garlands of spring flowers, many petaled tulips, and abundant peonies and fragrant roses from our gardens.

But Shavuot is so much more than a harvest holiday; this is the day which marks the giving of the Torah to Moses and the Jewish people at Mt. Sinai, after the Exodus. This was a new beginning for the Jews who moved from slavery to worshipping G-d and his commandments.

No Jewish festival is complete without food! Here is the holiday every vegetarian cherishes, because it is traditional to eat dairy foods for Shavuot. The Torah is likened to milk and honey in the Song of Songs and the Jews were on their journey to the Promised Land, a land of milk and honey.

So whether we serve creamy polenta with wild mushroom ragoût, baked brie and fruit, rich risotto, cheesecake in all its variations, your *Bubbe's* recipe for blintzes, Greek salad with salty feta cheese, fettuccine Alfredo or crème brûlée, for this two-day holiday which focuses on the Torah, forget concerns about cholesterol, forget your diet and … just enjoy.

SUGGESTED MENUS

SHABBAT

Challah

Hearty Vegetable Barley Soup

Refreshing Romaine Salad

My Favorite Shabbat Chicken

Zesty Green Beans

Kasha and Orzo Pilaf

Almond Cake

Passion Fruit Sorbet

Rosh Hashanah

DAY 1

Challah

Gefilte Fish With Horseradish

Safta's Chicken Soup With Mom's Floating Matzoh Balls

David's Romanian Eggplant Salad With Pita Chips

The Battle of the Brisket's Winning Recipe

Roasted Root Vegetables

Pecan Crusted Noodle Kugel

Jenny Fletcher's Apple Cake

Chocolate Walnut Brittle

DAY 2

Challah

Mamma Dora's Stuffed Cabbage

Asparagus Salad

Roast Turkey With Walnut Stuffing

Candied Sweet Potatoes

Cranberry Sauce With Apricots and Raisins

Green Beans With Black Sesame Seeds

Honey Cake

Poached Pears

Yom Kippur

PRE – FAST MEAL

Challah

Peasant Soup

Hearts of Palm and Spinach Salad

Chicken With Wine Sauce

Carrot Soufflé

Greek Rice With Chickpeas

Pumpkin Cake

BREAK – THE – FAST FOR A CROWD

Bagels and Lox

Platter of Sliced Tomatoes, Onions, and Cucumbers

Assortment of Cream Cheeses

Arlyn's Tuna Salad

Stuffed Mushrooms

Baked Blintz Soufflé

Lil's Noodle Kugel

Classic Caesar Salad

Orzo, Feta, and Cherry Tomato Salad

Rugelach

Holstein's Cheesecake

Best Brownies

SUKKOT

Gefilte Fish

Chicken Soup

Stuffed Zucchini

Festive Chicken

Butternut Squash and Apples

Strawberry Mango Mesclun Salad

Chocolate Chocolate Chip Cake

CHANUKAH

White & Sweet Potato Latkes With Applesauce

Sweet and Sour Stuffed Cabbage (Main Course)

Moroccan Chick Pea Carrot and Black Olive Salad

Tossed Green Salad With Salad Dressing #1

Sufganiyot

PURIM

Herring Salad With Pita Chips

Stuffed Eggs With Goat Cheese and Dill

Potato Salad

Salmon Florentine En Croûte With Caper Dill Sauce

Broccoli Salad

Hamantashen – Assorted Flavors

PASSOVER

SEDER 1

Nanny Gabby's Date Charoset

Lower East Side Chopped Liver

Safta's Chicken Soup With Matzoh Balls

Matzoh Farfel Kugel

Carrot Pudding

Grandma Rosie's Bilkes

Spiced Cranberry Sauce

Herb Baked Chicken

Roasted Red Snapper With Spinach and Tomatoes

Tossed Green Salad

Chocolate Mousse Torte

Forgotten Cookies

Passover Nut Cake

SEDER 2

Fancy Charoset

Gefilte Fish Mold

Safta's Chicken Soup With Foolproof Matzoh Balls

Farfel Bombs

Savory Passover Kugel

Roasted Asparagus

Rita's Hot Fruit Compote

Roasted Chicken With Garlic and Lemon

Veal in Wine Sauce

Tossed Green Salad

Mandel Bread

Sugar Pecans

Pineapple Orange Cake With Pineapple Sauce

SHAVUOT

Pasta With Roasted Red Pepper and Ricotta Sauce

Blintzes With Sour Cream

Greek Salad

Apple, Walnut, and Beet Salad

Crusty Loaf of Bread

Crème Brûlée

White Chocolate Croissant Bread Pudding (With Fresh Pears)

Beverages &
Appetizers

- *Read recipes thoroughly before you begin.*

- *Measure and prepare all ingredients before you begin.*

- *Eggs are always large if unspecified.*

- *Flour is all-purpose and unsifted unless specified.*

- *Fresh is best for fruits and vegetables whenever possible. Choose your menu based on what is in season.*

- *Adjust seasonings to personal taste.*

- *Be aware that oven temperatures may vary and adjust your cooking time accordingly.*

BEVERAGES & APPETIZERS

An hors d'oeuvre, a little nibble, finger food — or as our grandmothers might have said, *forshpayz* — food or drink before a meal to enhance and stimulate the appetite. Exciting the palate with that dip, herring, *knish* or meatball on a toothpick, or maybe an old favorite handed down from a previous generation, found in a magazine, traded with friends or made up with ingredients on hand. Whatever their origin, they set the mood for what is to follow.

For entertaining, have a variety of crackers and crusty breads on hand, as well as veggies for crudités and dips. Use vegetables and breads to dip or hollow out and use for bowls. You can even make a meal out of a variety of appetizers. Have fun and let your creative juices flow.

Add some pizzazz with a bowl of punch, an iced fruit sorbet ring containing whole fruit, or, on a cold night, a spicy hot chocolate treat.

In the 50's and 60's, cocktail parties were the rage. Sometimes, children were asked to be the servers, summarily dismissed after the cocktail hour with a plate of leftovers. Sitting at the top of the stairs, we spied on our parents who smoked, drank and laughed lustily — the men with the men who talked shop or sports, and the women — bragging about their children or the gossip picked up at the beauty parlor. If we were lucky, we got paper umbrellas and fancy plastic toothpicks as souvenirs.

Hot Chocolate from Mijas, Spain
DAIRY

2 teaspoons cornstarch
1½ cups whole milk, divided
½ cup water
10 ounces bittersweet chocolate, finely chopped
Pinch of salt

½ cup heavy cream
1 tablespoon unsweetened cocoa, divided
Whipped cream and shaved chocolate for topping

- Whisk cornstarch with 2 tablespoons milk in a small bowl; set aside.
- Bring water to a boil in a 2-quart saucepan. Decrease heat to medium-low and whisk in chocolate and salt until smooth.
- Add cream and remaining milk. Increase to medium heat and whisk until smooth and warm.
- Add half of cocoa and half of cornstarch mixture and whisk until thick. Add remaining cocoa and remaining cornstarch and whisk until smooth. Serve in small cups. Top with whipped cream and shaved chocolate.

Chocolate Hazelnut Hot Chocolate with a Kick
DAIRY

1½ tablespoons chili powder
6 cups whole or low-fat milk

1 cup chocolate hazelnut spread

- Combine chili powder and milk in a saucepan. Bring to a boil over medium heat. Whisk in chocolate spread until smooth.
- The longer this rests, the more intense the spice will be. Serve hot.
- 6 servings

Chocolate Caramel Cappuccino

DAIRY

1   cup hot water
¾   cup whole or low-fat milk
2   tablespoons chocolate syrup

3   tablespoons caramel ice cream topping
1   tablespoon instant coffee or instant espresso

- Combine all ingredients in a saucepan. Heat until hot and bubbly. Serve immediately.
- 2-3 servings

Banana Mango Smoothie

DAIRY

2   large ripe bananas, peeled
1   mango, peeled and cubed
3   cups regular or low-fat vanilla yogurt

½   cup pineapple or orange juice

- Freeze bananas and mango on a baking sheet for at least 1 hour or until firm.
- Purée frozen fruit with yogurt and juice in a blender until smooth.

For a slushy mixture, add ice and purée until ice is crushed. Other fruits such as raspberries, strawberries, peaches, etc. can be used.

OLD FASHIONED EGG CREAM
DAIRY

½   cup whole milk
1   cup seltzer

2   tablespoons chocolate syrup

- Stir milk and seltzer in a tall glass until foamy. Add chocolate syrup and quickly stir from the bottom only, clinking the spoon against the bottom of the glass. If this is done correctly, the bottom will be brown and the top will be white.
- 1 serving

APPLE RASPBERRY CIDER
PAREVE

12   cups apple cider
2   cups frozen raspberry juice concentrate, thawed

⅓   cup sugar
    Dash of cinnamon

- Combine all ingredients in a large saucepan. Simmer 15 minutes over medium heat, stirring occasionally. Serve hot.

PUNCH
PAREVE

1   (46-ounce) can pineapple juice
    Orange slices

1   (2-liter) bottle ginger ale
½   gallon cranberry juice

- Prepare an ice ring by pouring pineapple juice into a 4½-cup ring mold. Add orange slices. Freeze.
- When ready to serve, dip mold in warm water halfway up the side to loosen ice ring. Unmold ring into a large punch bowl.
- Pour ginger ale and cranberry juice over ice ring. The punch will be tasty but slightly tart.

Inexpensive sparkling champagne can be added. Garnish each glass with a slice of lime.

CHAMPAGNE PUNCH
PAREVE

1	(1-pound) package superfine sugar	1	quart champagne, chilled
1	cup strained fresh lemon juice	1	quart dry white wine, chilled
1	cup strained fresh orange juice	1½	quarts club soda, chilled
½	cup orange-flavored liqueur		Block of ice
2	(20-ounce) cans pineapple chunks, 1 can drained, other can with juice	1	quart strawberries, sliced for garnish

- The day before serving, combine sugar, lemon juice, orange juice, liqueur and pineapple in a large bowl. Refrigerate overnight.
- Just before serving, transfer mixture to a 2- to 3-gallon punch bowl. Add champagne, wine and club soda. Float ice block in punch bowl and add sliced strawberries.

POMEGRANATE MARTINI FOR FOUR
PAREVE

3	cups pomegranate juice	Splash of sparkling water (optional)
4	ounces lemon-flavored vodka	Lemon slices for garnish
2	ounces Cointreau or other flavored liqueur	Pomegranate seeds for garnish (optional)
	Ice	

- Shake pomegranate juice, vodka and liqueur with ice. Pour into serving glasses. Add sparkling water and lemon slices. Add pomegranate seeds for pizzazz.

BLOODY MARYS
PAREVE

1   (32-ounce) bottle vegetable or spicy vegetable juice, chilled

1¼   cups plain or lemon-flavored vodka

2   tablespoons lemon juice

2   tablespoons lime juice

1   tablespoon orange juice

1   tablespoon Worcestershire sauce

½   teaspoon salt

6   large stalks celery for garnish

- Combine all ingredients except celery in a large jar and shake.
- Serve over ice in large glasses and garnish with celery stalks.
- 4 large servings

FROZEN MARGARITAS
PAREVE

1   medium mango, peeled and cubed

1   cup tequila

½   cup cognac, passion fruit-flavored if available

½   cup fresh lime juice

3   tablespoons apricot jam, or to taste

- Combine all ingredients in a blender with ice and mix until smooth.
- 4-6 drinks

Keep washed celery stalks and carrot sticks in a tall glass of water in the refrigerator for a quick, healthy snack.

ADULT FROZEN AND FRUITY SLUSH
PAREVE

1½	cups vodka	Handful of pomegranate
2	cups orange juice	seeds (optional)
1	cup pomegranate juice	Orange or lime slices for garnish

- Combine vodka, both juices and pomegranate seeds in a 9x13-inch glass pan. Freeze 6 to 8 hours or overnight until slushy.
- Serve in wine or champagne glasses. Garnish with orange or lime slices.

Cranberry juice may be substituted for the pomegranate juice.
For the children, skip the vodka.

Pick a designated driver, then bring these in a cooler to the beach club for your cabana buddies.

RUM COOLERS
PAREVE

28	fresh mint leaves, divided	3	cups grapefruit juice
½	cup confectioners' sugar		Chilled club soda
¼	cup fresh lemon juice	8	grapefruit slices for garnish
¼	cup fresh lime juice		
2	cups rum		

- Crush 20 mint leaves with sugar, lemon juice and lime juice until sugar is dissolved. Add rum and grapefruit juice. Strain mixture into an airtight pitcher or container. Chill for up to 4 hours.
- When ready to serve, fill 8 glasses three-fourths full. Add ice and club soda to fill glasses. Garnish with remaining mint leaves and grapefruit slices.
- 8 servings

Pineapple juice may be used instead of grapefruit juice.

Cincinnati "Quick Pickles"

PAREVE

2	onions, sliced		1	tablespoon salt
¼	cup sugar		½	teaspoon cream of tartar
¾	cup vinegar		6	cucumbers, washed,
1	teaspoon mustard seed			peeled and sliced
1	teaspoon celery seed			

- Combine onion, sugar, vinegar, mustard seed, celery seed, salt and cream of tartar in a saucepan and bring to a boil.
- Pour mixture over cucumber slices and allow to cool.
- 6 servings

This recipe came from a friend in Cincinnati,
where sweet and sour cooking is famous — and mostly German.

Herring Salad

DAIRY

1	quart herring, drained of juice and onions		2	red onions, thinly sliced
2	red apples, unpeeled and thinly sliced		2	stalks celery, chopped
			1	cup walnuts or pecans
1	(16-ounce) can pineapple chunks, drained		1½	pints sour cream

- Combine all ingredients. Allow flavors to blend at least 6 hours or overnight.
- 8-10 servings

For a fun and decorative presentation, hollow out breads and vegetables of all shapes and sizes and use as a bowl to fill with your favorite dips, crudités or side dish.

AUNT RITA'S EGGPLANT CAVIAR
PAREVE

1	medium eggplant, peeled and diced	1/2	teaspoon dried oregano
1	large onion, chopped	1/2	teaspoon dried basil
1/2	green bell pepper, chopped	1	teaspoon sugar
2	cloves garlic, crushed	1	(6-ounce) can tomato paste
1/3	cup olive oil	1/4	cup water
1	teaspoon salt	1/4	cup vinegar
1/2	teaspoon black pepper	1/2	cup stuffed green olives
		1	(3-ounce) can mushrooms, drained and chopped

- Combine eggplant, onion, bell pepper, garlic and olive oil in a large skillet. Cover and simmer 10 minutes.
- Add salt, pepper, oregano, basil, sugar, tomato paste, water, vinegar, olives and mushrooms to skillet. Cover and simmer 20 minutes longer or until eggplant is cooked but not mushy. Chill. Serve cold with pita for a great hors d'oeuvre.
- 10 servings

MOCK CRABMEAT TOSTADAS
PAREVE

2	packages mock crabmeat sticks		Juice of 2 limes
4	carrots, peeled into thin strips	1	jalapeño pepper, seeds discarded, finely chopped
3	green bell peppers, very thinly sliced		Olive oil to taste, or olive oil mixed with canola oil
1	bunch scallions, finely chopped		Salt and pepper to taste
		1	sleeve tostadas, chipotle- or jalapeño-flavored

- Divide crabmeat sticks by hand into thin strips. Mix crabmeat with carrot strips, pepper, scallions, lime juice, jalapeño, olive oil and salt and pepper in a large bowl.
- To serve, pile some of mixture on a large tostada, or use as a dip.
- 15 servings

Spicy Salmon Tartar
PAREVE

1	pound salmon, cut into ¼-inch dice	¼	cup salted capers, rinsed
2	tablespoons Dijon mustard	⅓	cup chopped scallions
2	tablespoons puréed canned chipotle pepper	2	tablespoons olive oil
		3	tablespoons chopped fresh cilantro

- Combine all ingredients in a bowl. Serve on crackers or bread.
- 10 servings

Moroccan Carrots
PAREVE

2	pounds carrots, cut diagonally into ¼-inch thick slices	¾	teaspoon sweet smoked paprika
¼	cup olive oil	3	tablespoons red wine vinegar
2	cloves garlic		Salt and pepper to taste
¼	teaspoon cayenne pepper		Fresh parsley or cilantro for garnish
¾	teaspoon ground cumin		

- Blanch carrots for 1 minute in boiling water; drain.
- Heat olive oil in a saucepan. Add drained carrots and garlic cloves and sauté until carrots are softened. Remove from heat.
- Add cayenne, cumin, paprika, vinegar and salt and pepper to carrots. Transfer to a serving dish. Garnish with parsley or cilantro.

Skewer ideas for appetizers:

Use small skewers for spearing your favorite bites such as salami chunks with pineapple, cherry tomatoes with smoked turkey, assorted olives, assorted cheeses with grapes, tomatoes and herbs, etc. Skewers may be used with favorite hot nibbles as well, however, if using wooden skewers, it is best to soak them prior to use when heating.

Sephardic Jews from northern Africa use saffron, ginger, cumin and chiles in many of their recipes. In general, Sephardic cooking is quite aromatic, using plenty of herbs and spices.

RED PEPPER DIP

PAREVE

4	red bell peppers	2	tablespoons Pomegranate Molasses *(see recipe below)*
2	poblano peppers		
1½	cups toasted walnuts	½	teaspoon ground cumin
½	cup crushed wheat crackers	3	tablespoons olive oil
			Salt to taste
1	tablespoon lemon juice		Handful of toasted pistachios, chopped

- To roast bell peppers, char whole peppers on all sides under the broiler. Place roasted peppers in a bowl and cover with plastic wrap until cooled. Separately, roast poblano peppers and place in the same bowl to cool. When cooled, peel all peppers and discard seeds.
- Combine roasted peppers in a food processor with walnuts, crackers, lemon juice, Pomegranate Molasses, cumin, olive oil and salt. Process until mixed. Garnish dip with pistachios.

The reason for roasting peppers separately is that the skins have different thicknesses.

POMEGRANATE MOLASSES

PAREVE

3	cups pomegranate juice (if sweetened, reduce sugar in recipe to taste)	½	cup lemon juice
		½	cup sugar

- Combine all ingredients in a saucepan. Simmer until reduced to 1 cup. Chill.

Spinach Dip
DAIRY

1	(10-ounce) package frozen chopped spinach, thawed and squeezed dry	1	cup mayonnaise
1	cup sour cream	1	teaspoon dried oregano
½	cup chopped fresh parsley	½	cup chopped scallions
½	teaspoon dill seed	1	teaspoon salad seasoning
			Juice of ½ lemon

- Combine all ingredients. Refrigerate until chilled. Serve with pita chips or in a hollowed out loaf of pumpernickel bread.
- 10 servings

Avocado Mousse
DAIRY

2	large ripe avocados	½	cup medium salsa, or to taste
1	(8-ounce) package light cream cheese		Splash of lemon juice
1	teaspoon garlic salt		

- Combine all ingredients in a food processor and mix 3 minutes or until light and foamy.
- Prepare 8 ramekins with a splash of salsa on the bottom of each. Spoon avocado mixture into ramekins. Chill 1 hour before serving. (If chilled longer than 1 hour, cover with plastic to preserve color.)
- 8 servings

A delicious and showy appetizer suitable for company meals. You might try this with tofu cream cheese for a pareve version.

There is something wonderful about sitting around with friends and family noshing and talking ... a simple pleasure with which we should indulge ourselves more often. For your next get-together, try making several of these appetizers ... relax ... and forget about dinner!

MOCK CHOPPED LIVER #1

PAREVE

2-3	large onions, chopped	4-6	cubes bouillon
1	tablespoon olive oil	1	cup pulverized walnuts
1	cup dry lentils		Salt and pepper to taste
2½	cups water		

- Sauté onion in olive oil until glazed.
- Cook lentils in water with bouillon cubes until lentils are soft, adding a bit more boiling water if needed. Add walnuts.
- Combine lentil mixture with onion in a food processor and blend. Season with salt and pepper.

MOCK CHOPPED LIVER #2

PAREVE

5	onions, chopped	1	cup ground walnuts
¼	cup olive oil	1	(15-ounce) can tiny sweet
11	hard-boiled eggs, divided		peas, drained
			Salt and pepper to taste

- Sauté onion in olive oil for 5 minutes or until caramelized. Remove onion with a slotted spoon to a food processor, reserving oil.
- Peel 10 eggs and remove and discard yolks. Add egg whites to onion in food processor along with walnuts and peas. Process until smooth. Season as needed with salt and pepper. Add reserved oil by drops if mixture seems too dry.
- Press mixture into an 8-inch springform pan and chill. Unmold onto a bed of greens on a serving plate or pedestal. Peel and chop remaining egg and place in center of mold for garnish. Serve with crackers, pita or vegetables.

LOWER EAST SIDE CHOPPED LIVER
MEAT

4	tablespoons vegetable oil, divided
1	pound chicken livers, washed and patted dry
2	large onions, chopped
3	hard-boiled eggs, chilled and peeled
	Salt and pepper to taste

- Heat 2 tablespoons vegetable oil in a large skillet. Add livers and sauté 5 minutes or until firm and slightly pink in the center. Remove livers with a slotted spoon and set aside to cool.

- In a separate skillet over low heat, sauté onion in remaining 2 tablespoons oil for 30 to 40 minutes or until dark in color, reducing temperature as needed to prevent burning.

- Place cooked livers in a food processor and coarsely chop. Mash eggs with a fork, then add to processor with sautéed onion. Process to combine. Season with salt and pepper. Refrigerate several hours or overnight.

- 8 servings

UNCLE BILL'S DILL PICKLES
PAREVE

2-3	stems fresh dill
2	cloves garlic, smashed
2	teaspoons pickling spices
1	dried red hot pepper (optional)
	Extra dill seeds (optional if more flavor is desired)
6-8	whole pickling cucumbers (not waxed)
1/4	cup kosher salt, mixed into 1 quart water to make brine

- Fold dill stems and place into the bottom of a wide mouth jar along with garlic and spices. Tightly pack in whole cucumbers. Pour brine into jar to the top; not all brine may be used. Place a piece of plastic wrap on top of jar. Place lid over plastic and screw on loosely so fermenting liquid can ooze out. Place jar on a plate to catch overflow.

- Keep in a cool place for a week or two. It is normal for brine liquid to become cloudy and bubble. When ready, store jar in the refrigerator.

For sour pickles, keep longer if you can resist snacking.
Small green tomatoes may be substituted for cucumbers.

Remember when you were a child trying to choose the perfect pickle from the barrel or crock at the deli without getting caught by the man behind the counter? Or remember carefully deliberating which pickle looked the best to you from the big bowl on the table at your favorite eat-in deli?

HUMMUS WITH ARTICHOKES

PAREVE

2	cups canned chickpeas, drained	½	teaspoon paprika
1	cup canned artichoke hearts, drained	½	teaspoon ground cumin
6	cloves garlic	½	teaspoon kosher salt
	Juice of 1 lemon, or more to taste	½	teaspoon white pepper
		⅓	cup olive oil

- Combine all ingredients except olive oil in a food processor. Process until puréed. With motor running, slowly drizzle in oil. Serve with pita, veggies or crackers.
- 10 servings

Thanks Yuval!

YUVAL'S EGGPLANT SPECIAL RECIPE

PAREVE

2	large eggplants	1	onion, diced
2	teaspoons salt	1	red bell pepper, diced
1	(8-ounce) can tomato sauce	1	green bell pepper, diced
2	stalks celery, diced	2	cups canola oil for frying

- Cut unpeeled eggplants into 1-inch cubes. Sprinkle with salt and let stand overnight.
- Combine tomato sauce, celery, onion and bell peppers in a saucepan.
- Deep fry eggplant in canola oil until softened. Add eggplant to tomato sauce. Chill. Serve with pita or crackers.

Eggs Stuffed with Smoked Salmon and Caviar
PAREVE

1 tablespoon chopped fresh chives, plus extra for garnish	¼ cup salmon caviar
1 tablespoon olive oil	12 hard-boiled eggs, peeled, halved lengthwise and whites and yolks separated
1½ tablespoons fresh lemon juice	Black pepper to taste
12 ounces thinly sliced cold smoked salmon, finely chopped	Lemon wedges and assorted fresh herb sprigs for garnish

- Blend 1 tablespoon chives, olive oil and lemon juice in a bowl. Mix in smoked salmon. Fold in caviar.
- Chop 4 egg yolks and stir into salmon mixture. Season with black pepper.
- Pile generous amounts of salmon mixture into each egg white half-shell. Arrange stuffed eggs on a paper towel-lined rimmed baking sheet. Cover with plastic wrap and refrigerate up to 8 hours.
- When ready to serve, sprinkle extra chives over eggs and garnish with lemon wedges and herb sprigs.

Gefilte Fish Mold
PAREVE

1 jar gefilte fish, drained with liquid reserved	1 small jar horseradish
1 (3-ounce) package dry lemon gelatin	

- Slice fish horizontally and arrange loosely in a greased small, round ring mold, leaving space around each piece.
- Bring reserved fish liquid to a boil and mix with lemon gelatin. Add horseradish and mix well. Pour mixture over fish. Chill until set.
- Unmold and slice to serve. Serve with crackers or *matzoh* on Passover.
- 10 servings

It seems as though everyone loves stuffed or deviled eggs. One of the best known food writers in the world, Ruth Reichl, even included her friend Marion's "Deviled Eggs" recipe in the memoir "Tender to the Bone."

Marion's Deviled Eggs
PAREVE

4   hard-boiled eggs
¼   cup mayonnaise
1   teaspoon cider vinegar
1   teaspoon ballpark mustard
      Salt and pepper to taste

- Peel eggs, carefully cut in half lengthwise. Put yolks into a bowl and mash with a fork until smooth.
- Add remaining ingredients and mix well; mixture should be thick and creamy. Fill each egg white half with yolk mixture. Grate a bit of black pepper on top. Refrigerate until needed.

Makes 8 deviled eggs, or about 6 servings

Stuffed Eggs with Goat Cheese and Dill
DAIRY

6   hard-boiled eggs
2½   ounces fresh mild goat cheese, softened
1   tablespoon milk
¾   teaspoon Dijon mustard
¼   teaspoon coarsely ground black pepper
⅛   teaspoon salt
2½   tablespoons chopped fresh dill

- Halve eggs lengthwise and carefully remove yolks.
- Purée yolks, goat cheese, milk, mustard, pepper, and salt in a food processor until smooth. Add dill and pulse until finely chopped. Spoon mixture into egg white shells.

Avocado Feta Salsa
DAIRY

2   tomatoes, chopped
1   ripe avocado, peeled and chopped
¼   cup finely chopped red onion
1   clove garlic, minced
1   tablespoon chopped fresh parsley
1   tablespoon chopped fresh oregano
1   tablespoon chopped fresh cilantro
1   tablespoon chopped fresh basil
1   tablespoon olive oil
1   tablespoon red or white wine vinegar
2   ounces crumbled feta cheese

- Gently stir together tomato, avocado, onion and garlic in a bowl. Mix in parsley, oregano, cilantro and basil.
- Gently stir olive oil and vinegar into tomato mixture. Stir in feta. Cover bowl and chill 2 to 6 hours.
- 10 servings

Baked Brie in Puffed Pastry with Dried Fruit

DAIRY

1	(2-pound) wheel of Brie cheese	2	tablespoons chopped walnuts, lightly toasted
¼	cup brandy or other flavored liqueur	1	sheet frozen puff pastry, thawed
¼	cup chopped dried apricots	1	egg yolk, beaten with 1 tablespoon water to make an egg wash

- Freeze cheese wheel for about 20 minutes to make it easier to slice.
- Meanwhile, in a saucepan, bring brandy and apricots to a boil. Remove from heat and allow to cool. When cooled, mix in walnuts.
- Slice partially frozen Brie horizontally to make 2 circles. Spoon apricot mixture over the top of the bottom circle. Place top circle over apricot mixture.
- Roll puff pastry out onto a floured surface until large enough to wrap around the Brie. Place Brie in center of pastry and wrap pastry around cheese, sealing overlapping dough with egg wash. At this point, Brie can be refrigerated or frozen until ready to bake.
- Preheat oven to 400 degrees.
- Brie should be removed from refrigerator just before baking. If frozen, let stand at room temperature for about 10 minutes. Brush pastry with egg wash and place on a greased baking sheet. Bake 20 to 30 minutes or until golden.
- Serve on thinly sliced and toasted baguette or crackers.

NUT GLAZED BRIE
DAIRY

⅓	cup brown sugar	1	teaspoon water
¼	cup walnuts, pecans, almonds or combination, chopped	1	(14-ounce) round Brie cheese

- Preheat oven to 500 degrees.
- Combine brown sugar, nuts and water in a small mixing bowl.
- Place Brie cheese on an oven-proof platter or 9-inch pie pan or quiche dish; make sure dish is at room temperature.
- Bake cheese 4 to 5 minutes or until cheese is slightly softened. Spoon nut mixture over top and bake 3 or 4 minutes longer or until sugar is melted and cheese is heated through. Serve with toasted crackers.
- 16-20 servings

The nut mixture can be prepared and refrigerated up to 24 hours in advance.

SALMON SEVICHE
PAREVE

8	ounces sashimi grade salmon, cut into ½-inch pieces	1	mango, finely diced
	Juice of 2 oranges	¼	cup Coconut Mixture *(see recipe below)*
	Juice of 2 limes	4	tablespoons chopped cilantro, divided
1	cup pomegranate juice		

- Combine salmon, fruit juices, mango, Coconut Mixture and 2 tablespoons cilantro. Marinate in refrigerator for at least 2 hours.
- Garnish with remaining 2 tablespoons cilantro.

COCONUT MIXTURE

1	cup white wine	2	teaspoons Thai curry paste
1	small shallot, chopped		
¼	cup chopped lemongrass	1	(13-ounce) can coconut milk

- Combine all ingredients for coconut mixture in a saucepan. Simmer 15 minutes; strain and cool.

FETA CHEESE AND PEPPER DIP
DAIRY

1	pound feta cheese	½	teaspoon smoked paprika
2	red bell peppers, roasted, peeled and seeded	1	teaspoon lemon juice
2	teaspoons chili powder	¼	cup olive oil

- Combine all ingredients in a food processor and purée until smooth. Serve with celery stalks or crusty bread.

ROASTED PEPPERS

- Preheat broiler. Place whole peppers on a rack 4-inches from heat source. Turn peppers as they blacken so all sides are charred. Place hot peppers in a bowl and cover with plastic wrap. Cool, then peel over the bowl to collect accumulated juice. Discard peels, seeds and stems.

GUACAMOLE
PAREVE

½	red onion, thinly sliced	¼	cup chopped tomato
2	tablespoons lime juice	1	teaspoon salt
1	teaspoon ground cumin	2	avocados
1	small jalapeño pepper, finely chopped	2	tablespoons chopped cilantro
2	large cloves garlic, finely chopped		

- Marinate onion slices in lime juice with cumin. Cook onion slices on a grill until soft and slightly browned. Chop into bite-size pieces.
- Combine chopped onion, jalapeño, garlic, tomato and salt in a bowl. Cut avocados in half and scoop pulp into bowl. Mix well.
- Garnish with cilantro. Serve with chips, toasted pita bread or cold vegetables.

CORIANDER CURED GRAVLAX

PAREVE

½ cup kosher salt	2 tablespoons tequila
½ cup sugar	4 limes, divided
2 tablespoons peppercorns, crushed	Chopped jalapeño pepper for garnish (optional)
3 tablespoons coriander seeds, toasted and crushed	1 cup finely chopped red bell pepper
1 (2-pound) salmon fillet	1 cup finely chopped onion
1 bunch cilantro, coarsely chopped, some reserved for garnish	Mustard Sauce *(see recipe below)*

- Mix salt, sugar, peppercorns and coriander. Rub ¼ cup of mixture on the skin side of the salmon. Rub remaining mixture on flesh of salmon.
- Spread cilantro evenly over salmon. Sprinkle with tequila. Cut 2 limes into thin slices and lay over salmon.
- Cover with plastic wrap and weight down with a board and cans. Refrigerate at least 48 hours, turning every 12 hours.
- Scrape off limes, cilantro and salt mixture. Garnish with remaining 2 limes, thinly sliced, and cilantro. Serve with jalapeño pepper, bell pepper, onion and Mustard Sauce.

MUSTARD SAUCE

PAREVE

1½ teaspoons white wine vinegar	5 tablespoons Dijon mustard
1¾ tablespoons sugar	2 tablespoons chopped fresh cilantro
½ cup olive oil	1 tablespoon white pepper

- To make sauce, whisk vinegar and sugar together in a small mixing bowl until sugar dissolves. Slowly add olive oil, whisking well until all oil is incorporated.
- Blend in mustard and cilantro. Season with white pepper. Refrigerate until needed.
- Serve on pumpernickel toasts with cream cheese and dill, and a few capers on top.

TZATZIKI WITH BEETS
DAIRY

1   large clove garlic, minced
2   teaspoons lemon juice
1   teaspoon salt
1½ cups thick Greek plain yogurt

1   tablespoon olive oil
1½ cups grated roasted beets
2   tablespoons plus 1 teaspoon chopped fresh dill, divided

- Whisk together garlic, lemon juice and salt in a medium bowl. Whisk in yogurt and olive oil.
- Grate beets in a food processor or by hand and add to mixture. Mix in 2 tablespoons dill. Garnish top with remaining 1 teaspoon dill.
- 10 servings

When tasting this recipe for the first time, we thought it was pretty and that it looked festive on the table (it's pink). It was so delicious that we immediately looked at the ingredients. Beets!! Many of us don't like beets, but we loved this dip. If your guests don't ask – don't tell!

SALMON PASTRAMI
PAREVE

1   side fresh salmon, about 2 pounds, skin and bones removed
1   cup coarse kosher salt
½   cup sugar
3   tablespoons cracked pepper, divided
2   bunches fresh coriander
1   bunch fresh Italian parsley
½   pound shallots, peeled
½   cup molasses
2   tablespoons cayenne pepper
5   bay leaves
2   tablespoons paprika
2   tablespoons ground coriander
2   tablespoons black pepper
½   cup mustard oil
8   slices rye toast or crackers (1 per serving)

- Place salmon on a platter. Mix salt, sugar and 1 tablespoon cracked pepper and spread over both sides of salmon.
- In a food processor, mix coriander, parsley and shallots and purée until smooth. Coat both sides of salmon with shallot mixture, cover and refrigerate 2 to 3 days.
- Scrape marinade from fish and dry with paper towels.
- In a saucepan, combine molasses, cayenne pepper and bay leaves and bring to a boil. Simmer 1 minute. Allow to cool slightly. Brush mixture over both sides of salmon.
- Combine paprika, coriander, black pepper and remaining 2 tablespoons cracked pepper. Sprinkle mixture over both sides of salmon. Cover and refrigerate overnight.
- To serve, cut salmon on a bias into thin slices. Serve with mustard oil and rye toast or crackers.
- 8 servings

Goat Cheese and Sun-Dried Tomato Dip
DAIRY

¼	cup chopped sun-dried tomatoes, drained or patted dry	½	teaspoon dried thyme
3	ounces goat cheese	½	teaspoon coarsely ground black pepper
¼	cup chopped walnuts	2	tablespoons sour cream

- Mix tomatoes, goat cheese, walnuts, thyme and pepper in a mixing bowl. Stir in enough sour cream to make dip spreadable.
- Serve on slices of French baguettes or crackers.
- Makes ¾ cup

Blue Cheese and Shallot Dip
DAIRY

2	tablespoons olive oil	¾	cup mayonnaise
1	tablespoon butter	¾	cup sour cream
1¼	cups thinly sliced shallots (4 ounces)	4	ounces crumbled blue cheese, room temperature
1	tablespoon sugar		Salt and pepper to taste

- Heat olive oil and butter in a heavy medium saucepan over medium-low heat. Add shallots and sugar and cover. Cook, stirring occasionally, for 20 minutes or until shallots are deep golden brown, watching carefully so sugar does not burn. Cool.
- Whisk together mayonnaise and sour cream in a medium bowl until blended. Stir in blue cheese. Use a rubber spatula to mash cream mixture until smooth.
- Stir shallots into cream mixture. Season with salt and pepper. Cover and refrigerate 2 hours or until flavors are blended; the longer it chills, the better the flavor will blend.
- Serve at room temperature with pita crisps or crackers.

Dips are always easy and prepared ahead. What really makes them special is the presentation of your vegetables and fruits. Color and texture from our natural harvests are abundant. Think purple and red, think green, think orange and yellow. Think fresh herbs and spices.

Matbucha
Moroccan spicy tomato pepper dip
PAREVE

8	large tomatoes	2	jalapeño or other spicy peppers
5	red bell peppers		
4-5	green or yellow bell peppers	2	tablespoons olive oil
		5	cloves garlic, minced

- Dip tomatoes in boiling water to loosen skins; peel and dice.
- Bake or grill all peppers on each side; peel and dice.
- Sauté diced peppers in olive oil for 5 minutes. Add tomatoes and sauté. Add garlic and sauté until all liquid evaporates.
- Refrigerate until chilled. Serve with anything!

Chicken Wings in Peanut Sauce
MEAT

4	pounds chicken wings	1½	tablespoons peeled and minced ginger
1	tablespoon vegetable oil		
		1	clove garlic, minced

Sauce

2	tablespoons natural peanut butter	1	tablespoon sugar
		¼	teaspoon salt
1	tablespoon lime juice	¼	teaspoon red pepper flakes
1¾	teaspoons soy sauce		

- Preheat oven to 500 degrees.
- Pat wings dry and toss with oil, ginger and garlic. Arrange wings, thick-side up, in a single layer in a shallow pan.
- Bake 25 minutes. Turn on broiler and broil wings, turning once, until browned and crisp.
- Meanwhile, blend together all sauce ingredients.
- When wings are cooked, toss with sauce and serve.
- 10 servings

Chunks of boneless chicken breast can be substituted for the wings. Note: carefully watch baking and broiling time as they will decrease significantly.

ARTICHOKE DIP

DAIRY

1   (14-ounce) can artichoke hearts

1   (10-ounce) jar marinated artichoke hearts, drained

1   (4-ounce) can chopped chili peppers

1   tablespoon mayonnaise

1   (8-ounce) package shredded Cheddar cheese

- Preheat oven to 325 degrees.
- Pour a small amount of oil from marinated artichokes into a quiche dish.
- Chop canned and marinated artichokes and add to bottom of dish. Spread chili peppers over artichokes. Spread mayonnaise over top and sprinkle with cheese.
- Bake until cheese is melted. Best served with pita chips or nachos.

KOREAN DUMPLINGS

MEAT

½	small cabbage, finely chopped
1	zucchini, finely chopped
1	teaspoon salt
1	medium onion, finely chopped
3-4	cloves garlic, minced
4	scallions, finely chopped
2	carrots, finely chopped
½	pound ground turkey, veal or beef

	Salt and pepper to taste
50	dumpling wrappers (found in produce or Asian foods section of grocery store)
1	egg, beaten
1	tablespoon water
	Vegetable or peanut oil for frying

- Place cabbage and zucchini in a colander and sprinkle with salt. Let drain 20 minutes. Squeeze out as much liquid as possible. Combine cabbage and zucchini with onion, garlic, scallions, carrot, raw meat and salt and pepper. Mix well.
- Place 1 teaspoon vegetable filling in the center of each wrapper and fold over on the diagonal.
- Beat egg with water. Brush edges of each dumpling with egg wash.
- Heat about ¼-inch of vegetable oil in a skillet. Fry dumplings in oil until golden. Serve with your favorite dipping sauce.

A less caloric alternative is to drop dumplings into a large pot of boiling salted water for 8 to 10 minutes or until they float to the top.

SOY DIPPING SAUCE

⅓	cup low-sodium soy sauce
1	scallion, thinly sliced
2	tablespoons rice vinegar
2	teaspoons sesame oil

Crushed red pepper flakes (optional)
Ground ginger (optional)

- Combine all ingredients.

SICILIAN SPINACH STRUDEL
DAIRY

1 tablespoon olive oil
1 tablespoon minced garlic
1 pound fresh spinach, stems removed
¼ cup pine nuts
¼ cup golden raisins
2 ounces Gorgonzola cheese

Salt and pepper
4 sheets phyllo dough, cut into quarters
2 tablespoons melted butter
3 tablespoons Parmesan cheese

- Preheat oven to 375 degrees.
- Heat olive oil in a large skillet. Add garlic and sauté. Add spinach and sauté until barely wilted. Remove spinach and set aside.
- Add pine nuts to same skillet and cook and stir until toasted. Stir in raisins and Gorgonzola. Add mixture to spinach and season as needed with salt and pepper.
- To assemble, stack the 16 phyllo squares and cover with a moist cloth to prevent phyllo from drying out.
- Place 4 phyllo squares side by side on a work surface and quickly brush with melted butter. Sprinkle each with Parmesan cheese. Stack squares in a criss-cross pattern on each other.
- Place a small mound of spinach filling in the center and make a package by folding over the sides first, then rolling phyllo package forward to close. Brush top and sides of package with a little more butter to prevent drying out. Sprinkle Parmesan cheese on top and place on a greased baking sheet.
- Repeat assembly to make a total of 4 packages.
- Bake 10 to 12 minutes or until golden and crispy.
- 4 servings

Working with phyllo dough is easy as long as you keep it moist with a wet linen towel. It is available in almost any market freezer section. Simply thaw and follow the recipe. The dough is flaky and rich, as it is usually brushed with melted butter or olive oil, depending on the recipe. Any phyllo recipe makes an elegant presentation. Strudel is no longer reserved for the sweets table, but makes a wonderful appetizer or entrée as well.

STUFFED MUSHROOMS
DAIRY OR PAREVE

2   (14-ounce) packages
    cremini mushrooms
2   tablespoons butter or
    margarine
5   tablespoons olive oil,
    divided
2   carrots, grated

½   cup chopped walnuts
¼   cup chopped fresh parsley
¼   cup fresh bread crumbs
½   cup currants
¼   cup pine nuts, toasted

- Preheat oven to 350 degrees.
- Remove mushroom stems. Set mushroom caps aside and chop stems.
- Heat butter and 4 tablespoons olive oil in a large skillet. Add chopped mushroom stems, carrot, walnuts, parsley, bread crumbs, currants and pine nuts and sauté until mixture is moist.
- Stuff mixture into mushroom caps and place in a baking dish. Drizzle with remaining 1 tablespoon olive oil.
- Bake 25 minutes.

TOASTED MUSHROOM ROLLUPS
DAIRY

1   pound mushrooms
4   tablespoons butter
3   tablespoons flour
¾   teaspoon salt
½   teaspoon seasoned salt

1   cup light cream
2   teaspoons minced chives
1   teaspoon lemon juice
1   loaf sandwich bread
1½ sticks butter, melted

- Preheat oven to 400 degrees.
- Chop mushrooms until fine and squeeze dry in a paper towel. Sauté chopped mushrooms in butter. Blend in flour, salt and seasoned salt. Stir in cream and cook until thick. Mix in chives and lemon juice.
- Remove crusts from bread slices and flatten with a rolling pin. Spread mushroom mixture over flattened bread slices and roll up. Cut each roll into thirds.
- Dip each piece in melted butter.
- Bake 10 minutes or until golden.
- 4 dozen

POTATO KNISH
PAREVE

Filling

5	pounds all-purpose potatoes	3	pounds onions, chopped
		2	tablespoons canola oil

Dough

2	teaspoons baking powder	¼	cup canola oil
1	egg		Pinch of salt
½	cup hot water	2	cups flour

- Peel and quarter potatoes and cook in boiling salted water until fork tender; drain. Mash potatoes with a fork or put through a ricer.
- Sauté onion in canola oil until soft and brown, but not crisp. Mix onions into mashed potatoes; set aside.
- To make dough, combine baking powder, egg, hot water, canola oil and salt and mix well. Blend in flour. Divide dough into 4 parts.
- Roll out one part of dough on a lightly floured surface into a thin rectangle. Brush a thin layer of oil over surface of dough. Place ¼ of potato filling lengthwise on rectangle. Roll dough around filling into a log. Cut log into 1-inch pieces. Flatten each piece slightly between palms of hands after pulling the end piece of dough to cover what will then be the bottom of the knish.
- Preheat oven to 350 degrees.
- Bake 15 to 20 minutes or until golden brown.
- Repeat with remaining filling and dough.

The knish is a gift from our eastern European ancestors. Many cultures have their own versions -- pierogi, empanada and spanikopita to name a few. Once considered just a snack food, today we eat knishes as an entire meal or make them appetizer size for a crowd. Fillings are varied from mashed potatoes to chopped meat, sauerkraut and onions, kasha or cheese. Today very popular fillings include spinach and broccoli and even tofu.

Knishes are usually square but round ones are appealing as their filling sometimes appears out the top of the dough as a hint of the flavor we are about to taste.

GLAZED SALAMI APPETIZER

MEAT

1	large onion, chopped	1	pound dark brown sugar
2	cloves garlic, minced	3	tablespoons vinegar
2	tablespoons margarine or vegetable oil		Juice of ½ lemon
1	(12-ounce) bottle chili sauce	½	cup apricot preserves
1	chili sauce bottle of water	1	(2-pound) salami, or 2 (1-pound) salamis, cubed

- Preheat oven to 350 degrees.
- Sauté onion and garlic in margarine. Add chili sauce, water, brown sugar, vinegar, lemon juice and preserves.
- Place salami cubes in a baking dish. Pour sauce mixture over salami.
- Cover and bake 1½ to 2 hours. Serve with toothpicks.

FISH CAKES

DAIRY

3	tablespoons mayonnaise	½	teaspoon salt
1	egg, beaten	¼	teaspoon black pepper
¾	cup bread crumbs	⅛	teaspoon nutmeg
½	cup diced celery	3	dashes hot pepper sauce
½	cup thinly sliced scallions	1	tablespoon milk
1	tablespoon chopped fresh dill	1	pound cod, boiled and shredded after cooking
1	tablespoon lemon juice		Vegetable or peanut oil for frying
2	tablespoons Dijon mustard		

- Combine all ingredients except cod. Gently mix in cod. Form mixture into 1½-inch diameter patties for an appetizer, 3-inch patties for main course.
- Add ¼-inch vegetable oil to a skillet and heat. Fry fish cakes in hot oil for 5 to 6 minutes or until golden. Serve hot or at room temperature.
- Garnish with scallion slices. Serve with tartar sauce, rémoulade and or lemon wedges.

Zucchini Latkes
DAIRY

4	large zucchini	2	cloves garlic, minced
2	eggs, beaten		Salt and pepper to taste
¼	cup flour	2	tablespoons vegetable oil for frying, or as needed
¼	cup Parmesan cheese		
2	tablespoons chopped chives		Optional toppings: caviar, sour cream or crème fraîche or chopped scallion
1	tablespoon chopped fresh parsley		

- Grate 2 zucchini, purée other 2 zucchini. Combine all zucchini with eggs, flour, Parmesan cheese, chives, parsley, garlic and salt and pepper.
- Heat vegetable oil in a large skillet. Drop batter by spoonfuls into hot oil. Fry 3 to 4 minutes per side or until golden. Serve with optional toppings.

Crème fraîche is a richer and smoother variation of sour cream. Mix together 1 cup heavy cream, ¼ cup buttermilk and 1 tablespoon lemon juice. Cover and let stand at room temperature for 6 to 8 hours, then refrigerate.

Tempura Batter
PAREVE

5	eggs, beaten	4	teaspoons baking powder
1¼	cups club soda	½	teaspoon salt
1	cup flour		Vegetable oil for frying
½	cup cornstarch		

- Combine all ingredients except oil with a wooden spoon until mixed. Use batter to coat vegetables such as green beans, cauliflower, sweet potato, squash, zucchini or eggplant.
- Fill a skillet halfway with vegetable oil and heat until hot. Fry batter-coated vegetables until golden.

Serve battered vegetables with a variety of dipping sauces, such as soy sauce, sweet and sour sauce, wasabi or horseradish sauce.

Great recipe for the tradition of Chanukah.

MINI BLINTZES
DAIRY

2   (8-ounce) packages cream cheese, softened
½   cup sugar
2   egg yolks
2   (1-pound) loaves thin sliced white bread, crusts removed

2   sticks butter, melted
    Cinnamon sugar for topping

- Preheat oven to 400 degrees.
- Combine cream cheese, sugar and egg yolks in a mixing bowl and beat until smooth.
- Flatten each slice of bread. Spread cream cheese mixture over each slice. Roll up bread and dip in melted butter. Sprinkle with cinnamon sugar.
- If freezing, place in a single layer on a baking sheet and freeze. When frozen solid, transfer to plastic bags for storage.
- To serve, bake 10 minutes or until lightly browned. If frozen, bake a few minutes longer. Serve with flavored yogurt, sour cream or jam.

May substitute whole wheat or whole grain bread

CHEESE STUFFED MUSHROOMS
DAIRY

1   (14-ounce) package cremini mushrooms
4   tablespoons butter
5   cloves garlic, minced
2   tablespoons lemon juice

½   cup chopped fresh parsley
1   cup shredded cheese mixture, such as Gouda, Cheddar, Emek, etc.
    Salt and pepper to taste

- Preheat oven to 350 degrees.
- Clean mushrooms and remove stems. Set caps aside and chop stems. Sauté chopped stems in butter in a skillet. Add garlic and continue to sauté. Add lemon juice. Remove from heat and stir in parsley.
- Arrange mushroom caps in a glass dish. Pack shredded cheese into caps. Pour butter sauce over the top.
- Bake 20 minutes.
- 6 servings

Meatballs in Wine Sauce
MEAT

Meatballs

1	pound ground beef chuck or round	1	egg, lightly beaten
1	large apple, peeled and grated	1¼	teaspoon salt
		2	tablespoons vegetable oil
		¼	cup chopped onion

Sauce

¾	cup burgundy wine	½	teaspoon dried basil
¼	cup water	¼	teaspoon dried rosemary
2	(8-ounce) cans tomato sauce	¼	teaspoon sugar

- Combine beef, apple, egg and salt and shape into 1-inch diameter balls.
- Heat vegetable oil in a saucepan. Add meatballs and onion and cook over medium heat for 10 minutes or until meat is lightly browned on all sides. Drain grease.
- Combine all sauce ingredients and pour over meatballs. Cover pan and simmer 15 minutes.
- When ready to serve, reheat if needed. Transfer to a serving bowl and serve with toothpicks.

AREPAS

DAIRY

1½	pounds corn kernels		1	tablespoon Parmigiano-Reggiano cheese
4	tablespoons butter, melted		3	tablespoons ricotta salata, feta or queso blanco
1	egg		1	tablespoon butter
1	tablespoon milk		2	teaspoons oil
1	cup finely ground cornmeal			Crème fraîche
2	tablespoons sugar			Salt and pepper to taste
⅓	cup shredded Monterey Jack cheese			

- Combine corn, melted butter, egg and milk in a food processor and blend until puréed. Add cornmeal and sugar and pulse to combine. Let stand 20 minutes.
- Add cheeses to mixture in food processor and pulse to combine batter.
- Melt 1 tablespoon butter with oil in a large skillet over medium heat. Drop batter by heaping teaspoons into skillet. Cook about 4 minutes on each side, flattening after flipping.
- Serve immediately with crème fraîche seasoned with salt and pepper for dipping.

APPLESAUCE MEATBALLS
MEAT

Meatballs

1	pound ground beef	1	teaspoon lemon juice
½	cup bread crumbs	½	teaspoon salt
1	egg, beaten	⅛	teaspoon black pepper
½	cup applesauce	2	tablespoons oil for browning
2	tablespoons grated onion, or onion powder		

Sauce

½	cup ketchup	½	cup red wine (optional)
½	cup water		

- Preheat oven to 350 degrees.
- Combine beef, bread crumbs, egg, applesauce, onion, lemon juice, salt and pepper and mix lightly. Shape meat mixture into ½-inch diameter balls.
- Heat oil in a large heavy skillet. Brown meatballs in oil, moving frequently for even browning. Transfer meatballs to a shallow baking dish.
- Combine sauce ingredients. Pour sauce over meatballs and cover dish.
- Bake about 1 hour.

Instead of baking, meatballs can be cooked in a large saucepan on the stove.

Fried Mozzarella
DAIRY

1	pound mozzarella cheese	½	teaspoon ground cumin
½	cup flour		Pinch of salt
3	eggs		Pinch of black pepper
1	cup bread crumbs	8	ounces marinara sauce, chilled
½	teaspoon garlic powder		Vegetable oil for frying
½	teaspoon dried oregano		

- Cut mozzarella into sticks about ¼-inch thick and 1½-inches long. Coat sticks with flour, shaking off excess. Place eggs in a bowl and beat. Combine bread crumbs, garlic powder, oregano, cumin, salt and pepper in a separate bowl. Dip sticks in beaten egg, then dredge in bread crumb mixture. The coating on the first stick should be fairly dry when you finish the last stick. Repeat with another dip in egg then in bread crumbs.
- Deep fry coated sticks in batches in hot oil for 3 to 4 minutes or until coating is browned. Keep cooked batches warm in oven. Serve with chilled marinara sauce or salsa.

Vegetable Samosas
PAREVE

1¼	cups frozen mixed vegetables, cooked al dente and drained	¼	teaspoon dried hot pepper flakes
¼	cup chopped fresh cilantro	30	wonton wrappers (found in produce or dairy section of store)
½	teaspoon ground cumin		Vegetable oil for frying
½	teaspoon salt		Mango chutney

- Mix drained vegetables, cilantro, cumin, salt and pepper flakes.
- Brush edges of each wonton wrapper with water and place about 2 teaspoons vegetable filling on each wrapper. Fold in half diagonally and seal. Cook in hot vegetable oil until golden. Or, brush with oil and bake at 325 degrees for about 15 minutes. Serve with mango chutney.

Brunch &
Breads

BRUNCH & BREADS

If bread is the staff of life, brunch is the meal we would like to have everyday. Combining the best of breakfast and lunch, there are no rules that cannot be broken. Who says you can't have brunch for supper! Invite friends and family - ask them to make their favorite brunch dish.

Brunch is a late breakfast or an early lunch — a popular way to entertain. The choices are endless, and brunch works well before a matinee or an evening sporting event.

Bread consists of the end-result of mixing yeast with liquid, flour, sugar, salt and some form of shortening. Today, however, bread varies in taste, texture and wheat-grain combinations; and fruits, nuts and berries are added to enhance nutritional value and flavor.

Food presentation is an important part of brunch entertaining. Choose your most colorful platters, scatter greens and seasonal flowers around the table and decorate with crocks of jams, olives and condiments while using your most festive dinnerware and glasses. Mimosas or Bloody Marys served in large wine goblets and iced tea carafes with fresh mint ... the possibilities are endless - use your creativity!

APPLE FRENCH TOAST CASSEROLE
DAIRY

6	eggs	1	(1-pound) loaf French, cinnamon or cinnamon raisin bread, sliced 1½-inch thick
3	cups milk		
1	teaspoon vanilla		
¾	cup sugar, divided	5-6	apples, unpeeled and sliced
1	teaspoon cinnamon, divided	4	tablespoons butter

- Preheat oven to 400 degrees.
- Mix eggs, milk, vanilla, half the sugar and half the cinnamon.
- In a separate bowl, mix together the remaining sugar and cinnamon.
- Line a greased 9x13-inch baking dish with bread slices. Pour half the egg mixture over bread slices. Cover with apple slices. Pour remaining egg mixture over apple slices. Sprinkle with cinnamon sugar mixture and dot with butter.
- Bake 35 minutes. Remove from oven and cool 5 to 10 minutes. Serve warm.
- 6-8 servings

For an extra decadent delight, serve with a scoop of vanilla ice cream.

BAKED QUESO BLANCO
DAIRY

1	(1-pound) block queso blanco (white Spanish cheese)	¾	teaspoon black pepper
		1	teaspoon dried oregano
1	tablespoon olive oil	1	loaf crusty French bread, sliced
¾	teaspoon salt		

- Using a skewer, poke holes in block of cheese.
- Combine olive oil, salt, pepper and oregano. Pour mixture over cheese and allow to soak into holes in cheese. Marinate at room temperature for about 30 minutes.
- Place cheese in a microwave-safe dish and microwave on high for 2 to 3 minutes. Serve immediately with sliced French bread.

Queso blanco is a Latin cheese, a bit salty and similar in color and texture to farmer cheese.

An easy, quick and cheesy accompaniment to soup or salad. Also a great football game snack.

CINNAMON APPLE CUPS
DAIRY

2 (3-ounce) packages lemon gelatin
½ cup red cinnamon candies
2 cups boiling water
2 cups unsweetened applesauce (1-pound can)
1 tablespoon lemon juice
   Dash of salt (optional)
1 (3-ounce) package cream cheese, cut into small pieces
⅓ cup broken walnuts

• Dissolve gelatin and candy in boiling water. Stir in applesauce, lemon juice and salt. Chill until partially set. Stir in cheese and walnuts. Spoon mixture into small molds and chill until firm.

This is a nice side dish for a dairy brunch. It can be made in one large mold, but I prefer smaller, individual molds.

FRENCH TOAST CASSEROLE #1
DAIRY

1 loaf French, Italian or challah bread, cut into 1-inch slices
4 tablespoons butter, or as needed
8 eggs

3 cups milk
4 teaspoons sugar
1 tablespoon vanilla
¼ teaspoon cinnamon
   Maple syrup

• Lightly spread each bread slice with butter and arrange in a single layer in a greased 9x13-inch baking pan.
• Beat together eggs, milk, sugar, vanilla and cinnamon. Pour mixture over bread. Cover and refrigerate 4 to 36 hours, preferably overnight.
• When ready to bake, preheat oven to 350 degrees.
• Bake 45 to 50 minutes or until puffy and lightly browned. Remove from oven and let stand at room temperature 5 minutes. Drizzle maple syrup on top and serve.
• 12 servings

FRENCH TOAST CASSEROLE #2
DAIRY

1 loaf challah, torn into pieces
1½ (8-ounce) packages cream cheese, softened and cubed
8 jumbo eggs
¾ cup maple syrup

2 cups whole or low-fat milk
½ cup sugar
   Cinnamon
   Maple syrup, warmed (optional)

• Arrange half the bread pieces in a well-greased 9x13-inch glass baking dish. Scatter cream cheese cubes over bread. Top with remaining bread.
• Beat together eggs, syrup, milk and sugar until well blender. Pour mixture over challah. Cover and refrigerate overnight.
• When ready to bake, preheat oven to 350 degrees.
• Uncover casserole and sprinkle with cinnamon. Bake 45 to 60 minutes or until firm. Serve with warm syrup.
• 12 servings

BAKED BLINTZ SOUFFLÉ
DAIRY

A no-fail standby for your brunch table.

1	stick butter			Dash of salt
12	frozen blintzes		1	teaspoon vanilla
4	eggs		1	(16-ounce) package frozen berries, warmed
½	cup sugar			
1½	cups sour cream			

- Preheat oven to 350 degrees.
- Melt butter in a 9x13-inch baking pan. Arrange blintzes in pan.
- Beat together eggs and sugar until combined. Mix in sour cream, salt and vanilla. Pour mixture over blintzes.
- Bake 40 minutes. Serve with warm berries.

Recipe can be doubled.

For a citrus flavor, add ¼ cup orange juice to egg mixture.

BREAKFAST CASSEROLE
Assemble the night before!
DAIRY

Use your leftover potatoes and vegetables for omelets, frittata or quiche.

8	slices challah or French bread, cubed		1½	cups shredded Cheddar cheese
1½	cups chopped tomatoes		10	eggs
1½	cups sliced mushrooms		2	cups milk
4	scallions, thinly sliced		1	teaspoon powdered mustard
½	cup imitation bacon (optional)			Salt and pepper to taste

- The night before serving, arrange bread slices in a greased 9x13-inch baking pan. Sprinkle with tomato, mushrooms, scallions and imitation bacon. Top with cheese.
- Blend eggs, milk, mustard and salt and pepper. Pour mixture over casserole. Cover and refrigerate overnight.
- To serve, remove casserole from refrigerator and bring to room temperature.
- Preheat oven to 350 degrees.
- Bake, uncovered, for 40 minutes.

POTATO BRUNCH CASSEROLE

DAIRY

This sounds like a recipe from the 60's. Garnish with thinly sliced green onion and chopped parsley for a contemporary flair.

1 (2-pound) package frozen hash brown potatoes, unthawed	3 cups shredded Cheddar cheese
1 (10¾-ounce) can cream of celery soup, undiluted	1 cup sour cream
	1 cup finely chopped onion
	1 (6-ounce) can French fried onions

- Preheat oven to 350 degrees.
- Combine potatoes, soup, cheese, sour cream and chopped onion in a large bowl. Transfer mixture to a greased 9x13-inch glass baking dish.
- Bake 1 hour 10 minutes or until lightly golden on top.
- Sprinkle top with French fried onions and bake 5 minutes longer or until golden brown.
- 12 servings

CORNBREAD CASSEROLE

Very easy.

DAIRY

An easy enhancement for vegetarian or black bean chili.

1 (16-ounce) can whole-kernel corn, drained	1 stick butter, melted
1 (16-ounce) can cream-style corn	1 (8½-ounce) package corn muffin mix
1 cup sour cream	2 eggs, beaten

- Preheat oven to 350 degrees.
- Combine all ingredients in a bowl and mix well. Transfer mixture to a greased 9x13-inch or 8x8-inch baking pan.
- Bake 1 hour or until set and browned on top.

Recipe can be doubled and freezes well.

GREEK PIZZA
DAIRY

1	(16-ounce) box phyllo dough, thawed		1	bunch fresh basil
1	stick butter, melted		1	bag fresh baby spinach
1	pound mozzarella cheese, shredded		1-2	tomatoes, sliced
4	ounces crumbled feta cheese			Coarse salt and black pepper to taste
				Dried oregano to taste

- Preheat oven to 325 degrees.
- Thoroughly dampen a cotton towel to cover phyllo while working with dough. Layer phyllo in a greased baking pan, brushing melted butter over each layer. Be sure to cover unused dough with damp towel to prevent it from drying out.
- Top phyllo layers with mozzarella and feta cheese, basil, spinach and tomato slices. Season with coarse salt, pepper and oregano.
- Bake 20 to 25 minutes or until phyllo is puffy and lightly browned.

FRESH CORN QUICHE
DAIRY

3	eggs		1⅓	cups half-and-half
½	small onion, coarsely chopped		3	tablespoons butter, melted
1	tablespoon all-purpose flour		2	cups fresh corn kernels, or frozen, thawed
1	tablespoon sugar		1	deep-dish frozen pie shell, thawed
1	teaspoon salt			

- Preheat oven to 375 degrees.
- Combine eggs, onion, flour, sugar and salt in food processor and blend until onion is finely chopped. Add half-and-half and butter and process until just blended. Transfer mixture to a large bowl. Mix in corn. Pour mixture into pie shell.
- Bake 50 minutes or until filling is slightly puffed and top is golden. Transfer to a rack and cool slightly. Serve warm.
- 6 servings

- Melt butter over low heat. Skim off the top, foamy layer and discard. The next layer is the butter fat — pour this into a heatproof container. This is the clarified butter and may be used for sautéing or as directed in a recipe. Discard the milk solids left in the pan.

YELLOW SQUASH AND MOZZARELLA QUICHE WITH FRESH THYME

Slender wedges of this creamy quiche also make a wonderful appetizer.

DAIRY

Crust

1¼	cups unbleached all-purpose flour	4	tablespoons ice water, or more as needed
½	teaspoon salt		
1	stick unsalted butter, chilled and cut into ½-inch cubes		

Filling

1	tablespoon butter	1	cup heavy cream
12	ounces yellow crookneck squash, cut into ¼-inch thick rounds	¾	teaspoon salt
		¼	teaspoon black pepper
2	teaspoons chopped fresh thyme	¼	teaspoon hot pepper sauce
6	eggs	¾	cup packed coarsely grated mozzarella cheese

- For crust, blend flour and salt in a food processor. Add butter and pulse on and off until mixture forms coarse meal. Add 4 tablespoons ice water and pulse until dough comes together in moist clumps, adding more ice water, 1 teaspoon at a time, if dough is dry. Gather dough into a ball and flatten into a disk. Wrap dough and chill at least 1 hour or up to 1 day.

- Roll out dough on a floured surface to a 14½-inch round. Transfer crust to a 10-inch tart pan with a removable bottom. Fold in overhanging dough and press to form double-thick sides. Push sides up until dough rises ¼-inch above top of pan. Pierce crust all over with a fork. Freeze 10 minutes.

- When ready to bake dough, preheat oven to 375 degrees.

- Line dough with foil and add pie weights or dried beans. Bake 25 minutes or until all sides are set. Remove foil and pie weights. Bake 15 minutes longer or until crust is golden, piercing with a fork if crust bubbles. Transfer to a rack to cool completely. Reduce oven temperature to 350 degrees.
- For filling, melt butter in a heavy medium skillet over medium heat. Add squash and thyme and sauté 5 minutes or until squash is just tender and translucent. Cool to room temperature.
- Whisk together eggs, cream, salt, pepper and hot sauce in a bowl.
- Arrange squash in the bottom of the baked crust and sprinkle with grated cheese. Place tart pan on oven rack and pour egg mixture into crust, filling completely (some egg mixture may be left over.)
- Bake 35 minutes or until filling is golden and center is set. Transfer quiche to a rack and cool 15 minutes.
- 4 servings

WILD MUSHROOM TART
DAIRY

Pastry dough

2 cups flour
1 teaspoon salt
1½ sticks butter, chilled and diced

¼ cup vegetable shortening, chilled
½ cup ice water

Filling

1 tablespoon unsalted butter
1 tablespoon vegetable oil
12 ounces mixed fresh wild mushrooms, such as cremini, oyster and chanterelle, quartered lengthwise
2 tablespoons finely chopped shallot

1 teaspoon chopped fresh thyme
¾ teaspoon salt, divided
¼ teaspoon plus ⅛ teaspoon black pepper, divided
½ cup crème fraîche
½ cup heavy cream
1 egg
1 egg yolk

- Have all pastry ingredients ready to go. Combine flour, salt and butter in a food processor and pulse to roughly break up the butter. Add shortening and immediately, with the machine running, add ice water. Pulse 2 to 3 times. The dough should look lumpy at this point.

- Place dough on a work surface and knead with the heal of your hand, pushing dough together to form a 6-inch disc. Wrap dough in plastic and chill for at least 2 hours.

- Roll out pastry dough on a lightly floured surface with a lightly floured rolling pin into an 11-inch round. Fit dough round into a tart pan, trimming excess dough. Chill 30 minutes or until firm.

- Preheat oven to 375 degrees and position a rack in center of oven.

- Lightly prick bottom of pastry shell all over with a fork. Line shell with foil and fill with pie weights. Bake 18 to 20 minutes or until side is set and edge is pale golden. Carefully remove pie weights and foil and bake 10 to 15 minutes longer or until bottom of shell is golden. Cool completely in pan on a rack. Reduce oven temperature to 325 degrees.

- While shell bakes, prepare filling. Heat butter and oil in a heavy 12-inch skillet over medium-high heat until foam subsides. Add mushrooms, shallot, thyme, ½ teaspoon salt and ¼ teaspoon pepper and sauté 8 to 10 minutes or until mushrooms are tender and any liquid has evaporated. Transfer to a bowl and cool to room temperature.
- In a separate medium bowl, whisk together crème fraîche, heavy cream, egg, egg yolk, remaining ¼ teaspoon salt and remaining ⅛ teaspoon pepper until combined.
- Scatter mushroom mixture evenly over bottom of baked tart shell. Pour egg mixture over top.
- Bake at 325 degrees in pan on a baking sheet for 35 to 45 minutes or until custard is just set and slightly puffed.
- Cool in pan on a rack at least 20 minutes. Remove sides of pan. Serve tart warm or at room temperature.
- 8 appetizer servings or 6 main-course servings

Tart shell can be baked 1 day ahead, cooled completely and stored in pan at room temperature, wrapped well in plastic wrap.

Tart can be baked up to 2 hours ahead and kept, uncovered, at room temperature. Serve at room temperature.

SPINACH, RED PEPPER AND FETA QUICHE

Can be prepared in 45 minutes or less.
DAIRY

Crust

⅓	cup plus 3 tablespoons all-purpose flour
3	tablespoons unsalted butter, chilled

1	tablespoon vegetable shortening, chilled
	Pinch of salt
1½	tablespoons ice water, plus more as needed

Filling

⅓	cup sliced red bell pepper
1	tablespoon olive oil
2	cups packed fresh spinach leaves, trimmed and thoroughly washed

	Salt and pepper to taste
2	eggs
⅓	cup heavy cream or milk
⅓	cup crumbled feta cheese

- Preheat oven to 425 degrees.
- Use a pastry blender or small food processor to blend together flour, butter, shortening and salt until mixture resembles coarse meal. Add water and toss until incorporated, adding extra water, if needed, to form a dough. Pat dough into the bottom and one-half inch up the sides of a 7½-inch tart pan with a removable fluted rim or a 9-inch pie pan.
- Bake 7 minutes or until dough is set and pale golden.
- While crust bakes, prepare filling. Sauté bell pepper in olive oil in a large skillet over medium-high heat for 1 minute. Add spinach and sauté 1 minute or until wilted and tender. Remove skillet from heat and season with salt and pepper.
- In a small bowl, whisk together eggs and cream.
- Sprinkle feta cheese over the bottom of baked crust. Arrange spinach mixture on top. Pour egg mixture over spinach.
- Bake on a baking sheet in the center of the oven for 15 minutes. Reduce temperature to 350 degrees and bake 10 minutes longer or until set.

German Pancake

Pop it in the oven and watch it puff!

DAIRY

2	eggs
⅓	cup all-purpose flour
⅓	cup milk
¼	teaspoon salt
1	tablespoon butter or margarine

	Confectioners' sugar
2	tablespoons sliced almonds, toasted
½	cup currant jelly

- Preheat oven to 450 degrees.
- Beat eggs in a medium bowl with an electric mixer on high until frothy. Slowly add flour, beating on medium until well blended. Stir in milk and salt.
- Melt butter in a 10-inch ovenproof skillet. Pour egg mixture into hot skillet.
- Bake 15 to 16 minutes or until pancake is browned and puffed.
- Sprinkle with confectioners' sugar and almonds. Serve immediately with currant jelly.
- 2 servings

My family can eat pancakes for any meal of the day. They are simply made of batter poured into a pan or on a griddle, cooked on high heat and served with a variety of fruit sides, depending on the recipe. Americans call them hotcakes or flapjacks (large and round), crèpes (very thin and once French) or blinis (once Russian and smaller in size.)

GERMAN APPLE PANCAKE
DAIRY

Batter

4	eggs	1	cup milk
½	cup all-purpose or whole wheat flour	2	tablespoons butter, melted
1	tablespoon sugar	1	teaspoon vanilla
½	teaspoon baking soda Pinch of salt		Freshly grated nutmeg to taste

Filling

4	tablespoons butter	2	Granny Smith or other tart apples, peeled, cored and very thinly sliced
⅔	cup granulated sugar		
½	teaspoon cinnamon Freshly grated nutmeg (optional)		Confectioners' sugar

- For batter, combine eggs, flour, sugar, baking soda, salt and milk. Blend thoroughly using a mixer or blender. Add butter, vanilla and nutmeg and mix well. Let batter stand at room temperature for 30 minutes, or cover and refrigerate overnight.
- When ready to bake, preheat oven to 425 degrees.
- To make filling, melt butter in a 10-inch oven-proof skillet, swirling the butter to coat sides; remove from heat.
- Combine granulated sugar, cinnamon and nutmeg. Sprinkle half of mixture over butter in skillet. Add apple slices. Sprinkle with remaining cinnamon sugar mixture. Place skillet over heat only until mixture bubbles.
- Pour batter over apples in skillet and place in oven. Bake 15 minutes. Reduce oven temperature to 375 degrees and bake 15 minutes longer or until set.
- Slide pancake onto a heated platter and sprinkle with confectioners' sugar. Serve immediately.
- 4 servings

Souffléd Orange Crèpes

DAIRY

1 cup fromage blanc (mild white cheese)	Zest of 1 orange
¾ cup sugar, divided	¼ teaspoon salt
4 egg yolks	5 egg whites
1 tablespoon flour	8 crèpes (homemade or store bought)
1 teaspoon vanilla	Confectioners' sugar

- Preheat oven to 350 degrees.
- Whisk together fromage blanc, ½ cup sugar, egg yolks, flour, vanilla, orange zest and salt.
- Using an electric mixer with a whisk attachment, beat egg whites on medium until soft peaks form. Slowly add remaining ¼ cup sugar, increasing speed to high and beating until stiff, glossy peaks form. Fold half the egg whites into the cheese mixture until incorporated, then fold in remaining whites.
- Divide cheese mixture evenly among crèpes, placing mixture on one-fourth of each crèpe. Fold each crèpe into quarters. Place crèpes, overlapping slightly, in a greased oval ceramic gratin dish.
- Bake 20 minutes or until crèpes are golden and filling is set. Dust with confectioners' sugar.

CRÈPES

DAIRY

⅔ cup milk	¼ teaspoon salt
⅔ cup water	6 tablespoons butter, melted, divided
1 cup flour	
3 eggs	

- Whisk milk and water into flour until smooth. Whisk in eggs, salt and 3 tablespoons butter. Let rest 10 minutes.
- Heat a crèpe pan and brush with some of remaining melted butter. Pour ¼ cup batter into hot pan and tilt to cover. Cook 30 seconds or until brown. Turn crèpes and cook another 15 to 20 seconds.
- To store crèpes, transfer to a rack to cool. Stack cooled crèpes and place in a plastic storage bag. Refrigerate for up to 2 days or freeze for up to 1 month.

These crèpes can be used around, under or on top of almost everything - from entrées to desserts. Always have these on hand in your freezer.

BLINTZES
DAIRY

Filling

2	eggs	1	(2-pound) block farmer cheese
½	cup sugar, or to taste		

Batter

6	eggs	¼	cup canola oil
2	cups milk	¾	cup flour
1	teaspoon salt		Butter or oil for frying

- For filling, beat eggs until thoroughly mixed. Stir in sugar. Mix in cheese until well combined. Set aside.
- Prepare batter by beating eggs, milk, salt and oil together in a separate bowl. Blend in flour.
- Heat a little butter or oil in a shallow 6-inch skillet. Pour ¼ cup batter onto one side of the pan and tilt and rotate pan so batter covers entire pan. Any excess can be poured back into batter bowl. Cook until bottom is brown. Flip and cook only slightly on other side. Turn out onto a plate. Continue with rest of batter. If the batter becomes too thick, thin with a tablespoon of milk.
- Crêpes can be prepared up to 2 days ahead, wrapped in plastic wrap and refrigerated until needed. When ready to use, allow to stand at room temperature for 1 hour.
- Spoon 2 tablespoons of filling along one side of crêpe. Fold crêpe over once, tuck in sides and fold over again.
- Refry blintzes in butter, or for a large crowd, place blintzes on a greased baking pan, dollop butter on top and bake at 425 degrees until warm and brown. Serve with sour cream.

Blintzes freeze well.

FOURSOME PANCAKES
DAIRY

1 cup sour cream
1 cup cottage cheese
¾ cup flour
1½ teaspoons sugar

2 teaspoons vanilla
4 eggs, separated
Maple syrup
Cognac (optional)

The egg whites help to make these light and airy.

- Beat together sour cream, cottage cheese, flour, sugar, vanilla and egg yolks in a bowl.
- In a separate bowl, beat egg whites until stiff. Fold egg whites into batter.
- Ladle batter, about ⅓ cup for each pancake, onto a hot lightly greased griddle or large frying pan. Cook until browned on one side. Turn and cook on other side. Repeat until batter is used, stirring batter occasionally so batter maintains its consistency.
- Serve pancakes with maple syrup laced with cognac, if desired.
- Makes 16-24 pancakes, 4 servings

BAKED FRENCH TOAST
DAIRY

1 (15-inch) long French bread, cut into 1-inch slices
12 eggs
3 cups milk
2 cups light cream
2 teaspoons vanilla
½ teaspoon cinnamon

½ teaspoon nutmeg (optional)
1 stick butter, softened
1 cup light brown sugar
1 cup chopped walnuts
2 tablespoons light corn syrup
Maple syrup

- The night before serving, arrange bread slices in a single layer in a greased 11x14-inch casserole dish.
- In a medium bowl, combine eggs, milk, cream, vanilla, cinnamon and nutmeg. Mix well and pour over bread. Refrigerate overnight.
- The next day, preheat oven to 350 degrees.
- In a small bowl, combine butter, brown sugar, walnuts and corn syrup. Mix well and spread evenly over bread.
- Bake 40 minutes or until puffed and golden. Serve with maple syrup.

Recipe can be cut in half and baked in a 9-inch square pan.

Overnight Scrambled Eggs

DAIRY

Cheese Sauce

2	tablespoons butter	½	teaspoon salt
2½	tablespoons flour	⅛	teaspoon black pepper
2	cups milk		
1	cup shredded American cheese		

Filling

¼	cup chopped scallions	3	tablespoons butter, melted
8	ounces mushrooms, sliced	12	eggs, beaten

Topping

4	tablespoons butter, melted	2¼	cups plain bread crumbs
			Paprika to taste

- The night before serving, prepare cheese sauce by melting butter in a saucepan. Stir in flour until blended. Slowly mix in milk and cook until thickened. Add cheese and cook until melted. Season with salt and pepper.
- To make filling, sauté scallions and mushrooms in butter in a skillet. Add eggs and cook and stir to form large, soft curds. When set, stir in cheese sauce. Spoon mixture into a greased 9x13-inch baking pan.
- For topping, combine butter and bread crumbs and spread over eggs. Sprinkle with paprika. Cover and chill overnight.
- When ready to bake, preheat oven to 350 degrees.
- Bake, uncovered, for 30 minutes.

Corn Waffles
DAIRY

1 cup flour
1 cup stone ground cornmeal
1½ teaspoons baking powder
1 teaspoon baking soda
¼ cup sugar
¼ teaspoon salt
2 eggs
2 cups buttermilk
4 tablespoons unsalted butter, melted and cooled

- Preheat waffle iron.
- Whisk together flour, cornmeal, baking powder, baking soda, sugar and salt in a large mixing bowl.
- In a separate bowl, whisk together eggs and buttermilk. Mix in cooled, melted butter. Stir egg mixture into dry ingredients.
- Pour batter by spoonfuls into waffle iron. Cook 3 to 5 minutes or until waffles are crisp and brown.
- About 6 servings

Waffles freeze well.

For variety, add 1 cup corn kernels or 1 cup blueberries to batter.

Breakfast "Sausage" Patties
Healthy and delicious.
MEAT

1 pound ground chicken breast
⅓ cup peeled and diced red apple
2 tablespoons olive oil
2 tablespoons diced onion
1 tablespoon maple syrup
2 teaspoons dried sage
1 teaspoon salt
½ teaspoon black pepper
½ teaspoon minced garlic

- Combine all ingredients in a medium bowl and mix well. Form mixture into ⅓-cup patties.
- Sauté patties in a skillet over medium heat for 3 to 5 minutes on each side or until golden brown.
- 6 servings

These are delicious with scrambled or poached eggs on top of a toasted English muffin.

EASY GRANOLA
PAREVE

4	cups rolled oats	½	cup vegetable oil
1	cup wheat germ	1	cup honey
¾	cup sunflower seeds		
½	cup chopped walnuts (optional)		

- Preheat oven to 350 degrees.
- Combine oats, wheat germ, sunflower seeds and walnuts in a large mixing bowl.
- Heat vegetable oil with honey in a saucepan and cook until syrupy. Pour over dry ingredients and mix well. Spread granola on a jelly roll pan.
- Bake 20 to 30 minutes, stirring every 10 minutes.

BIRCHERMUESLI (SWISS MUESLI)
DAIRY OR PAREVE

2	cups old-fashioned oats or rolled oats	1-2	tablespoons honey (optional)
1-1½	cups soy or low-fat milk	¼	cup raisins, currants or dried cranberries

- Combine all ingredients in a bowl. Cover with plastic wrap and refrigerate overnight.
- The next morning, refresh mixture if needed with extra milk.

  Serve muesli in individual bowls topped with fresh fruit such as sliced bananas, peaches, berries, oranges, etc. Sprinkle with sunflower seeds or sliced almonds, and, if you want to be indulgent, drizzle with a little cream.

PICKLED SALMON
PAREVE

A zesty treat. Works well after the fast of Yom Kippur.

3-4   **pounds salmon fillet**
      Salt and pepper to taste
6   **ounces ketchup**
1   **cup vinegar**

½   **cup sugar**
2   **handfuls pickling spices (in spice section at supermarket)**
2   **thin slices onion**

- Poach fish in water to cover. Season with salt and pepper.
- Combine ketchup, vinegar, sugar and pickling spices in a small saucepan. Bring to a boil.
- Place onion slices in a glass baking dish. Arrange fish over onion and pour sauce over fish. Cover with foil.
- Refrigerate 5 to 14 days.
- Let stand at room temperature for 1 to 1½ hours before serving. Serve with mustard, capers or lemon slices.

CRANBERRY CORNMEAL MUFFINS

Great for Sunday brunch.

DAIRY

¾ cup fresh or frozen cranberries

1 cup cranberry juice cocktail

1 tablespoon orange liqueur or orange juice

2 eggs

1 egg yolk

½ cup milk

½ cup heavy cream

1 cup all-purpose flour

1 cup cornmeal

½ cup sugar

4 teaspoons baking powder

1 teaspoon salt

6 tablespoons unsalted butter, melted

½ teaspoon mace (optional)

2 tablespoons orange peel

- Combine cranberries, cranberry juice and liqueur in a small bowl. Cover and refrigerate overnight. The next day, allow to stand at room temperature for 30 minutes before adding other ingredients.
- When ready to bake, preheat oven to 425 degrees.
- Mix together eggs, egg yolk, milk and cream in a large bowl.
- In a separate bowl, combine flour, cornmeal, sugar, baking powder and salt. Mix dry ingredients with egg mixture and melted butter.
- Drain cranberries, discarding juice. Fold cranberries into batter.
- Spoon batter into greased muffin cups.
- Bake in center of oven for 14 minutes for tea-size muffins or 18 minutes for medium-size muffins. Remove from oven and allow to stand in tin for a few minutes before turning out of pan to cool on a rack.

Green Chile Corn Muffins

DAIRY

1 (8½-ounce) package cornbread mix
1 (8-ounce) can golden sweet corn, drained
1 cup shredded Cheddar cheese
1 (7-ounce) can chopped green chiles
¼ cup milk
2 eggs

- Preheat oven to 400 degrees.
- Combine all ingredients until just moistened; do not overmix. Spoon batter into greased muffin tins, filling each two-thirds full.
- Bake 15 to 20 minutes or until golden brown. Serve warm.

Cheddar Corn Muffins with Zip

DAIRY

1 cup all-purpose flour
1 cup yellow cornmeal
1 tablespoon baking powder
2 tablespoons chili powder
3 tablespoons sugar
½ teaspoon salt
1½ cups shredded Cheddar cheese, divided
1 egg, lightly beaten
1 cup milk
2 tablespoons butter, melted

- Preheat oven to 375 degrees.
- Combine flour, cornmeal, baking powder, chili powder, sugar and salt in a bowl and mix well. Toss in 1 cup cheese.
- In a separate bowl, combine egg, milk and melted butter. Combine mixture with dry ingredients and mix until moist.
- Spoon batter into greased muffin tins. Top with remaining ½ cup cheese.
- Bake 20 minutes. Serve warm.
- 12 muffins

Muffins freeze well.

BLUEBERRY MUFFINS
DAIRY

1 stick butter, softened	1 teaspoon baking powder
¾ cup sugar	¾ teaspoon baking soda
2 eggs	1 cup blueberries
2 cups flour, divided	¾ cup milk
¼ teaspoon salt	2 tablespoons vinegar
¼ teaspoon nutmeg (optional)	

- Preheat oven to 375 degrees.
- Cream together butter and sugar. Blend in eggs, one at a time.
- In a separate bowl, combine 1¾ cups flour, salt, nutmeg, baking powder and baking soda.
- Roll blueberries in remaining ¼ cup flour.
- Mix milk with vinegar.
- Add dry ingredients alternately with milk to creamed mixture. Fold in blueberries. Spoon batter into greased muffin tins.
- Bake about 25 minutes.

PEAR MUFFINS
DAIRY

2 cups peeled and cubed fresh Bartlett pears	1½ cups flour
¾ cup sugar	1 teaspoon baking powder
1 stick butter, melted and cooled	1 teaspoon baking soda
2 extra large eggs	½ teaspoon salt
1 teaspoon vanilla	¾ cup chopped pecans or walnuts

- Preheat oven to 350 degrees.
- Toss pears with sugar in a large bowl; set aside.
- In a separate bowl, blend butter, eggs and vanilla; set aside.
- In a third bowl, combine flour, baking powder, baking soda and salt. Stir in nuts.
- Stir egg mixture into pears until just combined. Add dry ingredients to pear mixture and stir until just combined. Spoon batter into greased or lined muffin tins.
- Bake 20 minutes or until a toothpick inserted comes out clean.
- 12 muffins

Lemon Scones
DAIRY

3 cups flour, plus more as needed for kneading

2½ teaspoons baking soda

⅓ cup sugar, plus extra for sprinkling on top

½ teaspoon salt

1 teaspoon lemon zest (orange zest may be substituted)

1½ sticks butter, cubed and chilled or placed in freezer for 30 minutes

1 cup buttermilk

1 cup currants (optional) Melted butter for brushing over scones

- Preheat oven to 425 degrees.

- Combine 3 cups flour, baking soda, ⅓ cup sugar, salt and lemon zest and mix well. Cut in butter using a pastry blender until mixture resembles ground cornmeal. Add buttermilk and mash with a fork until crumbly. Mix in currants, if using.

- Transfer dough to a cutting board and knead, adding up to ½ cup flour as needed, until dough is smooth. Separate dough in half.

- Press each dough half into a round. Brush rounds with melted butter and sprinkle with sugar. Cut each round into 6 wedges.

- Bake on a parchment paper-lined baking sheet or a silicone baking sheet for 20 to 25 minutes.

Be creative when baking muffins, scones and quick breads. Try adding raisins, blueberries, bananas, apples, lemon zest, cherries or chopped nuts.

SCONES

DAIRY

2	cups all-purpose flour	4	tablespoons butter, chilled and cut into slices
1	tablespoon baking powder	1	cup heavy cream
½	teaspoon salt	1	egg, beaten
¼	cup sugar, plus extra for sprinkling		

- Preheat oven to 375 degrees.
- Stir together flour, baking powder, salt and ¼ cup sugar. Work butter into dry ingredients with fingers or a pastry blender until mixture resembles coarse meal; do not overmix.
- With fingers, stir in cream and mix until combined. Gather dough into an 8- to 10-inch round, about 1 to 1½-inches thick. Cut into 12 wedges.
- Place wedges on a parchment-lined baking sheet. Brush tops with beaten egg and sprinkle with extra sugar.
- Bake 15 to 20 minutes.

Dough can be divided in half and rolled out to make smaller scones.

*For variety, try adding ¼ cup currants or
¼ cup mini chocolate chips or the zest of 1 orange.*

Honey Cornbread

A sweet cornbread that will crumble in your hand and melt in your mouth.

DAIRY

2	cups all-purpose flour	2	cups heavy cream
2	cups cornmeal	½	cup vegetable oil
½	cup sugar	½	cup honey
2	tablespoons baking powder	4	eggs, lightly beaten

- Preheat oven to 400 degrees.
- Stir together flour, cornmeal, sugar and baking powder in a large bowl.
- Make a well in the center of the dry ingredients. Add cream, oil, honey and eggs to well and stir to combine. Pour batter into 2 lightly-greased loaf pans.
- Bake 20 to 25 minutes or until a toothpick inserted comes out clean.
- 2 loaves

Cornbread with Manchego Cheese
DAIRY

1	cup yellow cornmeal	4	tablespoons butter, melted
1	cup flour	¾	cup buttermilk
1	teaspoon kosher salt	1	(8-ounce) can creamed corn
½	teaspoon baking soda	2	eggs, beaten
1	teaspoon baking powder	¾	cup shredded Manchego or Cheddar cheese
⅓	cup sugar		

- Preheat oven to 350 degrees.
- Combine cornmeal, flour, salt, baking soda, baking powder and sugar in a large bowl and mix well.
- In a separate bowl, stir together butter, buttermilk, corn and egg. Add mixture to dry ingredients and mix well. Fold in cheese. Pour batter into a greased 9x13-inch baking pan.
- Bake 20 to 25 minutes or until a tester inserted in the center comes out clean. Cut into squares and serve warm.

You have heard of the "Man from LaMancha", well Manchego is the "Cheese from LaMancha" Spain. It is golden in color, semi-firm and rather mellow. It melts easily for hot meals and children and adults alike snack on it.

MULTI-GRAIN BREAD WITH SESAME, FLAX AND POPPY SEEDS

PAREVE

½ cup unsweetened multi-grain cereal

2 cups boiling water

1 envelope dry yeast

4⅓ cups bread flour, divided, or as needed

1 tablespoon olive oil

1 tablespoon brown sugar

1½ teaspoons salt

2 teaspoons sesame seeds

2 teaspoons flax seeds, or any other small seed (available at health food stores)

2 teaspoons poppy seeds

2 cups water for baking pan

- Place cereal in a large bowl. Pour boiling water over cereal and let stand 20 minutes or until mixture cools to 105 to 115 degrees (warm to the touch).
- Sprinkle yeast over mixture. Add 1 cup flour, olive oil, brown sugar and salt and stir until smooth. Gradually mix in enough of remaining bread flour to form a dough. Cover and let rest 15 minutes.
- Turn dough out onto a floured surface. Knead 10 minutes or until smooth and elastic, adding more flour as needed until not sticky. Transfer dough to an oiled bowl, turning to coat top of dough. Cover bowl with a clean kitchen towel. Let dough rise in a warm place for 1 hour or until doubled.
- Punch down dough and turn out onto a lightly oiled surface. Knead briefly and shape into a 12x4-inch loaf.
- Combine sesame, flax and poppy seeds in a small bowl. Sprinkle 2 teaspoons of seed mixture over a baking sheet. Place loaf on top of seeds. Cover with towel and let rise in a warm place for 30 minutes or until almost doubled in size.
- Position a rack in center of oven. Position a second rack just below center of oven. Place an empty baking pan on lower rack. Preheat oven to 425 degrees.
- Brush loaf with water and sprinkle with remaining seed mixture. Using a sharp knife, make 3 diagonal slashes in surface of loaf. Place baking sheet with loaf in oven. Immediately pour 2 cups water into hot, empty baking pan. (Be careful as water will steam up.)
- Bake 35 minutes or until loaf is golden and crusty and an inserted tester comes out clean. Transfer to a rack to cool.

Bread can be baked up to 1 day ahead, wrapped in plastic and stored at room temperature.

WHOLE WHEAT BREAD
(Sponge Method)
DAIRY

2	packages dry yeast	½	cup molasses
½	cup warm water (105-115 degrees)	1	tablespoon salt
¼	cup brown sugar	2	tablespoons butter
3	cups water	4	cups whole wheat flour
½	cup honey	7-8	cups white flour

Topping

¼	cup dark corn syrup	¼	cup water

- Whisk together yeast, warm water and brown sugar and set aside.

- In a small saucepan, combine 3 cups water, honey, molasses, salt and butter. Heat until butter melts and honey and molasses are dissolved. Cool mixture to 115 degrees. Add to yeast mixture.

- Measure whole wheat flour into a large bowl. Whisk in liquid yeast mixture until well mixed; mixture will be thin. Let rise in a warm place for 30 minutes. When this mixture is ready, it is called a "sponge".

- Add white flour, 1 cup at a time. Knead dough until it is smooth and elastic. Place in a well-greased bowl, turning once to grease top of dough. Cover and let rise 2 hours.

- Punch down dough and let rise 1 hour longer. Cut dough into 4 equal pieces and shape into 4 loaves. Place in well-greased loaf pans and let rise 1 hour.

- When ready to bake, preheat oven to 350 degrees.

- Bake 30 minutes or until loaf sounds hollow when tapped on the bottom.

- While bread is still hot, brush top with a mixture of corn syrup and water. Let bread cool completely on a rack. Slice, toast and butter.

"Good bread is the most fundamentally satisfying of all foods; and good bread with fresh butter, the greatest of Feasts."
James Beard

FIVE BRAID CHALLAH

PAREVE

1½ tablespoons dry yeast	1 tablespoon salt
1 tablespoon plus ½ cup sugar, divided	8 cups flour, divided, plus ½ cup extra as needed
1¾ cups warm water (105-115 degrees)	Egg wash (1 egg plus 1 tablespoon water, beaten together)
1½ cups vegetable oil	Poppy seeds for garnish
1 cup eggs (about 4)	

- Mix yeast, 1 tablespoon sugar and warm water in the large bowl of an electric mixer. Let stand to proof for at least 5 minutes.

- Mix in oil, egg, salt and 2 cups flour and beat well. Add almost all of remaining 6 cups flour until dough holds together and pulls away from the sides of the bowl.

- Place dough onto a cloth-covered board sprinkled with some of remaining flour. Knead dough until smooth and elastic using as much of remaining flour as needed. Place dough in a large greased bowl, turning once to grease top of dough. Cover and let rise in a warm place for 1 hour. Punch down dough and let rise again for 30 minutes while you mentally prepare yourself for braiding this bread!

- Punch dough down and cut into 5 equal pieces (weigh it to be sure). Roll each piece into a snake anywhere from 12 to 16-inches long, keeping pieces the same length.

- Lay all 5 snakes parallel and connect at one end. Think of them as numbers 1 through 5 from left to right. The numbers remain sequential for each new step.

    Step 1: Move snake 5 between 1 and 2.

    Step 2: Move 1 between 3 and 4.

    Step 3: Move 2 between 3 and 4.

    Step 4: Move 5 between 1 and 2.

    Step 5: Move 1 between 3 and 4.

    Step 6: Move 2 between 3 and 4.

Repeat steps until finished. Place braid diagonally on a silicone-lined baking sheet, cover and let rise in a warm place for about 30 minutes.

- Preheat oven to 350 degrees.

- Brush gently with egg wash and sprinkle with poppy seeds.

- Bake 20 minutes or until loaf is golden and sounds hollow when tapped on the bottom. Cool slightly before slicing.

- If these directions make you crazy, make 4 small or 2 larger 3-braid loaves.

5 Strand Braided Challah — *Divide the dough into 5 strands and pinch together at the top. Number the strands 1-5, from left to right. Here's the order of the braiding; 2 over 5, 5 over 2 and 3 and 1 over 5. Repeat the pattern until the braid is complete.*

Proofing Yeast: Proofing tests yeast for freshness and potency. Dissolve the yeast in warm water (105 to 115 degrees) with a pinch of sugar. If the mixture foams after 5 to 10 minutes, the yeast is okay to use. Proofing also refers to the rising stage of the yeast dough.

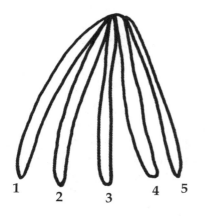

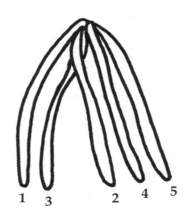

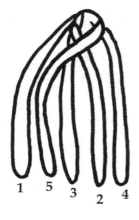

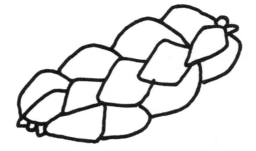

VEGETARIAN STUFFED BREAD

DAIRY

¾ cup regular or low-fat cream cheese, softened

1 tablespoon prepared olive spread

1 (2-pound) package frozen white or wheat bread dough, thawed in refrigerator 12 hours (2 loaves)

1 (12-ounce) jar roasted red peppers, drained

1 (10-ounce) package frozen chopped spinach, thawed and drained

1 (4-ounce) jar marinated artichoke hearts, drained and chopped

1 tablespoon olive oil

1 egg, lightly beaten

- Combine cream cheese and olive spread and mix until smooth.
- Roll each loaf of bread into a 5x12-inch rectangle on a floured board. Divide cream cheese mixture between the 2 rectangles and spread to within ½-inch of the edges. Arrange peppers, spinach and artichoke hearts on top.
- Starting with the long edge, roll each rectangle tightly, getting as much air out as possible. Pinch seams to seal and place, seam-side down, on a baking sheet that has been greased with olive oil. Let rise 1 hour or until doubled in size.
- When ready to bake, preheat oven to 375 degrees.
- Brush loaves with egg. Bake 35 minutes. Cool on a wire rack at least 5 minutes before slicing.

For heartier loaves, add any shredded cheese prior to rolling.

BANANA BREAD
DAIRY

2½ cups flour
½   cup granulated sugar
½   cup brown sugar
3   tablespoons vegetable oil
1   teaspoon baking powder
1   teaspoon salt

3-4 very ripe bananas, mashed
1   egg
⅓   cup milk
¾   cup nuts or chocolate
     chips (optional)

- Preheat oven to 350 degrees.
- Combine all ingredients in a bowl or food processor and blend well. Pour batter into 2 greased 8-inch loaf pans.
- Bake 45 minutes or until an inserted toothpick comes out clean.

PUMPKIN BREAD
PAREVE

4   eggs
2   cups oil
⅔   cup water
2   cups canned pumpkin
    (not pumpkin pie mix)
3   cups sugar

3½ cups flour
1   teaspoon cinnamon
1   teaspoon baking soda
1   teaspoon nutmeg
    (optional)

- Preheat oven to 350 degrees.
- Combine eggs, oil, water and pumpkin in a mixing bowl.
- In a separate bowl, mix sugar, flour, cinnamon, baking soda and nutmeg. Combine dry ingredients with pumpkin mixture and mix well. Divide batter among 3 greased loaf pans.
- Bake 1 hour or until a toothpick inserted comes out clean.

When I was a teacher at Gan Hayeled, this is the recipe we always used for fall pumpkin bread. My daughter makes it every year for our family's Thanksgiving get together.

GRANDMA'S CIBALLA KEICHEL (ONION COOKIES)
DAIRY

2	sticks butter, softened	1	teaspoon white pepper
3	eggs	3	large onions, grated to about 2 cups
2	teaspoons baking powder		Poppy seeds (optional)
1	teaspoon onion powder	4	cups flour
1	tablespoon kosher salt		

- Preheat oven to 350 degrees.
- Blend butter with eggs. Stir in baking powder, onion powder, salt, pepper, onion and poppy seeds with a wooden spoon. Add flour and mix thoroughly until dough is stretching.
- Roll out half the dough onto a floured board to about ½-inch thick. Cut into rounds using a drinking glass. Place rounds on a floured baking sheet and pierce each with a fork.
- Bake 15 to 18 minutes or until golden and hollow sounding when tapped.

ORANGE BREAD
PAREVE

2½	cups flour	4	tablespoons margarine, melted
1¼	cups sugar	½	cup orange juice
2	teaspoons baking powder	2	tablespoons orange zest
½	teaspoon baking soda	2	tablespoons water
½	teaspoon salt	1	cup chopped walnuts (optional)
2	eggs, beaten		

- Preheat oven to 350 degrees.
- Combine flour, sugar, baking powder, baking soda and salt in a mixing bowl.
- In a separate bowl, mix eggs, margarine, orange juice, orange zest and water. Add mixture to dry ingredients and stir quickly until all ingredients are moistened. Mix in walnuts, if using. Pour batter into a greased and floured 9x5-inch loaf pan.
- Bake 1 hour. Cool in pan 10 minutes before removing to cool on a wire rack. Slice and serve with cream cheese.

MULTIGRAIN WILD RICE BREAD
DAIRY OR PAREVE

2 packages dry yeast
½ cup warm water (105-115 degrees)
1 teaspoon sugar
1 cup multi-grain cereal
1 tablespoon salt
½ cup honey
4 tablespoons butter or margarine

2 cups boiling water
1 cup cooked wild rice (see note below)
2 cups whole wheat flour
4 cups white flour, divided
2 tablespoons seeds, equal amounts of flax, poppy and sesame

- Preheat oven to 350 degrees.
- Stir together yeast, warm water and sugar in the large mixing bowl of an electric mixer. Let stand 5 minutes to proof.
- Meanwhile, combine cereal, salt, honey and butter in a 2- to 3-quart bowl. Pour boiling water over the top and stir until butter is melted. Add cooked rice and whole wheat flour and stir. When temperature of mixture cools to 100 to 110 degrees, add cereal mixture to yeast in large bowl and stir well.
- Stir in 3½ cups white flour and mix with a blade attachment until all flour is incorporated. Place dough onto a well-floured, cloth-covered board and sprinkle with some of remaining white flour. Cover with a cloth and let rest for a few minutes until the stickiness is gone.
- Knead until bits of grain come out of the dough onto the cloth. Place in a well-greased bowl, turning once to grease top of dough. Cover and let rise in a warm place for 1 to 1½ hours or until dough doubles in size.
- Punch dough down and cut in half with a serrated knife. Shape into 2 oval or round loaves. Sprinkle some of the seed mixture onto a pie plate or other flat dish. Brush one side of a loaf with water and place wet side of loaf in seeds. Repeat with second loaf.
- Place on a silicone-lined baking sheet and let rise, covered with a towel, for 30 minutes or until doubled in size.
- Spray loaves gently with water before baking. Bake 40 to 45 minutes or until bread is golden and sounds hollow when rapped on the bottom. Cool before slicing.

To cook wild rice, bring ⅓ cup dry wild rice in a saucepan with ⅔ cup cold water to a boil. Simmer 30 minutes. Remove from heat and allow to cool before draining. Yields about 1 cup rice.

BLUEBERRY ORANGE COFFEE CAKE
DAIRY

1	(8-ounce) package light or regular cream cheese, softened	2	teaspoons baking powder
1	stick unsalted butter, softened	½	teaspoon baking soda
		¼	teaspoon salt
1½	cups sugar	¼	cup orange juice
1	tablespoon orange zest	1	cup plain yogurt
5	eggs	1½	cups fresh or frozen blueberries
2⅔	cups all-purpose flour	2	tablespoons confectioners' sugar

- Preheat oven to 325 degrees.
- Cream together cream cheese and butter using an electric mixer in a bowl. Gradually add sugar and orange zest and beat until light and fluffy. Beat in eggs, one at a time.
- In a separate bowl, combine flour, baking powder, baking soda and salt. Add dry ingredients alternately with orange juice and yogurt to creamed mixture, beating until thick and smooth. Stir in blueberries.
- Spoon batter into a greased and floured 10-inch fluted or plain Bundt pan, or plain tube pan.
- Bake 50 to 55 minutes or until an inserted wooden toothpick comes out clean. Let cool in pan on a rack for 15 minutes.
- Invert and remove pan. Just before serving, dust with confectioners' sugar.

Soups & Salads

SOUPS & SALADS

Soup, a savory blend of ingredients, is a comfort for a cold winter day. According to food historians in ancient Egypt, chicken soup was the prescription for the common cold, thus rendering the term "Jewish penicillin". Our European ancestors take the credit for its accompaniments, which include noodles, *matzoh* balls and *kreplach*.

Our mothers and grandmothers have given us their traditions and secrets for the perfect mushroom barley, split pea soup and *borscht*. Whether with a simple broth or hearty layers of flavors, the aroma of soup warms your senses as you ladle it into the bowl — it warms you inside and out.

When preparing broth or stock, make some extra for your freezer. Freeze in ice cube trays and use to enhance stews and sauces.

We continue to add our own tastes to these classic recipes. We add cold fruit soups and gazpacho to our summer menus. We move beyond our eastern European heritage to add curries, black beans and dried chile peppers to our soup pots.

There are no rules for soup. Use your imagination. Experiment with herbs and spices to create your own flavors.

Walking down the produce aisle of today's markets or grocery stores, we see a variety of bright colors. Whether straight from farms across the country, or triple-washed, bagged and ready for use, the choices are endless.

Try some new combinations with different ingredients. Add a piece of grilled chicken or fish for a light summer meal. Scoop chicken or tuna salads into lettuce cups for a buffet or single plate. Add rice or pasta, try a new potato salad — hold the mayo. Chop your salad using a mezzaluna or hand-chopper. Add capers, anchovies or a can of your favorite beans. Try a new dressing recipe or simply squeeze some fresh lemon with a drizzle of fine extra virgin olive oil.

COLD BLUEBERRY SOUP
DAIRY

2	pints blueberries	½	teaspoon cinnamon
½	cup water	2	cups plain yogurt
½	cup sugar	½	cup orange juice

- Cook blueberries, water, sugar and cinnamon in a saucepan for 15 minutes or until blueberries are soft and sugar is dissolved.
- Blend in yogurt and orange juice. Purée mixture in a blender or with and immersion blender. If soup is too thick, add more orange juice, yogurt or water. Serve chilled.

Save a few blueberries to garnish the top of individual servings.

Soup can be prepared up to 1 day ahead. Do not freeze.

SPICY GAZPACHO
PAREVE

1	large cucumber, peeled, divided	¼	cup olive oil
2	large ripe tomatoes, or 10 plum tomatoes, peeled, divided	⅓	cup vinegar
		¼	teaspoon hot pepper sauce
1	medium onion, diced, divided	¼	teaspoon dried red pepper flakes
1	green bell pepper, chopped, divided	1	clove garlic, diced
		2	tablespoons lemon juice
1	(14½-ounce) can crushed tomatoes, divided	2	tablespoons lime juice
			Salt to taste
12	ounces tomato juice, divided	1½	teaspoons freshly ground black pepper
			Croutons for garnish

- In a food processor or blender, process ½ cucumber, 1 large tomato, ½ onion, ½ bell pepper, ½ can crushed tomatoes, ½ cup tomato juice.
- Transfer purée to a large soup bowl. Stir in remaining tomato juice, olive oil, vinegar, hot sauce, pepper flakes, garlic and lemon and lime juices.
- Chop remaining cucumber, tomato, onion and bell pepper. Add chopped vegetables along with remaining half can of crushed tomatoes to soup. Season soup with salt and pepper. Cover and chill.
- Add croutons to individual bowls just before serving.

"Worries go down better with soup."
(Jewish proverb)

Cucumber Soup

DAIRY

5	cucumbers, peeled, halved lengthwise and seeded	¼	cup lemon juice
			Chopped fresh parsley
6	scallions, chopped	1	quart buttermilk
2	tablespoons chopped fresh dill	1	pint sour cream
			Salt and pepper to taste

- Season cucumber halves with salt and let stand 30 minutes.
- Coarsely chop cucumber in a food processor with a metal blade. Add scallions, dill, lemon juice, parsley, buttermilk and sour cream to food processor. Blend mixture on high speed.
- Chill before serving. Season as needed with salt and pepper.

Borscht

DAIRY

6	medium beets, peeled	3	eggs
10	cups cold water	1	cup milk
	Juice of 3 medium lemons	1	cup sour cream (optional)
3	tablespoons sugar	1	cucumber, peeled, seeded and diced for garnish
2	teaspoons salt		

- Cut beets in half and place them in a soup pot with 10 cups cold water. Bring to a boil. Reduce heat and simmer, partially covered, for 30 to 40 minutes or until beets are tender. Skim foam from cooking liquid as necessary.
- Remove beets from liquid with a slotted spoon and cool to room temperature. Grate beets and return to cooking liquid along with lemon juice, sugar and salt. Bring to a simmer and cook 15 minutes. Remove from heat and cool 15 minutes.
- Beat eggs and milk together in a bowl. Gradually whisk 3 cups of warm borscht into egg mixture, then pour mixture slowly back into remaining borscht.
- Cover and refrigerate soup until very cold. Adjust seasonings as needed to achieve desired balance between sweet and sour.
- Garnish individual servings with sour cream and cucumber.

Authentic Borscht
DAIRY OR PAREVE

1	small onion, chopped	2	bay leaves
2	small heads cabbage, sliced	½	teaspoon black pepper
1	medium carrot, shredded	2	teaspoons chopped fresh parsley
4	cloves garlic, minced	2	teaspoons chopped fresh dill
4	quarts vegetable broth		
2	medium beets, julienned	½	cup vinegar
2-3	large potatoes, peeled and cubed	⅓	cup sugar
1	(6-ounce) can tomato paste		Salt to taste
2	tomatoes, peeled and cubed		Sour cream for garnish (optional)

- Sauté onion, cabbage, carrot and garlic in a large soup pot until softened.
- Add broth, beets, potato, tomato paste, tomato, bay leaves, pepper, parsley, dill, vinegar and sugar and boil 3 minutes. Season with salt.
- Reduce heat and simmer 4 to 5 hours or until potatoes are softened. Serve with a dollop of sour cream.

BEET AND GINGER SOUP WITH CUCUMBER
PAREVE OR MEAT

2	pounds small beets
3	tablespoons olive oil
1	small leek, chopped
1	clove garlic, crushed
3	tablespoons chopped ginger

3	cups chicken or vegetable broth
3	cups water
	Kosher salt to taste
	Juice of 1 lemon
½	English cucumber, peeled, seeded and chopped into ⅛-inch cubes

- Preheat oven to 400 degrees.
- Place beets in an aluminum foil pouch and seal tightly. Roast in oven 1 hour or until a fork easily pierces beets. Cool, then peel and quarter.
- Heat olive oil in a soup pot over medium heat. Add leek and cook 5 minutes or until starting to soften. Add garlic and ginger and cook 2 minutes longer. Add beets, broth and water and simmer 10 minutes.
- Process soup in batches in a food processor until smooth, or use an immersion blender. Return to pot if using processor and season with salt and lemon juice. Adjust seasonings as needed. Just before serving, add cucumber cubes.

SPLIT PEA SOUP
PAREVE OR MEAT

5	soup bones with meat (optional)	2	tablespoons salt	
4	large celery stalks with leaves, thinly sliced	1	teaspoon black pepper	
		½	teaspoon herbes de Provence	
4	carrots, thinly sliced	1	(16-ounce) bag dried green peas	
1	medium onion, minced			
2	cloves garlic, minced	1	(16-ounce) bag frozen peas	
5	quarts water or chicken or vegetable broth		Garlic croutons (optional)	

- If using beef bones, sear and brown meat over high heat in an 8-quart stockpot; set aside bones. Pour off all but 2 tablespoons fat in stockpot.

- Add celery, carrot, onion and garlic to fat in stockpot. Sauté until vegetables are translucent. If using meat, return bones to pot along with water. Season with salt, pepper and herbes de Provence. Bring to a boil. Skim foam off top of soup. Add dried peas and simmer 1 hour.

- Remove bones from soup. When cool enough to handle, remove meat from bones and return to soup, discarding bones and fat.

- Adjust seasonings as needed. Add frozen peas and cook 5 minutes or until thawed. Garnish individual servings with garlic croutons.

Soup thickens if refrigerated and served the next day. It freezes well.

For a smoky flavor, use 2 smoked turkey drumsticks.

The Yiddish word for pea soup is "mitzapuny". It was a shtetl staple that is now on every dinner menu across America. When times were tough, many of our grandmothers learned to make this hearty soup with bone scraps and vegetables that had been discarded by storekeepers. It is made with or without a meat base, with or without barley and with vegetables in addition to peas.

LAMB SOUP
MEAT

2	tablespoons extra virgin olive oil	½	teaspoon saffron
1	large onion, chopped		Salt and pepper to taste
1	pound lamb shoulder or leg, cut into ½-inch cubes	8	cups water
		½	cup barley
1	(28-ounce) can diced tomatoes, undrained	2	cups canned chickpeas, drained
2	teaspoons smoked sweet paprika	½	tablespoon dried mint
½	teaspoon cayenne pepper	3	tablespoons chopped fresh Italian parsley

- Heat oil in a large saucepan. Add onion and lamb and sauté 5 minutes.
- Stir in tomatoes with juice, paprika, cayenne pepper, saffron and salt and pepper. Add water and simmer 45 minutes.
- Add barley and chickpeas and simmer 15 minutes. Add mint and parsley and cook 5 minutes longer.
- 6-8 servings

Soup freezes well.

PEASANT SOUP
PAREVE

2	tablespoons olive oil	1	stalk celery, thickly sliced
1	medium onion, chopped	1	tablespoon chopped garlic
2	shallots, chopped	4	quarts water
1½	cups dried navy beans		Salt and pepper to taste
3	carrots, sliced		Vegetable bouillon to taste
1	small head cabbage, cored and coarsely chopped	1	loaf sourdough bread
1	leek, sliced		

- Heat olive oil in a large heavy pot over medium heat. Add onion and shallots and cook 5 minutes or until slightly softened.
- Increase to high heat and add beans, carrot, cabbage, leek, celery and garlic. Stir in water and season with salt and pepper and bouillon. Bring to a boil. Reduce heat to low and gently simmer, partially covered, for 4 hours.
- Adjust seasoning. Serve with bread to soak up any leftover broth.
- 10 servings

FAVORITE LENTIL SOUP
DAIRY OR PAREVE

2	tablespoons olive oil	7	cups vegetable broth
2	cups chopped onion	1½	cups dried lentils, rinsed and picked over
3	carrots, coarsely grated		
¾	teaspoon dried marjoram, crumbled	½	teaspoon salt (optional)
		¼-½	teaspoon black pepper
¾	teaspoon dried thyme, crumbled	⅓	cup chopped fresh parsley, or 2 tablespoons dried
1	(28-ounce) can tomatoes, undrained and coarsely chopped	4	ounces Cheddar cheese, grated (optional)

- Heat oil in a large stockpot. Add onion, carrot, marjoram and thyme and sauté about 5 minutes. Stir in tomatoes, broth and lentils. Bring to a boil.
- Reduce heat and simmer, covered, for 1 hour or until lentils are tender.
- Add salt, pepper and parsley and simmer for a few extra minutes. Sprinkle individual servings with cheese.

Soup freezes well, but do not freeze with the cheese.

CARROT AND GINGER SOUP
PAREVE

3	tablespoons diced onion	¼	cup peeled and diced sweet potato
½	teaspoon olive oil		
1	tablespoon maple syrup	1	teaspoon salt
½	teaspoon honey	¼	teaspoon black pepper
1	tablespoon grated ginger	¼	teaspoon dried thyme
1	cup chopped carrot	¼	teaspoon minced garlic
3	cups vegetable stock		

- Sauté onion in olive oil until translucent in a medium pan over low heat. Add maple syrup, honey and ginger and cook 10 minutes or until onion turns golden brown.
- Stir in carrot, stock, sweet potato, salt, pepper, thyme and garlic and simmer 10 minutes or until carrot and potato are soft.
- Purée until smooth in a blender or with an immersion blender. Warm soup in a saucepan over medium heat before serving.

For an easy vegetarian meal, try a tabbouleh salad and a loaf of your favorite bread to accompany this light soup.

RIBOLLITA
DAIRY OR PAREVE

The soup should be thick. It is enhanced by sprinkling Parmesan cheese on top. It tastes better a day after it is made.

1 large bunch flat-leaf parsley, chopped
4 cloves garlic, chopped
2 bunches celery, chopped
1 pound carrots, chopped
4 medium-size red onions, chopped
¼ cup olive oil
1 (28-ounce) can plum tomatoes, undrained
4 pounds cavolo nero or Swiss chard, coarsely chopped

3 cups canned cannellini beans, undrained, divided
2 loaves stale hearty Italian bread, crusts removed, sliced or torn
Olive oil
Salt and pepper to taste
Freshly grated Parmesan cheese (optional)

- Sauté parsley, garlic, celery, carrot and onion in ¼ cup olive oil in a large pot for 30 minutes. Add tomatoes with juice and cook over medium to low heat for 30 minutes.
- Stir in cavolo nero and half the cannellini beans with enough juice from canned beans to cover. Simmer 30 minutes.
- Purée remaining half of beans in a food processor and add to soup. Add enough water to thin soup to desired consistency.
- Add bread pieces and extra olive oil and season with salt and pepper. Sprinkle with Parmesan cheese.

Safta's Chicken Soup

MEAT

1	whole kosher chicken, cut up	1	large or 2 small parsnips, chopped
6	carrots, chopped		Chicken bouillon to taste
3	stalks celery, chopped		Handful of fresh dill (optional)
1	onion, chopped		Salt to taste
1	leek, white part only, chopped		

- Combine chicken pieces, carrot, celery, onion, leek and parsnip in a large soup pot. Add water to cover and bring to a boil, skimming off foam from top as needed.
- Mix chicken bouillon with 1 cup of boiling soup broth and add back to soup when dissolved. Taste and add more bouillon as needed in same manner.
- Simmer, partially covered, for 1½ to 2 hours. Add dill during final 15 minutes of cooking. Remove chicken; skin, debone and chop and add meat back into soup. Season soup to taste with salt.

Our family always looks forward to Safta's chicken soup at all the Jewish holidays. She's been making it since we came here from Russia, and no matter how hard we try to duplicate it, it never quite tastes like Safta's. Her secret is that if her soup doesn't taste right to her, then she will continue to "scheit areine" (in Yiddish it means "pour in") more seasonings until it tastes just so.

Growing up in New Haven, I often accompanied my grandfather to Legion Avenue to buy chickens for Shabbat. The sawdust on the floors, chickens freshly butchered and plucked all arrayed was disquieting to a young child. That all changed when we got home and my grandmother took over. Her soup was rich and yellow in a way I cannot duplicate. The noodles - broad or thin, alphabets or small squares - shimmered in her old wide soup plates. All she used was chicken, carrots, celery, onion, salt and water. No parsnip and certainly no dill. Maybe it was the chicken feet.

MOM'S FLOATING MATZOH BALLS
MEAT

3	eggs	¾	teaspoon salt
6	tablespoons club soda (not water - this is the "float" part)		Chopped fresh parsley (optional)
6	tablespoons chicken fat	6	quarts chicken broth, or half broth and half water
¾	cup matzoh meal		

- Combine eggs, club soda, chicken fat, matzoh meal, salt and parsley in a small bowl. Refrigerate at least 3 hours. Prepare only 1 batch per bowl, do not double batch in same bowl.
- To test each batch, bring water to a boil in a small pan. Drop a walnut-size ball into boiling water. If it holds together, it is ready. If not, add a small amount of matzoh meal and retest. Repeat process until matzoh ball holds together.
- Heat chicken broth with enough water to fill an 8- to 10-quart saucepan three-fourths full. Bring to a boil. Drop in matzoh balls. Boil 20 minutes and check for desired texture. Drain and let stand on a broiler pan until ready to add to soup.
- 15 to 20 balls

Recipe may be used for Passover.

Common sense for mastering the texture of your matzoh ball ... the more you "patchke" with the balls, the heavier they will become (Aunt Lilly's cannon balls). To put it another way, the less you touch them to shape them, the fluffier they will turn out (Aunt Elaine's). In true Jewish tradition, there is debate over which way we eat them. There is a choice!

Knaidlach (matzoh balls) among Jews, quenelles in France, uszki in Poland, dumplings in America - each had their own soup accompaniment.

My Mom taught me to make each batch separately, and to test the matzoh balls for readiness. You either come from a "light as a feather" or a "deliciously dense" family when it comes to matzoh ball preferences. Ours float like feathers. This is a recipe in memory of my beloved mother.

Aunt Sylvia's rule - never remove the lid while cooking matzoh balls or else! (Use your imagination.)

SALMON KREPLACH FOR CHICKEN OR VEGETABLE SOUP

PAREVE

½	cup minced smoked salmon	1	teaspoon dried dill, or 1 tablespoon fresh
½	cup minced poached salmon	1	teaspoon lemon juice
1	shallot, minced	1	tablespoon white wine
½	teaspoon salt	1	egg
½	teaspoon black pepper	2	teaspoons water
¼	cup dry bread crumbs	1	package wonton wrappers

- Combine all salmon, shallot, salt, pepper, bread crumbs, dill, lemon juice and wine and mix well.
- Beat egg with water; set aside.
- Fill each wonton wrapper with 1 teaspoon salmon filling. Fold wrapper in half diagonally. Seal with egg mixture around all edges.
- Drop kreplach into boiling salted water and cook 10 to 12 minutes or until kreplach float to the top.

BEEF STOCK

MEAT

5-6	pounds beef soup bones	1	large potato, peeled and cubed
2	medium onions, quartered		
4	carrots, cut into chunks	10	whole peppercorns
12½	cups water, divided	5	sprigs parsley
3	stalks celery with leaves, cut into chunks	2	bay leaves
1	tomato, diced	1	tablespoon salt
1	cup chopped parsnip	2	teaspoons dried thyme
		3	cloves garlic, halved

- Preheat oven to 450 degrees.
- Place soup bones, onion and carrot in a roasting pan. Bake, uncovered, for 30 minutes.
- Drain fat. Place bones, onion and carrot into a large soup pot. Rinse roasting pan with ½ cup water and add this to the soup pot, scraping in all remains from bottom of pan.
- Add remaining 12 cups water, celery, tomato, parsnip, potato, peppercorns, parsley, bay leaves, salt, thyme and garlic. Bring to a boil. Reduce heat and simmer, covered, for 4 to 5 hours.
- Cool slightly, then strain stock through a cheesecloth and discard all solid remains. Chill or freeze until ready to use.

To remove all flecks from stock, combine ¼ cup cold water, 1 egg white and 1 crushed eggshell. Add to stock and boil. Remove stock from heat and let stand 10 minutes. Strain again through cheesecloth.

Vegetable Stock
PAREVE

2	tablespoons vegetable or safflower oil	3	parsnips, peeled and cut into chunks
8	carrots, cut into chunks	2	teaspoons dried thyme
8	stalks celery with leaves, halved	2	bay leaves
2	large onions, quartered	5	sprigs parsley
3	medium turnips, peeled and quartered	3	leeks, white part only, chopped
			Salt and pepper to taste

- Heat vegetable oil in a large soup pot. Add carrot, celery, onion, turnip and parsnip and sauté 5 minutes.
- Add thyme, bay leaves, parsley and leeks and enough water to cover by 3 to 4-inches. Season with salt and pepper.
- Bring to a boil. Reduce heat and simmer 1½ hours, skimming top occasionally. Cool slightly before straining through a cheesecloth.
- Refrigerate or freeze. Broth will keep 3 days in refrigerator or at least 3 months in a well-sealed container in the freezer.

Basic Chicken Stock
MEAT

2	pounds chicken parts	8	peppercorns
2	medium stalks celery, coarsely chopped	1	bay leaf
		10	sprigs parsley
2	medium carrots, coarsely chopped	4	sprigs dill, or 1 tablespoon dried
1	medium onion, quartered		Salt to taste
8	cups water		

- Combine all ingredients in a soup pot and bring to a boil. Skim off foam as it accumulates. Reduce heat and simmer 2 hours.
- Strain broth through a cheesecloth and discard all solids. Freeze if not using within 2 days.

It is always nice to have homemade stock on hand. Freeze in ice cube trays and use as needed for a little extra boost to soup, stews, sauces, pasta and more.

NORMA'S CABBAGE SOUP

MEAT

2	pounds short ribs or flanken
8	cups water
1½	heads cabbage, sliced
2	(28-ounce) cans whole tomatoes in juice or tomato purée

1	onion, chopped
½	cup brown sugar
½	cup granulated sugar
1	teaspoon sour salt
1	(12-ounce) bottle ketchup

- Place short ribs and water in a large pot. Bring to a boil. Skim fat from top of pot.
- Add cabbage, tomatoes, onion, both sugars, salt and ketchup. Cook several hours or until meat is tender. Taste broth frequently and add more sugar or salt as needed.

This recipe makes quite a bit of soup and freezes well.

NOT YOUR REGULAR CABBAGE SOUP

MEAT

1¼ pounds top round or flanken beef

1 medium onion, cut into ¼-inch dice

1 medium carrot, cut into ¼-inch dice

2 medium stalks celery, cut into ¼-inch dice

1 medium-size green bell pepper, cut into ¼-inch dice

½ cup rich red wine

½ cup steak sauce

2 tablespoons Worcestershire sauce

1½ teaspoons salt

½ teaspoon black pepper

1 teaspoon chopped fresh garlic

¼ teaspoon dried oregano, crushed

¼ teaspoon dried thyme, crushed

½ teaspoon whole caraway seeds

9 cups water

2 cubes beef bouillon, crumbled

½ head large green cabbage, cut into 1-inch pieces

1 (3-ounce) jar roasted red peppers, drained and chopped

Set aside an afternoon to let this soup simmer for several hours.

- Trim beef, reserving fat. Cut beef and fat into 1-inch cubes. Cook beef fat with meat cubes over medium heat in a large 6-quart pot until brown but not burned. Remove browned fat and set aside, leaving liquid fat in pot. Remove beef from pot and set aside.

- Add onion, carrot, celery and bell pepper to fat in pot and sauté 4 minutes or until softened. Add beef back to pot and sauté over medium heat for 3 minutes. Return browned fat to pot. Stir in wine, steak sauce, Worcestershire sauce, salt, pepper, garlic, oregano, thyme and caraway seeds. Add water and beef bouillon and stir well. Add cabbage and roasted peppers and bring to a boil. Reduce heat and simmer, skimming top regularly with a spoon, until scum stops accumulating on top. Partially cover and simmer 3 hours, stirring occasionally. Skim top as needed. Adjust seasoning. Add more water if soup is too thick.

POTATO LEEK SOUP
DAIRY OR PAREVE

8	large shallots, sliced ¼-inch thick	2	large russet potatoes, diced
6	tablespoons butter or margarine, divided	2	(14-ounce) cans vegetable broth
1½	tablespoons sugar	1	teaspoon dried thyme
8	leeks, chopped	2	bunches scallions, chopped
1	large onion, chopped		Salt and pepper to taste

- Preheat oven to 350 degrees.
- Place shallot slices on a pan lined with quick-release foil. Dot with 2 tablespoons butter and sprinkle with sugar. Bake 20 minutes to caramelize.
- Melt remaining 4 tablespoons butter in a large soup pot. Add leeks and onion and cook and stir until tender. Add potatoes and cook, stirring frequently, until soft. Add broth and bring to a boil. Reduce heat and simmer, covered, for 30 minutes.
- Blend soup until smooth with a food processor or with an immersion blender. Stir in thyme and scallions and season with salt and pepper.
- Garnish with carmelized shallots
- 4 servings

Zucchini Bisque

DAIRY

⅔ cup chopped onion
2 cups chopped zucchini (about 3 medium)
1½ cups vegetable stock

¼ teaspoon salt (optional)
¼ teaspoon curry powder
¼ cup plain low-fat yogurt

- Combine onion, zucchini and vegetable stock in a medium saucepan. Bring to a boil over medium-high heat. Reduce heat and simmer 10 minutes.
- Transfer mixture to a blender along with salt, curry powder and yogurt and process until smooth, or use an immersion blender. Serve hot or cold.
- Four (¾-cup) servings

Italian Zucchini Soup

DAIRY

2 tablespoons olive oil
1 large onion, thinly sliced
1 (16-ounce) can plum tomatoes, undrained
1 pound zucchini, cut into ½-inch rounds

1 large potato, peeled and diced
Salt and pepper to taste
Freshly grated Parmesan cheese to taste
Fresh basil leaves for garnish

A zucchini soup with an Italian flavor is also easy to make. There is such an abundance of this vegetable in the summertime.

- Heat olive oil in a saucepan. Add onion and sauté until clear. Add tomatoes with juice and cook 10 to 15 minutes or until thickened.
- Add zucchini and potato and enough water to cover. Season with salt and pepper. Simmer 30 to 40 minutes or until vegetables are softened. Serve hot with Parmesan cheese and garnish with basil leaves.
- 6 servings

MINESTRONE SOUP
PAREVE OR DAIRY

¼	cup vegetable oil	1½	cups cubed potato
1	cup chopped onion	1½	cups cubed sweet potato
½	cup chopped celery	1	quart vegetable broth
¾	cup chopped carrot	2	cloves garlic, minced
1	(19-ounce) can cannelloni beans, drained	2	tablespoons dried parsley, or 4 tablespoons fresh
1	cup shredded cabbage		
2	(14½-ounce) cans stewed tomatoes	1	teaspoon salt
1	(16-ounce) can chickpeas, drained	1	cup small pasta, such as elbow
2	tablespoons tomato paste	½-¾	cup Parmesan cheese (optional)

- Heat oil in a soup pot. Add onion, celery and carrot and sauté 5 minutes. Add beans, cabbage, tomatoes, chickpeas, tomato paste, all potatoes, broth, garlic, parsley and salt. Bring to a boil. Cover and reduce heat. Simmer 1 hour or until vegetables are tender.

- Add pasta and simmer 20 minutes longer. Adjust seasoning to taste and serve with Parmesan cheese.

Hearty Vegetable Barley Soup

MEAT

8	ounces lean ground beef	2	cups peeled and cubed potato, or more to taste
½	cup chopped onion		
4	cloves garlic, minced	2	cubes beef bouillon, or to taste
7	cups water		
1	(14½-ounce) can unsalted whole tomatoes, undrained and chopped	½	teaspoon dried basil, crushed
		1	bay leaf
½	cup medium barley	1	(16-ounce) package frozen Italian green beans
½	cup sliced celery		
½	cup sliced carrot		

- Brown beef in a 4-quart saucepan or a Dutch oven. Remove meat from pan, drain fat and wipe pan clean. Return beef to pan with onion and garlic and cook until onion is tender. Drain off any fat that has accumulated.

- Add water, tomatoes, barley, celery, carrot, potato, bouillon, basil and bay leaf to saucepan. Cover and bring to a boil. Reduce heat and simmer about 1 hour, stirring occasionally. Taste and add more bouillon if needed.

- Stir in green beans and cook 10 minutes longer or until beans are tender. Add more water if soup thickens while standing.

- 12 (1-cup) servings

VEGETABLE BARLEY SOUP

PAREVE

2	quarts vegetable broth		3	bay leaves
1	cup dry barley		1	teaspoon garlic powder
2	large carrots, chopped		1	teaspoon sugar
2	stalks celery, chopped		1	teaspoon salt
1	(14½-ounce) can diced tomatoes, undrained		½	teaspoon black pepper
1	zucchini, chopped		1	teaspoon dried parsley
1	(15-ounce) can garbanzo beans, drained		1	teaspoon curry powder
			1	teaspoon paprika
1	onion, chopped		1	teaspoon Worcestershire sauce

- Pour broth into a large pot. Add barley, carrot, celery, tomatoes, zucchini, garbanzo beans, onion and bay leaves. Season with garlic powder, sugar, salt, pepper, parsley, curry powder, paprika and Worcestershire sauce.

- Bring to a boil. Cover and simmer over medium-low heat for 1½ hours. Soup will be thick. Adjust thickness as desired by adding more broth or less barley. Remove bay leaf before serving.

- 8 servings

NANA'S MUSHROOM-BARLEY SOUP
DAIRY OR PAREVE

½	cup raw pearl barley	2	cloves garlic, minced
6½	cups stock or water, divided	1	heaping cup chopped onion
3-4	tablespoons tamari or soy sauce	1	pound fresh mushrooms, sliced
3-4	tablespoons dry sherry	½	teaspoon salt, or to taste
3	tablespoons butter or margarine		Freshly ground black pepper or to taste

- Cook barley in 1½ cups stock in a large soup pot until tender. Add remaining 5 cups stock, tamari and sherry.
- Melt butter in a skillet. Add garlic and onion and sauté until softened. Add mushrooms and salt and continue to sauté until mushrooms are softened.
- Add mushroom mixture and any accumulated juices to pot with barley. Season generously with black pepper. Simmer, covered, over low heat for 20 minutes. Adjust seasonings as needed.
- 6-8 servings

Tomato Carrot Soup
PAREVE OR MEAT

This soup can be served hot or cold or at room temperature in simple white bowls or in large wine goblets. Serve with White House Saltines.

3	leeks, white part only, chopped	1½	tablespoons tomato paste
½-¾	pound carrots, sliced	½	teaspoon dried thyme
3	tablespoons margarine	1	tablespoon brown sugar
1	(28-ounce) can crushed tomatoes	½	teaspoon dried red pepper flakes
3	ripe plum tomatoes, diced	2	tablespoons grated fresh ginger
1½	cups tomato juice	4	cloves garlic, crushed
5	cups canned chicken or vegetable broth	3	tablespoons chopped fresh cilantro for garnish

- Cook leeks and carrots in margarine over medium heat for 5 minutes or until softened, stirring from time to time.
- Stir in all tomatoes, tomato juice, broth, tomato paste, thyme, brown sugar, pepper flakes, ginger and garlic. Bring to a boil. Cover and simmer 40 minutes. Cool.
- Process in batches in a food processor until smooth. Garnish each serving with about 1 teaspoon cilantro.
- 8 servings

White House Saltines
(for soup)
PAREVE

24	saltine crackers Ice water	4	tablespoons margarine, melted

- Preheat oven to 400 degrees.
- Float saltines one at a time in ice water until well soaked, but not falling apart. Shake off excess water from each cracker and place carefully on a greased baking sheet. Use a soft pastry brush to coat top of crackers with melted margarine.
- Bake 15 minutes. Reduce oven temperature to 300 degrees and continue baking 45 minutes or until nutty brown. After heat is reduced, watch carefully as crackers can turn from charming brown to unattractive black very quickly.
- Cool completely before placing in an airtight container. Crackers will last in sealed container for at least a week.

CORN AND WILD RICE SOUP WITH KOSHER SMOKED SAUSAGE

MEAT

12½ cups canned low-sodium chicken broth, divided

1¼ cups dry wild rice (7½ ounces)

6¼ cups frozen white shoepeg corn, thawed, divided

2 tablespoons vegetable oil

10 ounces fully-cooked turkey or chicken sausage, cut into ½-inch slices

3 carrots, diced

2 medium onions, chopped

1½ cups non-dairy creamer or soy milk

Salt and pepper to taste

Chopped fresh chives or parsley for garnish

• Bring 5 cups broth to a simmer in a heavy medium saucepan over medium heat. Add wild rice and simmer, stirring occasionally, for 40 minutes or until all liquid evaporates and rice is tender.

• Meanwhile, purée 3¾ cups corn and 1½ cups broth in a food processor until thick and almost smooth.

• Heat vegetable oil in a heavy large saucepan or Dutch oven over medium-high heat. Add sausage and sauté 5 minutes or until sausage starts to brown. Add carrot and onion and cook and stir 3 minutes. Add remaining 6 cups broth and bring to a simmer. Reduce heat to low and simmer soup 15 minutes.

• Add cooked wild rice, corn purée and remaining 2½ cups corn to soup. Cook 15 minutes or until rice is very tender and flavors have blended. Stir in creamer and season with salt and pepper. Thin soup with extra broth if desired. Garnish with chopped chives or parsley.

Soup can be made up to 2 days ahead. Cool completely before refrigerating or freezing. May need to add more broth when reheating.

ROASTED VEGETABLE SOUP

PAREVE

3	medium carrots, quartered lengthwise	1	tablespoon olive oil
2	large tomatoes, quartered		Salt and pepper to taste
1	large onion, cut into 8 wedges	6	cups canned vegetable broth, or as needed, divided
½	small butternut squash, peeled, seeded and cut lengthwise into ½-inch thick wedges	4	cups finely chopped kale
		3	large fresh thyme sprigs
		1	bay leaf
6	cloves garlic, unpeeled	1	(15-ounce) can great Northern beans, drained

- Preheat oven to 400 degrees.
- Arrange carrots, tomatoes, onion, squash and garlic on a greased baking sheet. Drizzle with olive oil and sprinkle with salt and pepper. Toss to coat. Bake 45 minutes or until vegetables are brown and tender, stirring occasionally.
- Transfer carrots and squash to a work surface. Cut into ½-inch pieces; set aside. Peel garlic and place in a food processor. Add tomatoes and onion and purée until almost smooth. Pour ½ cup broth onto baking sheet and scrape up any browned bits. Transfer broth and vegetable purée to a large pot. Add remaining 5½ cups broth, kale, thyme and bay leaf to pot and bring to a boil. Reduce heat and simmer, uncovered, for 30 minutes or until kale is tender.
- Add beans and reserved carrots and squash to soup. Simmer 8 minutes to allow flavors to blend, adding more broth if needed to thin soup. Season with salt and pepper. Discard thyme sprigs and bay leaf. Soup can be made a day ahead, covered and chilled; bring to a simmer before serving.
- 6 servings

BLACK BEAN SOUP
PAREVE OR MEAT

1	(16-ounce) package dried black beans	1¼	teaspoons coriander
7	cups beef or vegetable broth	2	teaspoons cumin
2	teaspoons salt (or less to taste if using bouillon cubes)	1	(28-ounce) can tomatoes, undrained and chopped
		½	cup orange juice
3	tablespoons oil	¼	cup dry sherry
1½	cups chopped carrot	¼	teaspoon cayenne pepper
2	stalks celery, chopped	1	teaspoon lemon juice
1	medium onion, chopped	¼	teaspoon black pepper
2	cloves garlic, minced		Chopped onion for garnish

- Rinse beans, cover with water and soak at least 4 hours or overnight; drain.
- Place beans in a large soup pot. Add broth and salt and cook until beans are tender.
- Heat oil in a skillet. Add carrot, celery, onion, garlic, coriander and cumin and sauté. Add sautéed mixture along with undrained tomatoes to beans. Simmer over low heat for 30 minutes.
- Stir in orange juice, sherry, cayenne pepper, lemon juice and black pepper. Adjust seasonings as needed. Garnish individual servings with chopped onion.
- 12 servings

You may purée one-third of the soup and add it back to the pot. If vegetable broth is substituted for the beef broth, soup can be served with a dollop of sour cream — soup then becomes dairy.

Some Russian Jews made their way to Cuba when United States quotas for immigration had been met in the 1940's. Many had the foresight to leave Cuba before the Communist regime changed their way of life and brought to this country their Cuban-European recipes. Black beans, a Cuban dietary staple, are used in dips, over rice and in soups. They are the preferred protein of vegetarians.

CREAM OF ASPARAGUS SOUP

DAIRY

1	pound fresh or canned asparagus, chopped, tips reserved	3-4	sprigs fresh parsley, chopped
1	onion, finely chopped	6	cups vegetable stock
4	tablespoons butter, divided	2	tablespoons flour
	Salt and freshly ground black pepper to taste	1/4	teaspoon mace (optional)
		2	egg yolks, lightly beaten
		1/2	cup heavy cream
			Croutons

- For fresh asparagus, wash and peel spears and reserve tips for garnish. If using canned, reserve liquid for soup.
- Lightly sauté asparagus and onion in 1 tablespoon butter. Season with salt and pepper. Add parsley and stock. Cover and simmer 10 minutes or until asparagus is tender.
- Blend mixture in a food processor or with an immersion blender until smooth.
- Melt remaining 3 tablespoons butter in a saucepan. Stir in flour until smooth. Cook and stir 1 to 2 minutes. Blend mixture into soup.
- Bring soup to a boil. Reduce heat to a simmer. Add mace.
- In a small saucepan, cook asparagus tips 2 to 3 minutes or until tender.
- Add egg yolk, a few teaspoons at a time, to soup, stirring constantly. Gently stir in cream. Reheat soup, but do not allow to boil.
- Serve hot with croutons and reserved asparagus tips sprinkled on top.
- 4-6 servings

ANAT'S CURRIED SQUASH SOUP

PAREVE OR MEAT

2	teaspoons vegetable oil	1	cup apple cider
2	onions, chopped	½	cup dry white rice
3	cloves garlic, diced	2	pounds butternut squash, cubed
1	tablespoon curry		Salt and freshly ground pepper to taste
1	teaspoon cumin (optional)		
6	cups chicken or vegetable stock		

- Heat oil in a saucepan. Add onion and garlic and sauté until softened.
- Add curry, cumin, stock, cider, rice and squash to saucepan and cook 40 minutes. Season with salt and pepper.
- Blend soup in a food processor or with an immersion blender. Serve hot and thick.

VEGETARIAN HOT AND SOUR SOUP

PAREVE

8	dried mushrooms, such as Chinese, porcini, etc.	½	cup rice wine vinegar
10	cups vegetable stock	2	teaspoons sesame oil
10	slices fresh ginger	2	teaspoons dried red pepper flakes
1	teaspoon whole peppercorns	1	tablespoon soy sauce
8	scallions, sliced diagonally	¼	cup cornstarch mixed with 3 tablespoons water
1	red bell pepper, cut into strips	½	teaspoon sugar
		1	clove garlic, crushed
1	cup sliced mushrooms	3	drops hot pepper sauce, or more to taste

- Soak dried mushrooms in warm water for 20 minutes. Drain and squeeze dry, reserving liquid. Cut mushrooms into thin slices, discarding stalks.
- Bring reserved mushroom liquid, vegetable stock, ginger and peppercorns to a boil in a large saucepan. Reduce heat and simmer 10 minutes. Strain, discarding spices.
- Return strained broth to saucepan. Add scallions, bell pepper, all mushrooms, vinegar, sesame oil, pepper flakes, soy sauce, cornstarch mixture, sugar, garlic and hot sauce. Simmer 10 minutes. Serve with rice.`

HARIRA WITH LAMB OR CHICKEN

MEAT

¼	cup olive oil, or as needed
1	large yellow onion, chopped
2	medium-size red onions, chopped
4	cloves garlic, chopped
3	pounds skinless, boneless chicken thighs, or boneless lamb shoulder, cut into 1-inch cubes
2½	teaspoons ground turmeric
2	teaspoons freshly ground black pepper
2	teaspoons cinnamon
½	teaspoon ground ginger
¼-½	teaspoon cayenne pepper
	Salt to taste

1	cup chopped celery
1	cup chopped fresh cilantro
1	(29-ounce) can diced tomatoes, juice reserved
1	fresh tomato, chopped
12	cups water
1½	cups dried green lentils
2	(15-ounce) cans chickpeas, drained
6	ounces fine noodles or vermicelli, broken into 3-inch pieces
3	eggs, lightly beaten (optional)
	Juice of 2 lemons (optional)

Harira is a meat and vegetable soup traditionally eaten by Moroccan Jews after their Yom Kippur fast. Enjoy it on a cold day with a mixed green salad and a favorite loaf of bread.

- Warm olive oil in a large soup pot over medium heat. Add all onions and garlic and cook until softened. Remove onion mixture from pot and set aside.

- If needed, add a bit more oil to same pot and increase heat to medium-high. Add meat and brown, in batches, for 2 minutes per side.

- Add onion mixture along with turmeric, black pepper, cinnamon, ginger and cayenne. Cook, stirring occasionally, for 5 minutes. Season generously with salt. Add celery, cilantro, all tomatoes and simmer 15 minutes.

- Add reserved tomato juice, water and lentils and bring to a boil. Reduce heat and simmer, covered, for 2 hours. (If making ahead, stop here, cool and refrigerate until ready to reheat.)

- Increase heat to high and stir in chickpeas and noodles. Cook 10 minutes or until noodles are al dente. Adjust seasoning as needed.

- Traditionally, at this point, beaten egg is added to soup. Cook and stir until egg is cooked through. Squeeze lemon juice into soup and stir.

Recipe can be easily halved.
The soup tastes best when made a day before serving.

Strawberry Mango Mesclun Salad
DAIRY

¼ cup sugar
¼ cup canola or vegetable oil
½ cup balsamic vinegar
1 teaspoon salt
8 cups mesclun mixed greens
2 cups sweetened dried cranberries or blueberries

8 ounces strawberries, quartered
1 large mango, peeled and cubed
½ cup chopped onion
1 cup slivered almonds
¼ cup Gorgonzola cheese

- Combine sugar, oil, vinegar and salt in a jar. Cover tightly and shake.
- In a large bowl, combine greens, cranberries, strawberries, mango and onion and toss to mix.
- Add dressing to salad and toss to coat. Sprinkle with almonds and cheese.

Mesclun is a salad mix of young, small salad greens like mache, radicchio, frisée and arugula, to name a few. The colors and textures vary enough to make a pretty salad simply tossed with your favorite light dressing.

Other lettuce trivia ... head lettuces: crisphead is iceberg and butterhead is Bibb or Boston.

Arlyn's Tuna Fish Salad
PAREVE

2 (6-ounce) cans white albacore tuna, rinsed, drained and finely chopped
1 apple, peeled and cut into ¼-inch dice
2 stalks celery, chopped
2 tablespoons dried cranberries, chopped

1 teaspoon Worcestershire sauce
1 pinch freshly ground pepper
1 pinch onion powder
½ cup mayonnaise

- Combine tuna, apple, celery and cranberries in a serving bowl.
- Add Worcestershire sauce, pepper and onion powder and mix. Blend in mayonnaise. Refrigerate until serving.

REFRESHING ROMAINE SALAD
PAREVE

Dressing

1	teaspoon celery seeds	2	tablespoons honey
¾	teaspoon salt	⅓	cup cider or distilled
1	teaspoon dry mustard		vinegar
3	drops hot pepper sauce, or more to taste	⅔	cup vegetable oil

Salad

1	head romaine lettuce, outer leaves discarded, torn into bite-size pieces	½	green bell pepper, thinly sliced
3	navel oranges, peeled and cut into bite-size sections	3	scallions, white and light green parts only, chopped
½	cucumber, peeled and sliced	⅓	cup sliced or slivered almonds

- Coarsely crush celery seeds with the back of a spoon or a mortar and pestle.
- Combine crushed celery seeds, salt, mustard and hot sauce in a bowl. Add honey and vinegar and whisk briskly to combine.
- Slowly pour in oil, whisking constantly until thickened and well mixed. Store in a jar with a tight fitting lid.
- Combine all salad ingredients in a large bowl. Use ingredients listed and amounts as a general guide; add more or less of each ingredient as needed to suit taste and party size.
- Just before serving, shake jar of dressing vigorously and pour over salad; do not add too much dressing.

A light vegetable oil like canola is preferable to olive oil in this recipe. Lightly toasting the almonds at 300 degrees for 10 minutes, or until pale golden, brings out their flavor.

Romaine lettuce is crunchier than other lettuces. It has colorful dark green leaves on the outside and changes to lighter green-white leaves on the inside. It works nicely tossed with other softer varieties of lettuce.

Orzo, Feta Cheese and Cherry Tomato Salad

DAIRY

½	cup pine nuts
3	tablespoons olive oil, divided
1	pound orzo
2	large cloves garlic, chopped
1	cup chopped flat-leaf parsley

3	tablespoons red wine vinegar
	Salt and freshly ground pepper to taste
1	pint cherry tomatoes, cut into bite-size chunks
8	ounces feta cheese, crumbled

- Sauté pine nuts in 1½ tablespoons olive oil in a small skillet until golden brown. Transfer to paper towel to drain and cool.
- Cook orzo according to package directions; drain.
- Whisk together remaining 1½ tablespoons olive oil, garlic, parsley, red wine vinegar, and salt and pepper for a dressing.
- In a large salad bowl, combine tomatoes, feta, orzo and pine nuts. Pour dressing over the top and gently toss.

Tuna Salad - Hold the Mayo

PAREVE

1	(16-ounce) can cannelloni beans, drained and rinsed
1	(6-ounce) can albacore tuna, drained and broken into chunks
½	cup chopped cucumber
2	tomatoes, diced
¼	cup finely diced red onion

1	tablespoon fresh lemon juice, or more to taste
2	teaspoons Dijon mustard
¼	cup olive oil
¼	cup chopped fresh basil
	Salt and pepper to taste
	Lettuce leaves

- Combine beans, tuna, cucumber, tomato and onion in a large bowl.
- In a small bowl, mix lemon juice and mustard. Gradually whisk in oil and stir in basil. Drizzle dressing over salad and toss to mix. Season with salt and pepper.
- To serve, arrange lettuce leaves on a plate. Spoon tuna salad on lettuce.
- 2 servings

Couscous Salad for a Crowd
PAREVE OR MEAT

6	cups chicken or vegetable stock	1½	cups finely diced carrot
5	tablespoons olive oil, divided	1	cup chopped scallions
½	teaspoon ground ginger	½	cup finely chopped fresh parsley
¼	teaspoon saffron	2½	tablespoons fresh squeezed lemon juice
3	cups dry couscous	½	teaspoon cinnamon
¾	cup dried currants		Salt and pepper to taste
¾	cup chopped dates	¾	cup toasted pine nuts
2¼	cups finely diced celery		

- Bring stock, 2 tablespoons olive oil, ginger and saffron to a boil in a large saucepan. Add couscous and cook until liquid is absorbed. Remove from heat. Stir in currants and dates. Cover and let stand 15 minutes.
- Add celery, carrot and scallions to salad and mix well.
- In a small bowl, combine parsley, lemon juice, cinnamon and salt and pepper. Mix in remaining 3 tablespoons olive oil.
- Pour dressing over salad and toss, breaking apart any clumps with a fork. Cover and refrigerate overnight.
- When ready to serve, adjust seasonings and sprinkle with pine nuts.
- 10-12 servings

Couscous, granular semolina, is found in northern African diets. However, I learned that the Sephardim who fled to Italy after the Spanish inquisition brought this grain with them, so we see it used in Italian-Jewish recipes as well.

There is such a diverse assortment of vinegars in the marketplace. One should choose them according to flavor and strength (acidity). With tender lettuce, white wine vinegar or champagne vinegar is a good choice. With heartier lettuces, one should try a red wine vinegar or sherry vinegar or balsamic vinegar. Experiment combining vinegars for added sweetness, a little bite! There is a trend to add juices such as lemon, lime, orange and grapefruit for fresh flavor.

CHINESE PASTA SALAD
PAREVE

Dressing

½	cup rice vinegar		2	teaspoons dry mustard
¼	cup soy sauce		2	teaspoons sesame oil
¼	cup peanut butter		2	teaspoons grated ginger
2	tablespoons vegetable oil		2	teaspoons minced garlic
2	tablespoons sugar		¼	teaspoon dried red pepper flakes (optional)

Salad

1	pound spaghetti, or any shape pasta		½	cup carrots, diagonally sliced
1	teaspoon salt		½	cup bell peppers, color of choice, cut into bite-size pieces
1	teaspoon oil			
1	pound snow peas or sugar snap peas, trimmed		1	bunch scallions, thinly sliced
2	cups broccoli florets		1	cup dry roasted peanuts

- Combine all dressing ingredients in a blender and process until mixed.
- Cook pasta with salt and oil in boiling water until al dente; drain and rinse. Transfer pasta to a large salad bowl. Add one-third of the dressing and toss to mix. Chill until cooled.
- Meanwhile, blanch vegetables. Blanch snow peas in boiling water for 30 seconds or 1 minute for sugar snap peas. Blanch broccoli for 1 minute and carrot for 1½ minutes.
- Add peas, broccoli, carrot and bell pepper to salad and chill.
- Just before serving, toss salad with scallions and peanuts. Add remaining dressing and toss to coat.

Snow Pea and Corn Salad
PAREVE

1	pound fresh snow peas	12	leaves fresh tarragon
2	(11-ounce) can shoepeg corn	6	leaves fresh mint
2	medium shallots, minced	6	leaves fresh basil
2	tablespoons coarsely ground mustard	6	tablespoons sesame or peanut oil
2	tablespoons cider vinegar		Salt and freshly ground pepper to taste

- Blanch snow peas in boiling water for 1 minute. Quickly drain in a colander and rinse with ice cold water to stop cooking process. Transfer to a container along with corn.
- Combine shallot, mustard, vinegar, tarragon, mint and basil in a blender or food processor. Mix until smooth. With motor running, gradually add oil until dressing becomes creamy. Season with salt and pepper.
- Pour dressing over vegetables in container. Cover and refrigerate several hours or overnight to allow flavors to blend.
- 6 servings

Doubles or triples very well for a crowd. Using fresh herbs is important. Garnish with a red vegetable such as cherry tomatoes or radishes.

Always a hit!

Broccoli Salad
PAREVE

2-3	bunches fresh broccoli	1	cup dried cranberries
1	bunch scallions, sliced	1	cup mayonnaise
1	cup chopped walnuts	¼	cup cider vinegar
1	cup yellow raisins	½	cup sugar

- Break broccoli into small florets and slice stems. Transfer to a salad bowl. Add scallion, walnuts, raisins and cranberries.
- In a separate bowl, blend mayonnaise, vinegar and sugar for a dressing.
- Pour dressing over salad and toss well. Refrigerate overnight or up to 2 days.

DAVID'S ROMANIAN EGGPLANT SALAD

PAREVE

1	large eggplant	1	medium onion, chopped
½	cup olive or canola oil	½-1	(16-ounce) can chickpeas, drained (optional)
2	large green bell peppers, chopped	2	tablespoons wine vinegar
1	large red bell pepper, chopped	1	teaspoon sugar
2	cloves garlic, chopped		Salt and pepper to taste

- Preheat oven to 450 degrees.
- Wash eggplant, poke all over with a fork and place on a baking sheet. Bake 20 to 30 minutes or until soft. Cool. When cool enough to handle, scoop out flesh and chop, discarding skin.
- Heat oil in a skillet. Add all bell peppers, garlic and onion and sauté until soft, being careful not to burn.
- If using chickpeas, blend in a food processor to desired texture.
- Combine sautéed vegetables, chickpeas and chopped eggplant in a large bowl. Add vinegar, sugar and salt and pepper. Refrigerate several hours or overnight.

Garnish with pieces of bell pepper or veggies of choice, olives, etc.
Serve with your favorite crackers, toasted bread rounds or just enjoy as is.

"My friend David died recently. He always brought this dish to parties when he knew I would be there. We would share stories from our respective Romanian heritages. I present this eggplant recipe in his memory. It is a really delicious and healthy dish. Romanians call eggplant, "the poor man's meat."

Potato Salad
DAIRY

14 small new red potatoes
6 hard-boiled eggs, chopped
1 medium carrot, finely diced
2 medium scallions, thinly sliced
3 tablespoons chopped fresh dill
2 tablespoons chopped fresh flat-leaf parsley
½ teaspoon salt
½ teaspoon black pepper
¾ cup mayonnaise
¾ cup sour cream, or less to taste

- Cook potatoes in boiling water for 20 to 25 minutes or until just tender. Drain, cool and cut in half. Transfer potatoes to a large bowl.
- Add egg, carrot and scallion to potatoes. Mix in dill, parsley, salt and pepper and gently toss to combine.
- Combine mayonnaise and sour cream and gently fold into salad. Refrigerate several hours before serving to allow flavors to blend.
- 8 servings

Asparagus Salad
PAREVE

1½ pounds fresh asparagus, cut diagonally into 2-inch pieces
3 tablespoons sesame oil
4 teaspoons white wine vinegar
4 teaspoons soy sauce, regular or low-sodium
2½ teaspoons sugar
4 teaspoons sesame seeds or pumpkin seeds

- Cook asparagus in boiling water for 1 to 2 minutes. Immediately drain and run under cold water. Refrigerate.
- Combine sesame oil, vinegar, soy sauce, sugar and sesame seeds. Pour over asparagus and toss to coat.

Mixing nut oils with olive oil makes for a nice change in flavor. Sesame oils (dark and light), walnut or hazelnut oil are pantry staples for many cooks.

SALAD SURPRISE
DAIRY

Salad

1	head romaine lettuce	8	ounces asparagus
4	ounces mache lettuce	4	ounces haricot verts
1	head frisée		Juice and zest of 1 lemon
1	head radicchio	1	avocado, diced
1	fennel bulb, thinly sliced	4	ounces ricotta salata or fresh mozzarella, cut into 1/8-inch slices
4	ounces radishes, thinly sliced		
1	teaspoon salt	1	roasted beet, julienned
1/2	teaspoon black pepper		

Dressing

1/2	teaspoon salt		Juice of 2 lemons
1/4	teaspoon freshly ground pepper	3/4	cup olive oil
		1/4	cup white truffle oil

- Wash and tear romaine, mache, frisée and radicchio and place in a large salad bowl with fennel and radishes. Sprinkle with salt and pepper.
- Steam asparagus and haricot verts until tender. Chill on ice until cooled, then add to salad bowl.
- Squeeze lemon over avocado to prevent browning. Blanch zest from lemon in boiling water for 1 minute; set aside.
- Add avocado, ricotta and beet to salad. Sprinkle with lemon zest.
- Combine all dressing ingredients in a small jar, seal and shake to mix. Pour dressing over salad and toss.
- 4-6 servings

Moroccan Chickpea, Carrot and Black Olive Salad
PAREVE

Salad

2 cups cooked chickpeas, or canned and drained

12 kalamata olives, sliced

2 large carrots, diced

3 tablespoons chopped fresh cilantro

1 head romaine lettuce, thinly sliced

Dressing

1 medium shallot, minced

1 clove garlic, minced

3 tablespoons red wine vinegar

1 teaspoon ground cumin

½ teaspoon sweet paprika

¼ teaspoon cayenne pepper

¼ cup olive oil

1 tablespoon chopped fresh cilantro

Salt and freshly ground pepper to taste

- Combine all salad ingredients in a salad bowl and toss to mix.
- In a separate bowl, combine shallot, garlic, vinegar, cumin, paprika and cayenne pepper. Whisk in oil and cilantro and season with salt and pepper.
- Pour dressing over salad and toss.

How many teaspoons vinegar to oil? A usual guide would be 3 parts oil to 1 part vinegar. This needs to be adjusted to your individual taste prior to serving. Balancing flavors is the trick.

JAPANESE NOODLE SALAD
PAREVE

Dressing

⅔ cup rice wine vinegar
¼ cup light soy sauce
¼ cup vegetable oil
2 tablespoons sugar

1 teaspoon dry mustard
  Pinch of ground ginger
  Cayenne pepper to taste
  Few drops sesame oil

Salad

1 pound spaghetti or
  Japanese noodles
  Few drops sesame oil

1 bunch scallions, chopped
2-3 tablespoons sesame seeds

- Combine all dressing ingredients in a jar with a tight fitting lid. Dressing may be prepared a few days ahead.
- For salad, cook noodles according to package directions. Drain and while still warm, add a few drops of sesame oil to noodles and toss.
- Pour dressing over warm noodles and toss. Add scallions and toss. Sprinkle with sesame seeds. Salad is best if noodles are tossed with dressing a day before serving and scallions and sesame seeds are added just before serving.

Sesame seeds can be toasted, if desired.

Carrot Apple Salad
PAREVE

1	(6-ounce) can frozen orange juice concentrate, thawed	½	cup dark raisins
		½	cup golden raisins
1	(6-ounce) can cold water	½	cup coarsely chopped dry-roasted unsalted peanuts
2	pounds carrots, shredded		
3	Granny Smith (tart) apples, peeled and shredded		

- Mix juice concentrate with water in a glass or stainless steel bowl. Add carrot, apple and all raisins and mix well.
- Just before serving, sprinkle with peanuts.
- 8-10 servings

Summer Salad with Corn and Tomatoes
PAREVE

3	tablespoons extra virgin olive oil, divided		Salt and freshly ground pepper to taste
2	tablespoons chopped red onion	4	medium tomatoes, cut into bite-size pieces
1	tablespoon minced garlic	1	tablespoon freshly squeezed lemon juice
1	teaspoon chopped fresh thyme	2	cups arugula
2	cups fresh corn kernels (4 ears)		Chopped fresh chives or parsley

- Heat 2 tablespoons olive oil in a medium saucepan over medium heat. Add onion and garlic and cook 1 minute or until softened. Add thyme and corn and cook, stirring occasionally, for 10 minutes or until corn starts to brown. Season with salt and pepper.
- In a separate bowl, toss tomatoes with remaining 1 tablespoon olive oil and lemon juice. Season with salt and pepper.
- To serve, make a bed of arugula on each of 4 salad plates. Top each with a large scoop of corn mixture. Divide tomatoes with accumulated juices between salads. Sprinkle with chives or parsley.

Salads can be a main meal or side dish and provide a great opportunity to try new combinations of ingredients. Use leftovers or add simple grilled chicken or fish for a complete supper. Place your salad on a large lettuce leaf for a nice presentation.

G-d had a great day when he created tomatoes.

Serve Cilantro Vinaigrette with chunks of fresh mozzarella cheese and large bite-size slices of ripe red tomatoes over arugula.

Any of the 3 salad dressings listed can be used on a regular tossed salad or with fresh mozzarella and tomatoes.

SALAD DRESSING #1
PAREVE

1	tablespoon seasoned salt	⅔	cup salad oil
3	tablespoons lemon juice	1	heaping tablespoon
2	tablespoons cider vinegar		mayonnaise
	Dash of tarragon	1	clove garlic, crushed
1	teaspoon sugar (optional)		

• Combine all ingredients in a glass jar and refrigerate. Shake well before serving.

BASIL VINAIGRETTE SALAD DRESSING #2
PAREVE

1	clove garlic	2	teaspoons honey mustard
2	shallots	2	tablespoons balsamic
1	teaspoon salt		vinegar
1	teaspoon sugar	¾	cup extra virgin olive oil
¼	teaspoon black pepper	10	basil leaves

• Combine garlic, shallots, salt, sugar, pepper, mustard and vinegar in a blender or food processor and blend.
• With motor running, drizzle in olive oil. Add basil leaves and gently process until well blended.

CILANTRO VINAIGRETTE #3
PAREVE

3	cups fresh cilantro	1½	tablespoons minced garlic
3	tablespoons red wine vinegar	1½	tablespoons honey
1½	tablespoons lime juice	⅓	cup extra virgin olive oil
			Salt and pepper to taste

• Purée cilantro, vinegar, lime juice, garlic and honey in a food processor or blender.
• With motor running, slowly drizzle in olive oil until emulsified. Season with salt and pepper.

SALAD NIÇOISE
PAREVE

Salad

8	ounces baby red skin potatoes	2	(6-ounce) cans white tuna, drained
1	onion, thinly sliced	½	lemon
2	tablespoons olive oil	5	sprigs parsley or dill, chopped
	Salt and pepper to taste		
8	ounces green beans, trimmed	10	black or green olives
		5	anchovy fillets (optional)
1	head Boston lettuce	4	hard-boiled eggs, quartered
1	(16-ounce) package mixed salad greens	1	(12-ounce) package cherry tomatoes

Dressing

1	cup olive oil	1	clove garlic, minced
¼	cup red wine vinegar		Salt and pepper to taste

- Preheat oven to 375 degrees.
- Quarter potatoes and rinse to remove starch. Place potato wedges on a baking sheet. Top with onion slices. Drizzle with olive oil and season with salt and pepper.
- Bake 20 to 25 minutes; cool.
- Cook green beans in boiling salted water for 3 minutes; beans should still be crunchy. Drain immediately and cool under cold running water. Refrigerate until ready to use.
- Line the bottom of a chilled salad plate or bowl with lettuce leaves. Top with mixed salad greens.
- Break tuna into chunks into a mixing bowl. Squeeze juice from half of lemon over tuna. Sprinkle with sprigs of parsley. Spoon mixture into the center of the lettuce.
- Arrange olives, anchovy fillets, egg, tomatoes, green beans and potatoes around the tuna.
- Combine all dressing ingredients and mix well. Just before serving, mix dressing again and drizzle over salad.

Cucumber and Tomato Salad with Feta

DAIRY

1   large English cucumber, quartered lengthwise and sliced ¼- to ⅛-inch thin

2   large tomatoes, diced

1   (8-ounce) package crumbled feta cheese

Juice of 1 lemon

¼   cup olive oil

Salt and pepper to taste

Chopped fresh parsley (optional)

- Combine cucumber and tomato in a mixing bowl. Sprinkle feta cheese on top.
- Squeeze juice from lemon over salad. Drizzle with olive oil and sprinkle with salt and pepper. Top with parsley.
- Serve immediately; salad will wilt if made too far in advance.

Fresh Beet Salad

PAREVE

3-4   fresh beets

1   (11-ounce) can mandarin oranges, drained

1   bunch fresh mint, snipped with a scissors

2   tablespoons olive oil

½   tablespoon minced fresh ginger

1   tablespoon honey

1   tablespoon balsamic vinegar

Salt and pepper to taste

- Wash beets and cut off the ends. Bring water seasoned with kosher salt to a boil in a 2-quart saucepan. Add beets and cook until beets are tender when poked with a knife. Drain beets, gently peel away skin and cut into cubes.
- While still warm, combine beet cubes with mandarin oranges, mint, olive oil, ginger, honey, vinegar and salt and pepper in a medium mixing bowl. Toss to mix. Chill 1 hour before serving.

Classic Caesar Salad
DAIRY

Dressing

½   cup oil
1   tin anchovy fillets, chopped
2-3   cloves garlic, diced
1½   teaspoons Worcestershire sauce

⅓   cup fresh lemon juice
½   teaspoon spicy mustard
½   teaspoon black pepper
½   teaspoon kosher salt
1   coddled egg (optional)
     (see sidebar)

Salad

1   clove garlic
2   large heads romaine lettuce, washed and thoroughly dried

1   cup croutons
¼   cup freshly grated Parmesan cheese

- For dressing, combine oil and anchovy. Add garlic, Worcestershire sauce, lemon juice, mustard, pepper and salt. Whisk in coddled egg.
- To assemble salad, rub a garlic clove over the inside surface of a large wooden salad bowl. Tear lettuce into pieces and add to bowl.
- Drizzle dressing over salad and toss to mix. Add croutons and Parmesan cheese and serve immediately.
- 4-6 servings

Coddled Egg: Pour simmering water over an egg and let stand 10 minutes. You may also use an egg coddler. This kills any bacteria that may be present in an uncooked egg.

GREEN BEAN, FETA AND WALNUT SALAD

DAIRY

2	pounds green beans	1	head Bibb or Boston lettuce
1	cup extra virgin olive oil	1½	cups toasted walnuts, chopped
¼	cup chopped fresh mint		
⅓	cup white wine vinegar	1	small red onion, thinly sliced
¾	teaspoon kosher salt		
2-4	cloves chopped garlic	1	cup crumbled feta cheese
¼	teaspoon freshly ground pepper		

- Cook beans in 4 quarts of boiling water until crisp. Drain and immediately plunge into cold water to stop cooking. Drain again and pat beans dry with paper towel.
- Combine olive oil, mint, vinegar, salt, garlic and pepper in a food processor and blend.
- Arrange lettuce leaves on a plate. Place green beans on top. Sprinkle with walnuts, onion and feta cheese. Pour dressing over salad and serve.
- 4-6 servings

WILD RICE SALAD

PAREVE

2	(6-ounce) packages your favorite wild rice mixture, prepared according to package directions	¾	cup dried cranberries
		½	cup orange juice
		1½	tablespoons orange zest
1	(11-ounce) can mandarin oranges, drained	¾	cup chopped parsley
		¼	cup balsamic vinegar
½	cup sliced scallions	¼	cup extra virgin olive oil
½	cup chopped red onion		Salt and pepper to taste

- Combine all ingredients and refrigerate for up to 1 day in advance. Serve at room temperature.

CHICKPEA SALAD
PAREVE

1　(20-ounce) can chickpeas, drained
1　(6-ounce) jar mushrooms, drained
1　(6-ounce) jar Spanish olives, drained
1　(8.5-ounce) can artichoke hearts, drained and chopped

1　(8-ounce) jar sweet red peppers, thinly sliced
1　onion, minced
　　Minced garlic to taste
　　Chopped fresh parsley to taste
　　Tarragon vinegar to taste
　　Salt to taste

- Combine chickpeas, mushrooms, olives, artichoke hearts and peppers in a mixing bowl.
- Add onion, garlic, parsley, vinegar and salt and marinate overnight.

ORIENTAL SALAD
PAREVE

Salad

1　(16-ounce) package broccoli slaw or cole slaw
1　bunch scallions, chopped
1　cup sliced almonds, toasted

1　cup sunflower seeds
2　(3-ounce) packages Oriental ramen noodles, seasoning packets reserved for dressing

Dressing

½　cup oil
½　cup sugar
⅓　cup distilled vinegar

2　packages seasoning mix from Oriental ramen noodles

- Combine slaw, scallions, almonds and sunflower seeds in a salad bowl.
- Mix all dressing ingredients in a small jar. Seal and shake to mix. Pour dressing over salad.
- Crumble noodles over salad and toss to mix.
- 4 servings

Asparagus, Goat Cheese Mixed Green Salad

DAIRY

Salad

2	bunches fresh asparagus	6	ounces goat cheese, crumbled, divided
1	large head romaine lettuce, torn into small pieces	4	ounces pine nuts, lightly toasted
1	(10-ounce) package mesclun salad greens		Salt and freshly ground pepper to taste
1	red bell pepper, sliced		

Dressing

½	cup olive oil	Juice of ½ lemon
¼	cup balsamic vinegar	Pinch of sugar
1	tablespoon honey	

- Steam asparagus until slightly tender, drain and run under cold water until cool.
- Combine romaine lettuce, salad greens, cooled asparagus and bell pepper in a salad bowl. Add 4 ounces goat cheese and toasted pine nuts, reserving a few nuts for top of salad.
- Mix all dressing ingredients. Pour dressing over salad and toss gently.
- Sprinkle with remaining 2 ounces goat cheese and reserved pine nuts.
- 4-6 servings

String Bean Salad
DAIRY

1½	pounds fresh string beans, cut into 1-inch pieces	¼	teaspoon salt
⅔	cup olive oil	¼	teaspoon black pepper
1	teaspoon dried dill	1	cup chopped pecans, toasted
⅓	cup white wine vinegar	½	cup diced red onion
½	teaspoon minced garlic	1	cup crumbled feta cheese

- Cook beans in boiling water for 1 to 2 minutes, or steam in microwave; beans should still be crunchy. Immerse beans in cold water, drain and dry with paper towel. Refrigerate in unsealed plastic bags.
- Combine olive oil, dill, vinegar, garlic, salt and pepper. Chill until needed. Bring to room temperature when ready to serve.
- To serve, mix beans with dressing. Add pecans, onion and feta cheese just before serving.

Apple, Walnut and Beet Salad
PAREVE

3	medium beets, rinsed but not trimmed		Pinch of salt and black pepper
2	tablespoons walnut or peanut oil	1	head Bibb or Boston lettuce
3	tablespoons apple cider	3	tart medium apples, chopped
1½	teaspoons lemon juice	¾	cup walnut pieces
1½	tablespoons apple cider vinegar		

- Boil beets until tender; drain. When cool enough to handle, peel and cube.
- Mix oil, apple cider, lemon juice, vinegar and salt and pepper in a cruet or jar and shake well.
- Separate lettuce leaves and arrange on individual salad plates. Arrange apples, beets and walnuts on lettuce. Drizzle with dressing.

CHOPPED SALAD WITH BLUE CHEESE DRESSING
DAIRY

Salad

6	cups chopped iceberg lettuce	1	cup diced red bell pepper
2	cups cubed English cucumber	½	cup diced carrot
1	cup diced plum tomato	½	cup thinly sliced scallions
1	cup sliced celery	½	cup chopped fresh parsley
1	cup diced red onion	3	tablespoons capers, drained
1	cup sliced radish	1	teaspoon dried oregano

Dressing

⅓	cup buttermilk	1	teaspoon Worcestershire sauce
¼	cup crumbled blue cheese, or more to taste	½	teaspoon salt
1	tablespoon mayonnaise, regular or low fat	¼	teaspoon black pepper
1	tablespoon red wine vinegar		

- Combine all salad ingredients in a large salad bowl.
- Whisk together all dressing ingredients until smooth.
- Just before serving, drizzle dressing over salad and toss gently to coat.
- 12 (1-cup) servings

ORZO AND FETA SALAD
DAIRY

1	pound orzo pasta	1	cup tightly packed chopped spinach
⅓	cup balsamic vinegar	½	red onion, chopped
1	(6-ounce) package crumbled feta cheese	⅓	cup olive oil
¾	cup chopped fresh basil	¼	cup pine nuts or almonds, toasted
¾	cup rehydrated sun-dried tomatoes, chopped		Salt and pepper to taste
1	small tomato, chopped		

- Cook orzo according to package directions, being careful not to overcook; drain.
- While orzo is still hot, pour vinegar over pasta and mix. Let stand 10 minutes or until orzo fully absorbs vinegar.
- Add feta cheese, basil, all tomatoes, spinach, onion, olive oil and nuts. Season with salt and pepper and toss to mix. Chill.

GREEK SALAD
DAIRY

Salad

1	head romaine lettuce, torn into bite-sized pieces	1	red bell pepper, julienned
1	red onion, thinly sliced	2	large tomatoes, chopped, or 1½ pints grape tomatoes
¾	cup Greek olives		
1	green bell pepper, julienned	1	English cucumber, unpeeled and cubed
		1	cup crumbled feta cheese

Dressing

6	tablespoons extra virgin olive oil	Juice of 1 lemon
1	teaspoon dried oregano	Black pepper to taste

- Combine all salad ingredients in a large bowl.
- Whisk together all dressing ingredients and pour over salad. Toss to mix.

Caribbean Cole Slaw with Orange Mango Dressing
DAIRY

Dressing

1	medium mango, peeled, pitted and cubed	1	jalapeño pepper, seeded and minced
1	cup plain yogurt	1½	teaspoons minced fresh ginger
½	cup orange juice concentrate	½	teaspoon salt
¼	cup lime juice	½	teaspoon black pepper

Salad

8	cups green cabbage	1	medium-size yellow bell pepper, thinly sliced
2	large mangos, peeled, pitted and sliced	8	green onions, thinly sliced
1	medium-size red bell pepper, thinly sliced	½	cup chopped fresh cilantro

- Combine all dressing ingredients in a food processor and process until smooth; set aside.
- Combine all salad ingredients in a bowl. Add dressing and toss gently. Chill and serve.

CURRIED CHICKEN SALAD WITH MANGO CHUTNEY
MEAT

2	boneless, skinless chicken breasts, cut into large pieces	1	Bermuda onion, cut into chunks
1	teaspoon peppercorns	¼	cup mayonnaise
1	cube chicken bouillon	3	ounces mango chutney
2	bay leaves	1	tablespoon curry powder
			Salt and pepper to taste

- Poach chicken in a large pot of water with peppercorns, chicken bouillon and bay leaves. When cooked, remove chicken from broth and cool in a bowl. Add onion to cooled chicken.
- Meanwhile, combine mayonnaise, chutney, curry powder, onion and salt and pepper in a food processor. Pulse until mixed.
- Mix mayonnaise dressing with chicken and onion. Chill until serving.

For variety, add sliced grapes and sliced almonds.

Delicious in a wrap or on a bed of mesclun greens.

HEARTS OF PALM AND SPINACH
PAREVE

2	(16-ounce) bags fresh spinach	½	cup sliced almonds
1	(16-ounce) can whole hearts of palm, drained	½	cup sugar
1	pint cherry tomatoes	1	teaspoon salt
2	avocados, peeled and diced	½	teaspoon dry mustard
1	(10-ounce) package fresh mushrooms, sliced	½	teaspoon paprika
		¼	cup canola oil
		½	cup distilled vinegar
		½	cup ketchup
		2	cloves garlic, chopped

- Toss spinach, hearts of palm, tomatoes, avocado, mushrooms and almonds together in a large bowl.
- Combine sugar, salt, mustard, paprika, oil, vinegar, ketchup and garlic in a jar. Cover tightly and shake well.
- To serve, toss salad with dressing to coat.

FYI - this is the inner edible part of the stem of the cabbage palm tree!

Main Courses

Kosher meat

Take advantage of your local butcher, an expert on cutting for your cooking pleasure. He will also advise on the best cooking method for the type of meat that you are preparing.

Kosher beef: Neck, shoulder, foreshank, brisket, short plate, rib, chuck.

Kosher veal: Neck, shoulder, foreshank, breast, rib.

Kosher lamb: Neck, shoulder, shank, breast, rib.

Kosher poultry: Chicken, turkey, duck, Cornish game hens — "domesticated". The Torah names the species of fowl that are not kosher and includes predatory or scavenging species.

"Tastes and Traditions" provides a wide range of choices when deciding on a menu for a simple, well-balanced family dinner, a casual get-together with friends, or an elegant presentation for a formal dinner party.

This chapter is broken down into four categories — meat, poultry, fish and vegetarian - and with a well-stocked freezer and pantry, any number of these recipes can be prepared without enormous effort.

How many ways can you prepare chicken without repeating yourself? You'd be surprised at the variety — marsala, piccata, Florentine, with a spicy peanut sauce or fruit salsa!

Beef is a favorite standby, and narrowing down the many brisket recipes was no easy task. Testing and tasting them, however, was a treat.

A fresh piece of fish is often overlooked as a main course option. Tasty preparation, including simple pan grilling, or adding a savory rub is surprisingly delicious.

Vegetarian choices are also satisfying alternatives. *Cholent*, a traditional *Shabbat* lunch meal, can also be prepared meatless, or you can go international with a southwest bean stew, eggplant parmesan, spinach phyllo tart or a tofu stir-fry.

Shepherd's Pie Vegetarian

PAREVE

1	cup dry lentils, or 2 cups cooked	1	(8-ounce) can tomato sauce
1	large onion, chopped	1	(15-ounce) can diced tomatoes
2	carrots, chopped	2	tablespoons soy sauce
½	cup sliced celery	2-3	tablespoons chopped fresh parsley
2	cloves garlic, chopped		Salt and pepper to taste
2-3	tablespoons olive oil	4	medium potatoes, cooked and mashed
1	teaspoon mixed dried herbs of choice, such as marjoram, thyme, basil or sage		Paprika to taste

- Preheat oven to 350 degrees.
- Simmer lentils gently in enough water to cover until softened.
- Sauté onion, carrot, celery and garlic in olive oil in a skillet until softened. Add dried herbs, tomato sauce, tomatoes, soy sauce, parsley and salt and pepper. Mix in lentils. Transfer mixture to a baking dish.
- Spread mashed potatoes evenly over top. Sprinkle with paprika.
- Bake 45 minutes.

TOFU STIR-FRY WITH NOODLES
PAREVE

1	(14-ounce) package extra firm tofu	2	cloves garlic, slivered
2	tablespoons vegetable oil, divided	1/2	teaspoon dried red pepper flakes
1 1/2	teaspoons kosher salt, divided	2 1/2	tablespoons smooth peanut butter
2	red bell peppers, thinly sliced	1/4	cup hot water
1	small head green cabbage, quartered and thickly sliced	1/2	cup soy sauce
		1/2	cup rice vinegar
		6	ounces dry spaghetti, cooked al dente and drained

- Drain tofu and pat dry with paper towel. Cut tofu into 1/2-inch cubes. Heat 1 tablespoon vegetable oil in a nonstick skillet. Add tofu and 1 teaspoon salt and sauté 8 minutes or until golden. Transfer to a plate.

- Heat remaining 1 tablespoon oil in same skillet over medium-high heat. Add bell pepper, cabbage, garlic, pepper flakes and remaining 1/2 teaspoon salt. Toss to coat. Sauté 10 minutes or until vegetables are crisp-tender.

- Meanwhile, prepare a sauce by blending peanut butter and hot water until smooth. Stir in soy sauce and vinegar.

- Add sauce, tofu and drained spaghetti to vegetables in skillet. Simmer 2 minutes or until well heated.

VEGETARIAN CHOLENT
PAREVE

½ cup dried white beans
½ cup dried kidney beans
½ cup dried pinto beans
8 cups cold water
2 tablespoons olive oil
3 large onions, chopped
3 cloves garlic, minced

½ cup dry barley
Salt and pepper to taste
3 large white potatoes, peeled and coarsely chopped
1 (15-ounce) can diced tomatoes with garlic and basil

- Sort and rinse all beans and place in a large pot. Add 8 cups cold water and bring to a boil. Cook 2 to 3 minutes. Cover and remove from heat. Let stand at least 1 hour (quick-soak method), but preferably 4 hours; 24 hours maximum. (The longer soaking time is recommended to allow a greater amount of sugar to dissolve, thus helping the beans to be more easily digested.) Whether you soak the beans for 1 hour or several, drain beans in a colander and rinse, discarding soaking liquid. Rinse pot.

- Heat oil in same large pot over medium heat. Add onion and garlic and sauté until onion is softened and transparent. Add drained beans and barley. Add enough cold water to cover by 2-inches. Generously season with salt and pepper. Bring to a boil. Reduce heat, cover and simmer 30 minutes.

- Add potatoes and tomatoes and simmer, covered, for 30 minutes longer. Transfer to a crockpot. Cook overnight on low heat.

- If not using a crockpot, continue to simmer about 3 hours longer. Turn off stove and let stand on burner overnight. The next day, cook another few hours or until hearty and thick.

Cholent (stew) was born of the Orthodox observance of the Sabbath when we could not light fires (or later turn on stoves). If a family did not want to leave a low flame lit overnight, the woman would carry her pot down to the village baker and let the food cook overnight in his ovens. When Irene was a little girl, she remembers walking to the bakery with her grandmother and asking her how would she know which pot was hers when tomorrow came. Her grandma smiled and said, "See this red twine on the handle? I am very clever because it is easy to tell my pot from the others." No other woman had thought to do this!

LAYERED VEGETABLE TERRINE

PAREVE

Vegetable oil or vegan margarine

2-3 onions, sliced

1 (1-pound) package extra-firm tofu, sliced

3 tomatoes, sliced

3 portobello mushrooms, stems removed, sliced

1 jar organic vegetarian tomato sauce

1 package sliced soy cheese

- Preheat oven to 350 degrees.
- Generously grease a 9x5-inch loaf pan with vegetable oil or vegan margarine.
- Heat vegetable oil in a large skillet. Add onion and sauté until golden; remove and set aside.
- Add tofu to skillet and brown lightly on both sides.
- In prepared pan, layer in order listed: tomato slices, tofu, onion and mushrooms. Pour tomato sauce over all. Lay slices of cheese on top.
- Bake 30 minutes. Transfer to broiler and cook a few minutes to brown top.

Assembly can be done ahead of time and refrigerated until ready to bake.
Do not freeze.

FLAKY SPINACH PIZZA
DAIRY

2   pounds baby spinach leaves

7   (12x7-inch) sheets phyllo dough, thawed

6   tablespoons unsalted butter, melted

½   cup Parmesan cheese

¾   red onion, thinly sliced

2   tablespoons chopped fresh basil

Salt and pepper to taste

1   cup crumbled feta or goat cheese

2   tablespoons extra virgin olive oil

- Preheat oven to 400 degrees.
- Gently pour boiling water over spinach in a bowl and soak 1 to 2 minutes to wilt; drain well.
- Cover phyllo dough with plastic wrap or a damp paper towel to keep moist while working with it. Place 1 sheet dough on a large, heavy baking sheet. Lightly brush with melted butter and sprinkle with 1 tablespoon Parmesan cheese. Continue to layer phyllo dough with butter and cheese, gently pressing layers together.
- Bake phyllo crust 5 minutes or until lightly browned.
- Leaving a 1-inch border around sides, cover crust with wilted spinach. Scatter onion and basil on top. Season with salt and pepper and sprinkle with crumbled cheese. Drizzle olive oil over all.
- Bake 15 minutes or until cheese is melted and pizza looks done. Cut into squares and serve immediately.

SOUTHWESTERN TOFU WITH COUSCOUS

PAREVE OR DAIRY

2   tablespoons olive oil
1   medium onion, chopped
1   teaspoon ground cumin
1   teaspoon chili powder
¾   teaspoon salt
2   cloves garlic, minced
½   jalapeño pepper, minced

1   (14½-ounce) can Mexican-style stewed tomatoes, undrained
1   cup water
⅔   cup dry couscous
1   (14-ounce) package firm tofu, finely chopped
¼   cup chopped fresh cilantro

- Heat olive oil in a large skillet over medium heat. Add onion, cumin, chili powder, salt, garlic and jalapeño and sauté 5 minutes or until softened.
- Add tomatoes with juice and water. Bring to a boil. Stir in couscous and tofu and cover. Remove from heat and let stand 5 minutes.
- Fluff with a fork and stir in cilantro. Mix well.

Serve as is or in warmed taco shells with shredded lettuce and cheese.

Tofu Stir-Fry with Fresh Herbs
PAREVE

1 (14-ounce) package soft tofu, drained	1½ cups stir-fry sauce (Szechuan, sweet and sour, teriyaki, etc.)
1 teaspoon sesame oil	1 teaspoon chopped fresh basil
1 tablespoon chopped garlic	
1 tablespoon chopped fresh ginger	1 tablespoon chopped fresh mint
1 (12-ounce) package Oriental mixed vegetables (bean sprouts, celery)	2 tablespoons chopped fresh parsley
1 cup sliced fresh mushrooms	1 red bell pepper, cut into small strips
	4 cups steamed rice

- Heat tofu in oven or microwave.
- Heat sesame oil in a wok or skillet over high heat. Add garlic and ginger and cook and stir constantly until light brown. Add mixed vegetables and mushrooms and cook 2 to 4 minutes or to desired crispness of vegetables. Stir in sauce and bring to a boil.
- Just before serving, add half of fresh herbs and pour mixture over warmed tofu. Garnish with remaining herbs and bell pepper strips. Serve with steamed rice.

Black Bean Stew
PAREVE

2 (15½-ounce) cans black beans, rinsed and drained
1 (29-ounce) can stewed tomatoes
1 (8-ounce) can tomato sauce
1 medium butternut squash, peeled, seeded and cut into 3-inch cubes
1 green bell pepper, quartered
   Sprig of cilantro
1 medium onion, peeled and left whole
1 tablespoon minced garlic
1 tablespoon salt
6 tablespoons olive oil

- Combine all ingredients in a 7-quart pot. Cover and cook over medium heat for 30 minutes or until squash is tender.
- With the back of a large spoon, gently mash squash against the side of the pot. Stir mashed squash back into stew, creating a thick sauce.

Serve over brown or white rice with avocado slices or sweet plantains on the side.

To prepare squash, cut into 3-inch strips with a sharp knife. Scoop out seeds and cut off outer hard skin.

Spinach and Pasta Bake
DAIRY

1 pound fresh spinach, or a 10½-ounce package frozen chopped spinach
8 ounces dry ziti or penne pasta, cooked and drained
8 ounces ricotta cheese
1 (15½-ounce) jar marinara sauce, or more to taste
2 eggs, lightly beaten
⅓ cup freshly grated Parmesan cheese
2 tablespoons chopped fresh parsley
1 teaspoon salt
¼ teaspoon freshly ground pepper

- Preheat oven to 350 degrees.
- If using fresh spinach, cook just until wilted, drain and chop. For frozen spinach, thaw and squeeze dry.
- Combine all ingredients in a large mixing bowl until thoroughly blended. Transfer to a generously greased 6-cup casserole or baking dish.
- Bake 30 to 45 minutes or until top is golden brown and sauce is bubbly.

EGGPLANT PARMESAN
DAIRY

1	large eggplant (about 1½ pounds)	2	(15-ounce) cans tomato sauce
2	eggs, lightly beaten	1½	teaspoons dried oregano
1½	cups seasoned bread crumbs	½	teaspoon salt
½	cup peanut, canola or vegetable oil, or as needed	½	cup Parmesan cheese
		8	ounces mozzarella cheese, thinly sliced

- Preheat oven to 350 degrees.
- Peel eggplant and slice crosswise into ½-inch rounds. Dip slices in beaten egg, then dredge in bread crumbs, coating each slice completely.
- Heat oil in a large skillet over medium heat, making sure bottom of skillet is covered by oil. Add eggplant to oil, a few slices at a time, and cook until browned on both sides, adding more oil to skillet as needed. Drain eggplant well on paper towel.
- In a well greased, shallow 8-inch square baking pan, layer one-third of fried eggplant, then one-third each of tomato sauce, oregano, salt and cheeses. Repeat layers twice.
- Bake, uncovered, for 45 minutes or until sauce is hot and cheeses are melted.
- 4-6 main course servings, or 8 side servings

For a low-fat version, bake eggplant instead of fry. Place eggplant slices in a single layer on a lightly greased baking sheet. Spray or lightly drizzle with olive oil. Bake at 425 degrees for 20 to 30 minutes or until crisp. Proceed with recipe.

EGGPLANT LASAGNA
DAIRY

2 tablespoons unsalted butter

2 tablespoons all-purpose flour

1 cup milk
 Salt and pepper to taste

1 cup tomato or marinara sauce, homemade or store-bought

1½ pounds prepared (fried) eggplant slices from the market

1 cup shredded mozzarella cheese

- Preheat oven to 375 degrees.
- Melt butter in a saucepan. Blend in flour and cook and stir over low heat for about 5 minutes. Add milk, whisking to remove all lumps. Increase heat slightly and cook until white sauce thickens. Season with salt and pepper and remove from heat.
- Pour a little tomato sauce over the bottom of a 10- to 12-inch glass casserole dish. Arrange one-third of eggplant slices on top. Cover eggplant layer with a little more tomato sauce and some of white sauce. Sprinkle with a third of the cheese. Repeat layers twice.
- Bake 30 minutes or until hot and bubbly.
- 4 main course servings, or 8 side servings

Stir Fry Sha-Wo-Fun Noodles

PAREVE OR MEAT

6 tablespoons peanut or vegetable oil

1 clove garlic, thinly sliced

1 pound Chinese baby bok choy, bottom trimmed, washed and drained

6 fresh water chestnuts, peeled and sliced into 3-4 pieces

1 pound tofu, cubed

¼ cup soy sauce

¼ cup rice vinegar

¼ cup hoisin sauce

1 pound Asian sha-wo-fun noodles, cut into 1-inch wide strips, or fettuccine pasta

- Heat oil in a skillet. Add garlic and bok choy and stir-fry 1 minute or until slightly wilted. Add water chestnuts and mix well. Stir in tofu. Add soy sauce, vinegar and hoisin sauce and stir well.

- Lay noodles on top and cover skillet. Cook over low heat, allowing the noodles to steam, for 5 minutes. Mix and serve.

You can also use chicken in this recipe, either alone or with the tofu. Slice it into thin strips and sauté first to brown. Remove from pan and proceed with recipe, adding chicken back in just before adding noodles.

The noodles can be found in a Chinese grocery.

GREEN OR RED OR YELLOW PEPPERS STUFFED WITH EGGPLANT
DAIRY

3-4 medium eggplants, peeled and diced into 1-inch cubes	½ cup Parmesan cheese, grated
¼ cup olive oil	1-1½ cups fresh bread crumbs or matzoh meal
3-4 cloves garlic, crushed	Salt and pepper to taste
1 bunch fresh basil, chopped	4 bell peppers, color of choice

- Preheat oven to 350 degrees.
- Sauté eggplant in olive oil, in batches if needed, until eggplant is brown and soft but not mushy. To prevent burning, add garlic towards the end of cooking the eggplant. Stir in basil and cook until wilted. Mix in cheese and bread crumbs and season with salt and pepper.
- Cut off top of peppers and remove seeds. Spoon eggplant stuffing into peppers and place in a baking dish.
- Bake 30 minutes or until filling puffs up and top is browned.

After baking, each pepper can be topped with a slice of mozzarella cheese and marinara sauce. Bake 5 minutes longer or until cheese is melted.

Tomatoes Stuffed with Rice
DAIRY OR PAREVE

8	large beefsteak tomatoes		1	tablespoon tamarind paste
1	medium-size yellow onion, chopped		1½	teaspoons sugar
				Salt and pepper to taste
3	tablespoons olive oil		2	teaspoons dried mint, or fresh if available
1¼	cups dry short-grain or Italian rice		3	tablespoons pine nuts
2	cups water			

- Preheat oven to 350 degrees.
- At the stem end of each tomato, cut a slice to make a cap for tomato. Spoon out center and seeds, leaving each tomato with a thick outer shell so tomato does not fall apart.
- Sauté onion in olive oil until golden. Add dry rice and stir until translucent. Mix in water, tamarind paste, sugar and salt and pepper. Stir until paste is completely dissolved.
- Cover and simmer 15 minutes or until water is absorbed. Mix in mint and pine nuts.
- Spoon rice stuffing into tomato shells. Replace tomato cap on top and place in a baking dish.
- Bake 40 minutes or until tomatoes are soft.

To stuff with cheese, prepare tomato shells as above. Mix cottage cheese and another favorite cheese such as feta, with a lightly beaten egg to hold mixture together. Season with a little sugar and nutmeg ... it is almost like a kugel filling.

STUFFED ZUCCHINI
PAREVE

8	small to medium zucchini	1	cup apricots (about 30 dried), soaked overnight in water, water reserved
2	cups cooked rice		
½	teaspoon cinnamon		Juice of 1 lemon, or more to taste
2	tablespoons pine nuts		
	Salt and pepper to taste		

- Cut zucchini in half lengthwise. Scoop out inside of zucchini, leaving a firm shell. Discard inside of zucchini or use for zucchini bread.
- Combine rice, cinnamon and pine nuts. Season with salt and pepper and blend well. Chop soaked apricots and add to mixture. If stuffing mixture seems too dry, add a little of apricot water.
- Spoon stuffing into zucchini shells and place in a heavy heat-proof casserole dish or stainless steel braiser/roaster. Sprinkle with lemon juice. Pour about 1 cup of apricot water over zucchini.
- Simmer 45 to 60 minutes or until zucchini are tender, adding more apricot water as needed.

SPRING VEGETABLE STIR FRY
PAREVE

1	teaspoon oil	4	ounces sugar snap peas, ends trimmed
1	clove garlic, sliced		
½	teaspoon finely chopped fresh ginger	4	ounces young asparagus, cut into 3-inch pieces
4	ounces baby carrots	8	scallions, sliced
4	ounces squash or zucchini, cubed	¼	cup wine
		2	tablespoons water
4	ounces green beans, ends trimmed		

Dressing

	Juice of 2 limes or lemons	1	teaspoon sesame oil
1	tablespoon honey	2	tablespoons white wine
1	tablespoon soy sauce		

- Heat oil in a wok or skillet. Add garlic and ginger and stir-fry over medium-high heat for 1 minute, being careful not to burn garlic.
- Increase heat to high and add carrots, zucchini and beans and stir-fry 3 to 4 minutes. Add peas, asparagus and scallions and stir-fry 2 minutes longer.
- Combine all dressing ingredients and pour over stir-fry. Cook 2 to 3 minutes longer or until just crisp tender.

  Serve over brown rice. Add tofu to stir-fry for extra protein.

Mexican Cheese Bake
DAIRY

2	cups roasted red peppers, commercial or homemade, drained, divided	4	eggs
2	tablespoons olive oil	¼	cup flour
1	large onion, chopped	1	(8-ounce) package cream cheese, softened
1	clove garlic, minced	2	cups salsa of choice
½	teaspoon dried oregano	2	cups frozen or canned corn
1	teaspoon ground cumin	½	cup shredded mozzarella cheese
¾	teaspoon salt	½	cup shredded Cheddar cheese
¼	cup chopped fresh parsley		

- Preheat oven to 350 degrees.
- Arrange half of peppers in a single layer in the bottom of a greased 9x13-inch glass baking dish.
- Heat olive oil in a skillet. Add onion and garlic and sauté until softened. Stir in oregano, cumin, salt and parsley; set aside.
- In a food processor, blend eggs. Add flour and process until combined. Add cream cheese and mix until smooth; set aside.
- To assemble, cover layer of peppers, in order listed, with half each of the onion mixture, salsa, corn, egg mixture and cheeses. Repeat layers starting with remaining peppers.
- Bake 30 minutes or until golden brown. Cool 5 to 10 minutes before slicing.

VEGETABLE PAELLA
PAREVE

Pinch of saffron
3 tablespoons water
Salt to taste
1 medium eggplant, cubed
3 tablespoons olive oil
1 onion, chopped
2 cloves garlic, crushed
1 yellow bell pepper, diced
1 red bell pepper, diced
2 tablespoons paprika
1 cup dry Arborio rice
2½ cups vegetable broth
1 (19-ounce) can diced tomatoes, drained
Black pepper to taste
1 cup mushrooms, sliced
1 cup green beans, cut into 1-inch pieces
1 (19-ounce) can chickpeas, rinsed and drained

- Sprinkle saffron over 3 tablespoons water and let stand. Sprinkle salt over eggplant and let drain in a colander for 30 minutes. Rinse and drain.

- Heat oil in a large skillet. Add onion, garlic, bell peppers and eggplant and sauté 5 minutes. Sprinkle with paprika and stir. Add rice, broth, tomatoes and saffron water. Season with salt and pepper to taste. Bring to a boil. Reduce heat and simmer, uncovered, for 15 minutes, stirring frequently.

- Mix in mushrooms, green beans and chickpeas. Cook 15 minutes longer. Serve immediately.

SALMON WITH POTATO ARTICHOKE HASH

PAREVE

8	small red new potatoes, sliced ¼-inch thick	1	tablespoon olive oil, divided
1	(14-ounce) can artichoke hearts (not marinated), drained and halved	1	teaspoon salt, divided
		¼	teaspoon or more black pepper
1	tablespoon fresh chopped thyme, or 1 teaspoon dried	1½	pounds skinless salmon fillet

Sauce

½	cup chopped fresh parsley	½	teaspoon salt
1	tablespoon Dijon mustard		Pinch of black pepper
1	tablespoon white wine vinegar	1	tablespoon water

- Preheat oven to 475 degrees.
- Combine potatoes, artichoke hearts, thyme, ½ tablespoon olive oil, ½ teaspoon salt and pepper in a large roasting pan and toss to coat. Arrange vegetables around sides of pan.
- Place salmon in center of pan. Sprinkle with remaining ½ tablespoon oil, ½ teaspoon salt and pepper to taste.
- Roast, turning vegetables once, for 20 minutes or until salmon is cooked through and vegetables are nicely browned.
- Meanwhile, prepare sauce. Stir together parsley, mustard, vinegar, salt and pepper. Add water and mix well.
- To serve, slice salmon into serving-size pieces. Drizzle sauce over salmon and vegetables.

SPICE RUBBED SALMON

PAREVE

3	tablespoons chili powder	1	tablespoon salt
2	tablespoons brown sugar	2	tablespoons olive oil
1	tablespoon ground cumin	2½	pounds skinless salmon
1	tablespoon dried thyme		fillet or steaks

• Combine chili powder, brown sugar, cumin, thyme, salt and olive oil. Spread seasoning rub generously over all surfaces of salmon. This can be rubbed on just prior to cooking, but the longer it is on, the more flavor it imparts. However, it is probably not a good idea to marinate fish in rub longer than a few hours.

• Broil in a broiling pan or grill on a greased rack, for 5 minutes per side or according to thickness of fish and desired doneness.

Perfect on its own, or especially good with a homemade salsa or good quality store bought salsa such as peach, mango or other fruit salsa.

This can be served warm or at room temperature, so it is especially good for buffets if made with a large fillet. Rub can also be used on any mild white fish to be used for fish tacos. Adjust seasonings according to your taste. Keep in mind that a "hot" chili powder may be excessive.

Some chili powders are spicier than others. Choose one that suits your taste.

Salmon en Croûte

DAIRY

1	sheet frozen puff pastry dough, thawed	1	(1-pound) salmon fillet
1	egg, beaten	¼	teaspoon salt
1	(5-ounce) package baby spinach	¼	teaspoon black pepper
		2	tablespoons prepared pesto

- Preheat oven to 375 degrees.
- Roll pastry on a floured surface to ⅛-inch thick. Brush egg lightly around the edges. Place half the spinach lengthwise down the center of the pastry.
- Season salmon with salt and pepper and place over spinach. Spread pesto over fish and top with remaining spinach.
- Wrap salmon in the pastry, folding in the sides to seal completely, then the top and bottom. Place on a baking sheet and brush with egg.
- Bake 25 to 30 minutes or until the pastry is golden brown. Serve immediately.

Other thick fish fillets, such as snapper,
cod or tuna, could be substituted for the salmon.

Pesto

DAIRY

3	cups basil leaves	⅓	cup olive oil
3	large cloves garlic	⅓	cup Parmesan cheese
⅓	cup pine nuts, lightly toasted		Salt and pepper to taste

- Blend together in a food processor.
- Use over pasta or as recipe indicates.

SPECIAL WILD SALMON
PAREVE

¾ cup soy sauce

¾ cup honey

3 tablespoons wasabi powder

1 pound wild salmon

2 tablespoons sesame seeds

2 tablespoons sesame oil

2 tablespoons chopped scallions

- Preheat oven to 350 degrees.
- Mix soy sauce, honey and wasabi powder together in a pan or plastic zip-top bag. Reserve some of mixture prior to adding salmon for a dipping sauce. Add salmon and marinate 1 hour, turning a few times to coat fish.
- Remove salmon from marinade, discarding marinade. Coat both sides of salmon with sesame seeds.
- Heat sesame oil in an ovenproof pan over medium-high heat. Sear skin-side of salmon in oil for up to 3 minutes. Turn and cook salmon on other side for 1 minute.
- Transfer to oven and bake 6 to 10 minutes or to desired degree of doneness; do not overcook.
- Garnish salmon with scallions. Place reserved dipping sauce in a bowl and sprinkle with a few scallions as well. Serve dipping sauce with salmon.

CRANBERRY GINGER GRAPEFRUIT RELISH
PAREVE

1 (16-ounce) package fresh cranberries

2 cups sugar

½ cup chopped fresh ginger

Zest of 1 grapefruit

¼ cup grapefruit juice

½ cup blanched slivered almonds, toasted

- Combine cranberries, sugar, ginger, zest and juice in a saucepan. Cover and bring to a boil. Reduce heat to low and cook 10 minutes or until cranberries pop. Remove from heat and stir in almonds. Cool.

Cajun Broiled Salmon
PAREVE

3	tablespoons paprika	1	tablespoon orange zest
1	tablespoon onion powder	2	teaspoons salt
1	tablespoon garlic powder	¾	pound or more salmon, red snapper or tilapia fillets
1	tablespoon cayenne pepper, or to taste		
2	teaspoons white pepper		Lemon wedges

- Combine paprika, onion powder, garlic powder, cayenne pepper, white pepper, orange zest and salt in a shaker jar.
- Cover a baking sheet with aluminum foil and spray with cooking spray. Cut salmon into individual portions and place on foil. Sprinkle salmon generously with seasoning mixture.
- Place under an unheated broiler. Turn broiler on and cook exactly 7 minutes; salmon may be slightly blackened. Turn broiler off, move pan to a lower shelf in oven and leave exactly 2 minutes. Serve with lemon wedges on the side.

Jewish folklore tells us that fish is a symbol of fertility, prosperity and knowledge.

Fish with Tomatoes and Coriander
PAREVE

1-2	red bell peppers, cubed	1	teaspoon paprika
6-8	fresh tomatoes or 2½ cups canned tomatoes, chopped	½	teaspoon cayenne pepper (optional)
4-5	cloves garlic, minced	½	teaspoon salt, or to taste
1	tablespoon vegetable oil	2	pounds cod or scrod
½	teaspoon ground cumin	½	bunch fresh coriander
½	teaspoon turmeric		

- Sauté bell pepper, tomato and garlic in vegetable oil for 15 minutes. Add a little water and continue to sauté until tomato and pepper soften.
- Add cumin, turmeric, paprika, cayenne pepper and salt and sauté 10 minutes longer over low heat.
- Add fish to mixture and place coriander on top. Cover and simmer 15 minutes or until fish is cooked through.
- 4-6 servings

This dish is ideal for Shabbat dinner as the appetizer, great instead of gefilte fish.

Peppered Roulade of Salmon with Puréed Roasted Peppers

DAIRY

1	(3-pound) center-cut fresh salmon fillet	¼	teaspoon cayenne pepper
2	leeks, julienned	2	tablespoons olive oil
1	tablespoon butter		Cracked black pepper
1½	teaspoons kosher salt	2	tablespoons or more peanut or canola oil
3-4	roasted red peppers		
2	tablespoons light cream (optional)		

- Trim salmon fillet and remove any excess bones. Slice horizontally to 1-inch from the thick end and open fillet like a book. Cover with plastic wrap and pound to an even ½-inch thick rectangle.

- Sauté leeks in butter over low heat until limp.

- Remove plastic wrap from salmon and sprinkle with salt. Scatter leeks evenly over surface to make a sparse covering. Using parchment paper under the salmon, roll salmon up into a very tight cylinder. Unroll and roll again in the parchment paper. Twist ends of paper and tie with twine to secure. Refrigerate in a plastic bag for 2 hours.

- Purée roasted peppers, cream and cayenne pepper together in a food processor; set aside or refrigerate.

- Lay a sheet of aluminum foil on countertop. Lightly coat entire surface of foil with olive oil. When salmon roulade is well chilled, cut off ends of parchment paper with a scissors and unwrap fish onto foil. Sprinkle with black pepper, pressing it all over the surface. Wrap foil very tightly around roulade and twist ends to seal.

- Heat peanut oil over medium-high heat in a skillet until very hot. Add foil-covered roulade to hot oil and roll around in skillet for 4 to 5 minutes. Cool to room temperature.

- To serve, slice roulade with foil on, then remove foil. Spoon roasted pepper sauce onto serving plates and place sliced roulade on top.

Salmon Florentine en Croûte with Caper Dill Sauce

DAIRY

Sauce

½ (1¾-ounce) jar capers
½ bunch dill
½ bunch scallions
½ bunch parsley

Juice of 1 lemon
1 cup sour cream
½ cup mayonnaise
Salt and pepper to taste

Salmon

1 sheet frozen puff pastry dough, thawed
1 (10-ounce) package frozen spinach, thawed and squeezed dry

1 side of salmon (about 3 pounds), rinsed and dried with paper towel
Salt and pepper to taste
1 egg, beaten
Sprigs fresh parsley

- For sauce, place capers, dill, scallions and parsley in a food processor and chop. Add lemon juice, sour cream and mayonnaise and blend. Season with salt and pepper; set aside

- For salmon, lay pastry on a parchment paper-lined baking sheet. Spoon spinach in center of dough and top with salmon. Season with salt and pepper.

- Wrap pastry around fish and turn so seam-side is down. Brush with egg. Place parsley sprigs around pastry for decoration.

- Bake 30 minutes or until golden brown. Serve with dill sauce.

- 8-10 servings

Salmon in Papillote with Basil Butter
Dairy or Pareve

15	fresh basil leaves		Salt and pepper to taste
1	tablespoon chopped garlic	4	salmon steaks
½	teaspoon cayenne pepper	8	slices tomato
1	stick unsalted butter or margarine, softened	4	slices lemon
	Few drops lemon juice	4	bay leaves
			Paprika to taste

- Preheat a grill or an oven to 325 degrees.
- For basil butter, blend basil, garlic, cayenne pepper, butter, lemon juice and salt and pepper in a food processor.
- Place steaks on separate pieces of double-thick aluminum foil. Top steaks with tomato, lemon and bay leaves. Season with paprika, salt and pepper. Add one-fourth of basil butter to each piece of salmon. Fold foil over salmon and seal well.
- Place packages on grill and cook, covered for 25 to 30 minutes, or bake in oven for 30 minutes.
- 4 servings

Grape Leaf-Wrapped Snapper
Pareve

4	whole snapper (about 1½ pounds), scaled and cleaned	8	sprigs fresh rosemary
	Salt and freshly ground pepper to taste	1	tablespoon extra virgin olive oil, plus extra for brushing
8	cloves garlic, thinly sliced	2-3	small jars grape leaves (available in supermarkets or Middle Eastern stores)
12	lemon slices		

- Prepare fire in a charcoal grill.
- Rinse fish under cold running water and pat dry. Season fish cavities with salt and pepper. Stuff cavities with garlic, lemon slices and rosemary. Drizzle olive oil into cavities.
- Wrap fish in grape leaves, completely covering body of fish but leaving head and tail exposed. Use any remaining grape leaves to garnish serving platter.
- When coals are medium-hot, brush wrapped fish with olive oil and place on grill. Cook about 10 minutes. Turn carefully with a long spatula and cook another 10 minutes or until done.

Instead of grilling, fish can be baked at 350 degrees for 20 minutes.

Preserved Lemons
Pareve

8	lemons
1	cup kosher salt
1¾	cups fresh lemon juice
3	tablespoons olive oil

- Blanch lemons in boiling water for 5 minutes and drain. Cool and thinly slice, discarding seeds.
- Toss with salt and tightly pack into a 2-quart jar. Add lemon juice to cover and seal. Let stand at room temperature for 5 days, shaking gently 1 to 2 times daily. After 5 days, add oil and refrigerate.

Great for cocktails, soups, salads and grilled fish. If chilled in a jar with a tight fitting lid, these lemons will keep for up to 1 year.

Much easier than you would think and perfect for Rosh Hashanah. Traditionally, many people wish to eat a fish with the head on for the head of the year!

APRICOT CRANBERRY RELISH WITH A KICK

DAIRY

2 tablespoons
   unsalted butter
½ cup finely diced red
   onion
2 tablespoons finely
   julienned peeled
   fresh ginger
2 jalapeño peppers,
   seeded and minced
2 (16-ounce) packages
   fresh cranberries,
   divided
2 cups fresh orange
   juice
2 tablespoons brown
   sugar
½ cup honey
¼ cup dried apricots,
   julienned
1 tablespoon curry
   Salt and freshly
   ground black pepper
   to taste

- Melt butter in a
  medium saucepan
  over medium heat.
  Add onion, ginger,
  jalapeño pepper and
  1 package cranberries.
  Cook 5 minutes.

- Increase to high heat
  and add orange juice,
  brown sugar and
  honey. Bring to a
  boil. Reduce heat to
  medium and simmer
  10 minutes.

- Add remaining
  package of cranberries
  and simmer about
  5 minutes. Stir in
  apricots, curry and
  salt and pepper. Mix
  well and remove
  from heat. When cool,
  pour into a bowl and
  refrigerate up to 3
  days.

GRILLED MAPLE SALMON

PAREVE

¼ cup maple syrup
3 tablespoons soy sauce
6 tablespoons olive oil
½ teaspoon minced garlic

1½ tablespoons Dijon
   mustard
1 (3-pound) side of salmon
   with skin on, boned and
   cut into 6 equal portions

- Preheat a grill; brush rack with oil to prevent sticking.

- Whisk together maple syrup, soy sauce, olive oil, garlic and mustard
  in a small bowl. Drizzle half of mustard mixture over salmon; set
  remaining mustard mixture aside. Allow salmon to marinate 10 to
  15 minutes.

- Remove salmon from marinade, discarding marinade. Place salmon,
  skin-side down, on hot grill. Grill 4 to 5 minutes. Turn carefully
  using a wide spatula. Grill 4 to 5 minutes longer. The salmon will
  be very pink but will continue to cook as it stands.

- Transfer salmon onto a plate. Spoon remaining mustard mixture
  on top. Allow to rest 10 minutes. Serve warm, at room temperature
  or chilled.

- 6 servings

Poached Salmon with Cucumber Dill Sauce

DAIRY

Salmon

2	cups dry white wine	6	sprigs fresh dill
2	cups water	2	stalks celery, halved
1	tablespoon powdered vegetable bouillon	1	medium onion, quartered
½	teaspoon white pepper	6	salmon fillets, or 1 large fillet, ½-inch thick

Sauce

½	cup chopped English cucumber	3	tablespoons chopped fresh dill
½	cup plain regular or low-fat yogurt	2	teaspoons Dijon mustard
½	cup regular or low-fat sour cream		Fresh dill for garnish

- Combine all salmon ingredients in a large skillet or a fish poacher. Bring to a boil. Cover and reduce heat. Simmer 10 minutes. Transfer salmon to a serving platter and chill.
- Mix all sauce ingredients together; set aside.
- To serve, spread sauce over fish, or serve sauce on the side. Garnish with dill.

SALMON IN PUFF PASTRY

DAIRY

2	(16-ounce) cans salmon, drained	1	stick butter or margarine, melted
½	cup crushed round butter crackers	2	tablespoons lemon juice Pinch of garlic salt
1	large onion, chopped	1	(16-ounce) package frozen puff pastry, thawed
1	cup sour cream	2	egg yolks, beaten

Sauce

1	cup sour cream	1	teaspoon Dijon mustard
½	cup mayonnaise	1	teaspoon dill

- Preheat oven to 425 degrees.
- Combine salmon, cracker crumbs, onion, sour cream, butter, lemon juice and garlic salt and mix well.
- Place one pastry on a baking sheet. Spoon salmon mixture on top and pat down. Place second pastry sheet over salmon mixture and pinch closed. Brush top and sides with egg yolk.
- Place in preheated oven. Immediately reduce heat to 400 degrees. Bake 20 to 25 minutes.
- Meanwhile, combine all sauce ingredients and mix well.
- To serve, cut salmon puff pastry into squares. Place a dollop of sauce on each square, or serve sauce on the side.

Chilean Sea Bass

DAIRY

2	tablespoons butter
2	tablespoons olive oil
4	(6-ounce) Chilean sea bass fillets

Cajun or Creole seasoning
Salt and pepper to taste

- Melt butter with olive oil in a large skillet. Coat fillets with seasoning and season generously with salt and pepper. Cook in skillet for 4 minutes on each side or until golden. Watch carefully to not overcook; this fish is delicate.

Baked Sea Bass with Porcini and Sun-Dried Tomatoes

PAREVE

¾ ounce dried porcini mushrooms

1 tablespoon olive oil, plus more for cooking
Sea salt and freshly ground pepper to taste

1 (6- to 8-pound) whole sea bass or grouper, filleted
Few sprigs fresh thyme

⅓ cup sun-dried tomatoes in oil

- Preheat oven to 400 degrees.
- Soak mushrooms in warm water for 30 minutes; drain.
- Sauté mushrooms in 1 tablespoon olive oil until lightly browned. Season with salt and pepper.
- Line 2 rimmed baking sheets with heavy foil. Brush foil with olive oil. Place a fillet on each sheet, skin-side down.
- On one fillet, scatter mushrooms and a few sprigs of thyme. Season with salt and pepper and drizzle with olive oil. On second fillet, do the same, substituting tomatoes for the mushrooms. Fold foil around fillets into loose but airtight packages.
- Bake 20 minutes. Place foil packages on a serving dish. Unwrap at the table.

Other large fillets of fish can be substituted.

The mushrooms and tomatoes can be combined and placed atop both fillets, if desired.

FRAN'S TILAPIA
PAREVE

1   pound tilapia fillet, or
     other white fish
     Cajun spices to taste
6   sun-dried tomatoes,
     chopped

½   (6-ounce) jar marinated
     artichoke hearts, juice
     reserved
     Handful pitted kalamata
     olives
     Juice of 1 lemon
¼   cup water

- Preheat oven to 400 degrees.
- Place tilapia in a baking dish. Sprinkle with Cajun spices. Scatter tomatoes, artichoke hearts and olives over the top.
- Mix lemon juice, water and a little juice from marinated artichoke hearts, if desired. Pour mixture over fish.
- Bake, covered, for 25 minutes.
- 4 servings

Fresh tomatoes, mushrooms, parsley and capers can be used in place of the sun-dried tomatoes, artichoke hearts and olives.

ROLLED STUFFED FISH
DAIRY

2   tablespoons butter, plus
     extra for dotting
⅔   cup finely chopped celery
1   large onion, finely
     chopped
4   ounces fresh mushrooms,
     chopped
1   (16-ounce) can red salmon,
     drained

½   cup bread crumbs
     Salt and freshly ground
     pepper to taste (optional)
1   tablespoon lemon juice
¼   teaspoon dried dill
½   teaspoon ground allspice
1   egg, lightly beaten
8   thin flounder or sole
     fillets

- Preheat oven to 350 degrees.
- Heat 2 tablespoons butter in a skillet. Add celery, onion and mushrooms and sauté until softened. Stir in salmon, bread crumbs, salt and pepper, lemon juice, dill, allspice and egg.
- Spread salmon mixture over fish fillets. Roll up fillets and place on a lightly greased baking sheet. Dot with butter.
- Bake 25 to 30 minutes.
- 4 servings

Iris's Baked Sole
DAIRY

12   small flounder or sole fillets (about 1½ pounds)
     Salt and pepper to taste

2   tablespoons finely chopped fresh dill

2   teaspoons imported mustard

2   tablespoons bread crumbs

4   tablespoons melted butter

3   tablespoons lemon juice

1   teaspoon soy sauce

3   tablespoons chopped scallions (optional)

- Preheat oven to 350 degrees.
- Arrange half of fillets, skin-side down, in a greased baking dish. Top with half each of dill, mustard, bread crumbs and melted butter. Add remaining fillets and top with remaining dill, mustard, bread crumbs and butter.
- Blend lemon juice and soy sauce and pour around and between fillets.
- Bake 15 minutes. Transfer to a broiler and broil on low for 4 to 6 minutes or until bubbly. If broiler does not have a low setting, position at least 8-inches from heat source.
- Sprinkle with scallions. Baste with pan juices and serve.

Take favorite vegetables, fish and a lot of garlic, sauté or bake and serve over rice with a little spice!

GREEK STYLE FISH WITH TOMATO, FENNEL AND FETA

DAIRY

1½-2	pounds fish fillets, such as haddock, cod or flounder	1	large onion, diced
½	teaspoon salt, or more to taste	¾	teaspoon fennel seeds, lightly crushed with back of spoon
½	teaspoon freshly ground pepper, or more to taste	3	cups peeled and diced tomatoes, fresh or canned
3	tablespoons extra virgin olive oil	1½	teaspoons dried basil
		8	ounces good quality feta cheese
3	large cloves garlic, minced	½	cup finely chopped fresh parsley

- Preheat oven to 375 degrees.
- Rinse fish fillets and pat dry with paper towel. Season lightly with salt and pepper; set aside.
- Heat olive oil in a large skillet over medium heat. Add garlic, onion and fennel and sauté 5 minutes or until wilted but not browned. Add tomato and cook over medium-high heat for 5 to 10 minutes or until thickened. Add basil. Season to taste with salt and pepper and cook over low heat 5 to 10 minutes to develop flavor.
- Lightly grease a casserole dish large enough to hold all fish in one layer. Spread half of tomato sauce in bottom of dish. Place fish on top and cover with remaining sauce. Sprinkle with feta cheese and parsley.
- Bake 15 to 20 minutes, depending on thickness of fillets; sauce should be bubbly and fish should be opaque.
- 4-6 servings

Excellent substitutions or additions include:

A few tablespoons drained capers

2 teaspoons lemon zest

1 tablespoon dried dill in place of basil

PECAN ENCRUSTED FILLET OF FISH
PAREVE

May substitute matzoh meal for crumbs and use for Passover.

3   cups ground pecans
2   cups bread crumbs or panko (Japanese bread crumbs), plus extra for dipping
2   tablespoons mustard powder
2   teaspoons wasabi powder

1   tablespoon salt
1   tablespoon dried dill
    Generous amount of black pepper
4-5 eggs, beaten
10-12 white fish fillets, such as tilapia, red snapper, etc
    Canola oil for sautéing

- Preheat oven to 375 degrees.
- Mix pecans, 2 cups crumbs, mustard powder, wasabi powder, salt, dill and pepper in a wide bowl or pan to create a pecan crumb mixture; set aside.
- Put enough crumbs in a separate wide bowl or pan to coat fish. Place egg in another wide bowl or pan.
- On the counter top, line up crumbs, egg, pecan crumb mixture and then a foil-lined baking sheet.
- Dip fish fillets first in plain crumbs and shake off any excess. Dip fillets in egg to coat and shake off excess. Finally dip in pecan crumb mixture and place in a single layer on prepared baking sheet.
- Heat oil in a skillet or iron griddle. Add fish and sauté on each side until lightly browned. Return fillets to baking sheet.
- Bake 5 to 10 minutes.

ASIAN FISH PACKETS

PAREVE

1	cup cooked brown or white rice
2	cups coarsely chopped fresh greens, such as bok choy, kale, Swiss chard, mustard greens, spinach or combination
2	(5- to 6-ounce) fish fillets, such as salmon, snapper, or filet of sole
2	scallions, chopped

Shiitake mushrooms, sliced (optional)

Water chestnuts, sliced (optional)

1	tablespoon vegetable oil
1	tablespoon grated fresh ginger
1	clove garlic, minced
2	tablespoons soy sauce
2	teaspoons sesame oil

Chili oil to taste (optional)

- Preheat oven to 350 degrees.
- Place two 12-inch square pieces of heavy aluminum foil on countertop, or use two 12x24-inch sheets regular foil folded over to make double-thick squares.
- Divide rice between foil squares and spread. Add greens, fish, scallions, mushrooms and water chestnuts.
- In a small bowl, combine vegetable oil, ginger, garlic, soy sauce, sesame oil and chili oil. Pour half of sauce over each serving. Fold foil into airtight packets.
- Bake 20 minutes. Carefully open packets, avoiding hot steam, and transfer onto plates or into large bowls.
- 2 servings

Roasted Red Snapper with Spinach and Tomatoes
PAREVE

1	teaspoon chopped garlic	1	tablespoon soy sauce
2	pounds baby spinach	1	tablespoon sesame oil
	Olive oil for sautéing	1	pint cherry tomatoes
1	pound red snapper or salmon	1	(8- to 10-ounce) package mushrooms
2	pinches kosher salt		Juice of 1 lemon
	Black pepper to taste		

- Preheat oven to 400 degrees.
- Sauté garlic and spinach in a small amount of olive oil until spinach is just wilted. Drain any accumulated juices and place spinach in a casserole dish.
- Lay fish over spinach. Sprinkle with salt and pepper. Coat fish with soy sauce and sesame oil. Scatter tomatoes and mushrooms in dish. Squeeze lemon juice over fish.
- Bake 20 to 30 minutes.

Serve with sweet potato purée.

Tuna with Blue Cheese
DAIRY

1-2	red onions, coarsely chopped	1	pound tuna, or other firm, meaty fish
1	tablespoon olive oil	4	teaspoons butter, melted
1	tablespoon seasoning mixture of dried thyme, oregano, basil and salt	1	large tomato, seeded and coarsely chopped
		¼-½	pound blue or Gorgonzola cheese

- Preheat broiler.
- Toss onion with olive oil and seasoning mixture in an ovenproof pan. Broil onion until charred but not burnt; set aside.
- Brush tuna with melted butter. Broil 5 minutes. Turn tuna and place cooked onion, tomato and cheese on top.
- Transfer to oven setting and bake at 350 degrees for 10 to 15 minutes or until tuna reaches desired degree of doneness and cheese is melted; do not overcook.

Horseradish Encrusted Cedar Planked Trout

DAIRY

Sauce

24	peppercorns
3	bay leaves
	Juice of 3 lemons
¾	cup white wine
1½	teaspoons chopped fresh thyme

¾	cup heavy cream
6	tablespoons butter, chilled and cut into cubes
	Salt and pepper to taste

Essence

2½	tablespoons paprika
2	tablespoons salt
2	tablespoons garlic powder
1	tablespoon black pepper
1	tablespoon onion powder

1	tablespoon cayenne pepper
1	tablespoon dried oregano
1	tablespoon dried thyme

Trout

	Zest and juice of 6 lemons
	Zest and juice of 6 oranges
6	tablespoons grated fresh horseradish, or bottled
6	tablespoons chopped fresh parsley
6	tablespoons chopped fresh cilantro

	Kosher salt to taste
	Sugar to taste
6	(8-ounce) trout fillets, skin removed
	Olive oil to drizzle
6	(10-inch) untreated cedar planks, soaked in water for 1-2 hours before using

- Preheat oven to 400 degrees.
- For sauce, combine peppercorns, bay leaves, lemon juice, wine and thyme in a saucepan. Bring to a boil and cook 2 to 3 minutes. Add cream and return to a boil. Cook until reduced by half.
- Whisk in butter, a few cubes at a time. Season with salt and pepper. Strain sauce and keep warm until serving.
- Combine all essence ingredients and mix thoroughly.

- Bring a small saucepan of salted water to a boil. Blanch lemon and orange zest in boiling water for 1 minute. Remove zest and place in ice water to stop cooking process. Pat zest dry.
- Mix zest with lemon and orange juices, horseradish, parsley and cilantro to make a crust. Season with salt and sugar.
- Rub essence mixture into trout. Drizzle oil over cedar planks and place planks on a baking sheet. Place a trout fillet on each plank. Divide crust mixture evenly between fillets and spread to cover top of trout.
- Bake 12 to 15 minutes or until crust is golden and fish is cooked through, or cook on a grill. Serve with warm butter sauce on the side.
- 6 servings

Fresh Tuna Stew

PAREVE

5   tablespoons olive oil, divided

3   anchovy fillets, chopped

2   sweet onions, chopped

2   carrots, diced

3-4 cloves garlic, chopped

3   russet potatoes, coarsely chopped

½   head green cabbage, coarsely chopped

1   (28-ounce) can plum tomatoes, quartered

3   roasted red peppers, chopped

2   cups dry white wine

Zest of 1 lemon, cut into strips

½   cup torn fresh basil leaves

½   bulb fennel, trimmed, cored and sliced

2   teaspoons kosher salt, divided

1   teaspoon black pepper, divided

2   pounds very fresh tuna, cut into 1½-inch cubes

1   tablespoon Dijon mustard

1   tablespoon chopped fresh basil

1   tablespoon chopped fresh cilantro

- Heat 4 tablespoons olive oil in a large skillet over medium heat. Add anchovies, onion, carrot, garlic, potato, cabbage, tomato and roasted peppers. Cook and stir 15 minutes.
- Add wine, zest, ½ cup torn basil, fennel, 1 teaspoon salt and ½ teaspoon black pepper. Reduce heat to low and cook stew for 2 hours.
- Just before serving, combine tuna, mustard, 1 tablespoon chopped basil, cilantro, remaining 1 teaspoon salt and remaining ½ teaspoon black pepper in a bowl.
- In a new skillet, heat remaining 1 tablespoon olive oil. Add tuna mixture and quickly brown on all sides, cooking no more than 2 to 3 minutes; do not overcook, tuna should be rare to medium-rare.
- Add tuna to stew and combine.
- 6-8 servings

GRILLED TUNA WITH FRESH FIG SAUCE
Perfect for Sukkot
PAREVE OR MEAT

Fig Sauce

2 tablespoons olive oil
1/4 Spanish onion, chopped
2 cinnamon sticks
2 tablespoons imitation bacon bits
1/2 cup fresh orange juice
4 fresh figs, quartered through the stem, leaving root intact

1/2 cup chicken broth, regular or low sodium or pareve powdered mix
2 tablespoons balsamic vinegar
2 tablespoons honey

Tuna

2 tablespoons chopped fresh ginger
1/4 cup pomegranate molasses (available in Middle Eastern stores and kosher markets)
4 scallions, thinly sliced
2 tablespoons za'atar (available in Middle Eastern stores and kosher markets)

4 (8-ounce) very fresh bluefin or yellowfin tuna steaks, 1½ to 2-inches thick
1 teaspoon kosher salt
1/2 teaspoon black pepper

- To make sauce, place a large skillet over medium-high heat. Add olive oil. Add onion, cinnamon sticks, imitation bacon bits, orange juice, figs, broth, vinegar and honey, stirring well after each addition. Bring to a boil and cook 5 minutes.

- Place ginger, molasses, scallions and za'atar in a shallow bowl and stir to mix well. Add tuna and cover with marinade. Cover bowl and refrigerate 1 hour.

- Preheat a grill.

- Remove tuna from marinade, discarding marinade. Sprinkle tuna with salt and pepper.

- Grill tuna about 3 to 4-inches from heat source for 4 minutes on each side or until outside is charred and inside is very rare. Spoon fig sauce over tuna and serve immediately.

Traditionally, our grandmothers did not go outside the home to work. Their jobs were more likely to keep house, shop daily, and keep the children in line. When they did work it was usually to help our grandfathers. Many times our grandparents lived over the store or around the corner. Baby boomers' mothers may have worked before children, part-time while children were in school. In either case, circumstances may have been such that moms became the sole income providers or their incomes were necessary to keep their families afloat. More recently, moms and dads work full-time and families, in general, keep hectic schedules that require precise timing and mapping to survive. For some that may mean a large library of take-out menus, frozen dinners and stops at diners or other quick meal restaurants.

Quick home-cooked meals require a well-stocked pantry and a repertoire of easy marinades, sauces, rubs, herb pestos and salsas to use with grilled chicken, steaks and chops or fish. Buy these at your grocery store and look for those that are labeled organic and have the lowest salt content. Some, like salsas, may be found in refrigerated areas of the store and may have a short shelf life.

Outdoor grilling or a heavy-weighted and well-seasoned stove top grill pan help produce low fat and nutritious meals in less than an hour. Vegetarian meals of quick pastas, stir fry or risottos can also assure a wholesome home cooked meal in short order.

Marinades can be as simple as opening a bottle of a good vinaigrette dressing. Use resealable plastic bags for easy clean-up. Add ¼-½ cup white wine (use red wine for beef or lamb), dried or fresh herbs and Dijon mustard. Worcestershire sauce is another typical basic add in flavor.

- Asian variations: add ¼ cup soy sauce and or 2 tablespoons hoisin sauce and two cloves of minced garlic.

- Barbecue sauces are usually thick and are often better used in the last few minutes of cooking as they burn. You can add a tablespoon or two to a marinade so that the flavor is part of the cooking. Add more at the end or as a condiment on the table.

- Fish is more delicate; a marinade of lemon or lime juice with a small amount of soy sauce is needed for only a short time. Fish gets "cooked" by the acids in the juices, so do this just before cooking.

NOTE: Never use the marinade a second time once you have put your meat in it! You can make extra and separate it in two portions before adding your protein.

General grilling: Drain marinade, season with salt and pepper prior to cooking. Let rest while grill or pan heats. Spray grill pan with a bit of oil to prevent sticking. Make sure it is hot by holding hand above the pan - when you feel the heat at about 5-inches from the pan, it is hot. Lay meat, fish or poultry on a diagonal for best grill marks. Do not move or turn for at least 2 minutes or until bottom has a good sear.

- Boneless chicken breasts: grill about 6 minutes per side, or longer if breasts are thick.

- Lamb chops: grill 3 to 5 minutes per side, depending on thickness.

- Steaks or veal chops: grilling time will depend on the cut, thickness and desired degree of doneness. London broil or skirt steaks cook quickly in about 3 minutes per side. Thick rib cuts take about 6 minutes per side.

Fish: Use firm fish to grill in this manner. Halibut, cod and tuna are good choices. The thinner the fish, the harder it is to turn when grilling. For this reason, broiling or baking grouper, tilapia or snapper is easier. Fresh fruit salsas are great with fish!

If you like tuna, cut into 2- to 3-inch wide pieces. Use a bit of oil to coat all sides and then dip in a spice rub of your choice. Grill 2 minutes on each side for rare or longer if desired.

THE BATTLE OF THE BRISKETS WINNING RECIPE

MEAT

Many years ago, a group of friends decided to compare our favorite brisket recipes. This recipe won the Battle of the Briskets and has been on our holiday tables ever since.

- *Cook meat at least a day before you plan to serve it.*

- *The brisket freezes well, but do not freeze sweet potatoes.*

- *For a smaller piece of meat, adjust other ingredient amounts accordingly, but cooking time will stay the same.*

- *If making this for Passover, substitute ½ teaspoon ground ginger for the ginger snaps.*

5	pounds first-cut brisket, well trimmed of fat
	Kosher salt and freshly ground pepper to taste
	Sweet Hungarian paprika to taste
½	cup ketchup
½	cup water
½	cup lemon juice
1	cup dark brown sugar
8-10	small ginger snaps, crumbled
3	cloves garlic, chopped
3	medium-large onions, chopped
5	large carrots, thickly sliced on the diagonal
½	(10-ounce) package pitted prunes, or more to taste
3-5	sweet potatoes, peeled and thickly sliced

- Season brisket by rubbing generous amounts of salt, pepper and paprika into both sides of meat. Brown brisket well on both sides in a large Dutch oven or heavy skillet. If needed, use a small amount of vegetable oil to prevent sticking.

- Stir together ketchup, water, lemon juice, brown sugar and ginger snaps and pour over meat in pan. Scatter garlic, onion and carrot on top.

- Bring to a boil. Reduce heat and simmer, tightly covered, for at least 3 hours. After cooking for 1 hour, stir mixture and add prunes, cover and continue cooking.

- You may taste and adjust seasoning as needed, but it will taste much richer the following day. Cool and refrigerate overnight.

- The next day, remove meat from pan and slice, against the grain, with an electric knife. Place slices in a large casserole dish.

- With a slotted spoon, cover meat with carrot, onion and prunes as well as some of the pan juices. Cover with aluminum foil and refrigerate until ready to reheat.

- Add sweet potatoes to remaining juice in pan. Cover and simmer 20 minutes or until tender but not mushy. When cooked, sweet potatoes can be added to dish with meat or served in a separate dish.

- When ready to reheat, preheat oven to 350 degrees.

- Reheat meat and sweet potatoes, in covered dishes, for at least 30 minutes; being careful not to overcook meat as it will dry out.

Poppy and Grandma's Brisket

MEAT

2	tablespoons oil	2	tablespoons ketchup or tomato paste
4	pounds fresh brisket		
4	large carrots, cut into chunks	1	teaspoon grape jelly, or 1 tablespoon sugar
3	medium onions, cut into chunks	1	teaspoon lemon juice
1	bay leaf	¼	teaspoon black pepper
2	cups water	¼	teaspoon salt
1	(12-ounce) can beer	1	teaspoon paprika
1	(10-ounce) bottle tomato-based chili sauce	1	clove garlic, minced

- Heat oil in a heavy stew pot. Add brisket and brown on all sides. Add carrot, onion, bay leaf, water and beer. Cover and simmer on stove top, or bake in a 350 degree oven, for 1½ to 2 hours. Check liquid level while cooking and add more water as needed.

- Stir in chili sauce, ketchup, jelly, lemon juice, pepper, salt, paprika and garlic. Cook 2 to 4 hours longer or until meat is fork-tender.

- Transfer meat to a platter to cool and slice. Remove bay leaf from pot. Mash carrot and onion and stir back into pan juices to make a rich gravy. (For a thicker gravy, dissolve 1 tablespoon cornstarch in ¼ cup cold water. Add mixture to gravy and simmer 10 minutes or until thickened.) Serve gravy with meat.

Chilling onions before slicing will reduce tears.

HOROWITZ FAMILY BRISKET

MEAT

1	(12-ounce) can frozen orange juice concentrate	1	large first-cut beef brisket Salt and pepper to taste
3	orange juice cans water	3	large yellow onions, chopped
1	(1-ounce) package dry onion soup mix	1	(24-ounce) bottle ketchup
2	tablespoons canola oil		

- Preheat oven to 400 degrees.
- Mix juice concentrate, water and onion soup mix in a large pitcher.
- Heat canola oil in a large roasting pan. Add brisket to oil and sear over high heat for 1 to 2 minutes or until just browned. Season on both sides with salt and pepper.
- Pour about 2-inches of orange juice mixture into roasting pan. Cover brisket with onion and top with ketchup.
- Bake, uncovered for 30 minutes. Reduce temperature to 350 degrees and bake, covered, for 3 hours. Turn meat once per hour while baking and add more orange juice mixture if needed. Uncover and bake 30 minutes longer.
- If gravy is too thin when uncovered for the last 30 minutes of baking, add more ketchup. Gravy should be thick and rich, not thin and drippy.

Brisket can be made the night before serving and reheated.

BRISKET WITH SUN-DRIED TOMATOES
MEAT

1	(5-pound) brisket	4	carrots, sliced ½-inch thick
	Salt and freshly ground pepper to taste	½	cup chopped fresh parsley
2	red bell peppers, coarsely chopped	¼	cup ketchup
		1	cup beef broth
2	white onions, coarsely chopped	3	tablespoons brown sugar
3	tablespoons olive oil	1	cup sun-dried tomatoes

- Preheat oven to 350 degrees.
- Season brisket with salt and pepper and place, fat-side up, in a roasting pan.
- Sauté bell pepper and onion in olive oil until lightly browned. Scatter mixture over brisket along with carrot and parsley.
- Combine ketchup, broth and brown sugar in a measuring cup. Add enough water to equal 2 cups liquid. Stir in sun-dried tomatoes. Pour mixture around brisket. Cover pan tightly with a lid or heavy foil.
- Bake 2½ hours.
- Remove brisket from pan to cool. Trim away visible fat. Slice meat diagonally against the grain. Return to pan with vegetables and gravy.
- Reheat in 350 degree oven for 30 minutes.

SWEET AND SOUR STUFFED CABBAGE
MEAT

2	tablespoons olive oil	1	pound ground bison or lean beef
1	large onion, halved and sliced	¼	cup dry kasha
3	medium carrots, sliced	1	teaspoon black pepper
3	cloves garlic, thinly sliced	1	teaspoon garlic powder
3	large mushrooms, sliced	½	teaspoon curry powder
½	cup raisins, divided	2	(8-ounce) cans tomato sauce, divided
1	large head cabbage, separated into leaves	1	cup ketchup, divided
1	pound ground turkey	2	cups water
			Juice of ½ lemon

- Pour olive oil in the bottom of a 6- to 8-quart pot. Add onion, carrot, garlic, mushrooms and ¼ cup raisins and mix.
- Add 10 or more cabbage leaves to a 2-quart saucepan of boiling water and cook until softened.
- Combine ground meats, kasha, black pepper, garlic powder and curry powder. Form mixture into balls to fill cabbage leaves. Roll leaves around meat balls and secure with toothpicks if needed.
- Place a layer of cabbage rolls over onion mixture in pot. Mix 1 can tomato sauce with ½ cup ketchup and pour over first layer of rolls. Use remaining cabbage rolls to form a second layer. Mix remaining can of tomato sauce with remaining ½ cup ketchup and pour over the top. Sprinkle with remaining ¼ cup raisins.
- Add 2 cups water to pot and bring to a boil. Reduce heat to a simmer and cover. Cook 1½ hours.
- Add lemon juice and cook, covered, for 30 minutes longer.

This recipe was created by making variations on the original, such as adding curry powder and kasha instead of the traditional rice. The cabbage rolls can be prepared ahead and refrigerated until ready to cook.

Mamma Dora's Stuffed Cabbage

MEAT

1	head cabbage	1	small apple, chopped, divided
	Veal bones (optional)	3	tablespoons ketchup, divided
2	pounds ground beef and veal combination	4	tablespoons golden raisins, divided
2	cloves garlic, finely chopped	1½	cups tomato juice
½	cup cooked rice	1	tomato, chopped
1	small onion, chopped, divided		
5	tablespoons honey, divided		

As a simple sauce substitution, you can mix together a 26-ounce jar marinara sauce and a 14-ounce can whole cranberry sauce.

- Cut out cabbage core and blanch head of cabbage in boiling water for 5 to 10 minutes to make the leaves soft and flexible. Separate leaves and cut away the toughest part of each leaf.
- If using veal bones, simmer bones in boiling water to get foam part off the bones before placing them in the bottom of a large pot that you will be cooking the cabbage rolls in.
- Combine ground meat, garlic, rice, ½ chopped onion, 2 tablespoons honey, ½ chopped apple, 1 tablespoon ketchup and 1 tablespoon raisins in a bowl.
- Place a meatball-size amount of meat mixture in a cabbage leaf and roll up, tucking sides in. Repeat with remaining meat mixture and cabbage leaves. Place rolls, seam-side down, in large pot, arranging in layers.
- Add tomato juice, tomato, remaining ½ onion, remaining 3 tablespoons honey, remaining ½ apple, remaining 2 tablespoons ketchup and remaining 3 tablespoons raisins to pot. Add extra ketchup and tomato juice if more moisture is desired.
- Bring to a boil. Reduce heat to medium-low and cover pot with a lid. Cook 1 to 2 hours or until done.

THELMA BRASS STUFFED CABBAGE

MEAT

1 large head cabbage, cored	1 onion, chopped
1 pound lean ground beef	2 cups diced canned or
Salt and pepper to taste	fresh tomatoes
1 small onion, grated	2 tablespoons distilled
½ cup cooked rice	vinegar
1 egg, lightly beaten	3 tablespoons sugar

- Place cabbage head in a large pot and pour boiling water over top. Let stand until leaves are flexible and can be separated from head. Remove 8 large leaves, trim center vein to remove bulge and to make leaves easier to roll; set aside.

- Season meat generously with salt and pepper. Add grated onion, rice and egg and mix well.

- Place a cabbage leaf on the counter with rounded-side down so leaf "cups" the filling. Place a few spoonfuls of meat filling at the bottom of the leaf and roll up one turn. Tuck in sides and continue to roll up. Place roll, seam-side down, in a large stockpot. Repeat with remaining cabbage leaves and filling.

- Add chopped onion, tomato, vinegar and sugar to pot along with a little water or tomato juice. Chop remaining cabbage and add to pot.

- Simmer, covered, for about 1 hour. Taste and adjust sugar and vinegar as needed.

- 4 servings

Taste improves if made a day ahead.

A small can of sauerkraut can be used in place of the vinegar.

MEATBALLS IN BEER SAUCE
MEAT

Meatballs

2	pounds beef or veal	2	eggs, beaten
½	cup bread crumbs, soaked in water	1	medium onion, grated
			Salt and pepper to taste

Sauce

1	(24-ounce) bottle ketchup	1	teaspoon dry mustard
1	(12-ounce) bottle chili sauce	3	tablespoons dark brown sugar
1	(10-ounce) jar sweet relish	1	(12-ounce) can beer
1	teaspoon Worcestershire sauce		

- Preheat oven to 350 degrees.
- Combine all meatball ingredients and form into balls. Place balls on a greased baking sheet.
- Bake until meatballs are cooked through.
- Mix all sauce ingredients except beer in a pot. Bring to a simmer. Add cooked meatballs. Pour in beer and heat.

Cocktail franks can be added, if desired.
The meatballs can also be served as an appetizer.

SLOPPY JOES

MEAT

1	pound ground chuck	1	teaspoon Dijon mustard
½	cup chopped onion	1	teaspoon paprika
1	cup ketchup	1	tablespoon dark brown sugar
1	tablespoon distilled vinegar		Salt and pepper to taste
1	tablespoon fresh lemon juice	4	hamburger buns
1	teaspoon Worcestershire sauce		

- Sauté ground chuck and onion in a large skillet over medium-high heat, stirring occasionally. Break up the lumps and cook 8 minutes or until meat is no longer pink.
- Stir in ketchup, vinegar, lemon juice, Worcestershire sauce, mustard, paprika, brown sugar and salt and pepper. Cook, uncovered, over low heat, stirring occasionally for 30 minutes or until mixture has thickened.
- Divide mixture among hamburger buns.
- 4 servings

CUBAN PICADILLO
(Savory Ground Beef)
MEAT

2	tablespoons olive oil	¼	cup vino seco (dry white wine)
1	medium onion, chopped		
½	green bell pepper, diced	2	tablespoons sliced stuffed Spanish olives
1	clove garlic, minced		
1	pound extra-lean ground beef	1	tablespoon capers, drained
1	(8-ounce) can tomato sauce	1	bay leaf
¼	cup raisins (optional)	½	teaspoon ground cumin
			Salt and pepper to taste

- Heat olive oil in a large, heavy skillet over medium heat. Add onion and bell pepper and sauté 3 to 5 minutes or until onion is translucent. Add garlic and cook a few minutes longer.
- Add beef and cook and stir, breaking up lumps with a fork or spatula until beef is browned without letting beef stick to bottom of pan.
- Reduce heat to low and stir in tomato sauce, raisins, wine, olives, capers, bay leaf, cumin and salt and pepper. Simmer at least 20 minutes or until mixture thickens. For optimal flavor, simmer longer.

For a healthy substitution, use ground turkey, veal or chicken in place of the beef.

In order to have a real Cuban meal, serve the picadillo with plenty of fluffy white rice, black beans, plantains and or tostones.

Every Cuban cook has a special way of making picadillo. Some omit the capers and add raisins. Others add cubed, fried potatoes and top each serving with a fried egg.

Picadillo has always been Cuban comfort food and food for my soul. It brings back memories of Sunday get-togethers with my large Cuban Jewish family in Miami. With the accompaniments, it makes a plentiful meal that serves many and is even better as a leftover.

Asian Glazed Short Ribs

MEAT

1 tablespoon Chinese five-spice powder

2 teaspoons kosher salt

2 teaspoons brown sugar

1 teaspoon toasted and ground coriander seed

½ teaspoon toasted and ground cumin seed, or use more coriander

½ teaspoon black pepper

4 pounds short ribs (use about 1 pound per person)

3 tablespoons peanut or olive oil, divided

2 large onions, coarsely chopped

Salt and pepper to taste

3 large cloves garlic, mashed

2 tablespoons coarsely chopped fresh ginger

1 (12-ounce) bottle beer

1 cup low-salt beef or chicken broth

2 tablespoons soy sauce

1 bay leaf

¼ cup honey

2 tablespoons orange juice

2 tablespoons ketchup

1 teaspoon fish sauce (Chinese section of grocery store)

- Combine five-spice powder, salt, brown sugar, coriander seed, cumin seed and black pepper in a bowl. Rub mixture over short ribs. Place on a long baking dish, cover with plastic wrap and refrigerate 12 to 24 hours.

- Preheat oven to 300 degrees.

- Heat 2 tablespoons oil over medium heat until hot in a heavy, oven-proof pot with a lid. Brown ribs in hot oil for 3 to 4 minutes per side, turning frequently to evenly brown all sides. Transfer ribs to a platter.

- Pour off most of fat from pot. Add remaining 1 tablespoon oil to pot. Add onion and season with salt and pepper. Cook 5 to 7 minutes or until soft and brown. Add garlic and ginger and cook 2 minutes longer. Stir in beer and bring to a boil. Cook 2 minutes, scraping bottom to dislodge brown bits. Add broth and soy sauce and return to a boil. Reduce to a simmer and add bay leaf.

- Return ribs to pot in a single layer. Crumble a large sheet of foil over pot and cover with lid. Transfer to oven.

- Bake on lower rack of oven for 2½ hours or until fork tender, turning every 45 minutes. Transfer ribs to a large, oven-proof pan and cover with foil to keep warm.

- Strain pan juices through a sieve into a large measuring cup, pressing solids with a spoon to remove all liquid. Skim fat.
- To make a glaze, measure honey into a measuring cup. Add orange juice, ketchup and fish sauce and whisk together.
- Preheat broiler and place rack 6-inches from heat source.
- Brush top of ribs with glaze. Broil 4 minutes or until glazed.
- Serve ribs with strained pan juices on the side.

Toast coriander and cumin seeds in a pan in the oven,
then grind in a coffee grinder.

CHINESE BEEF
MEAT

2	tablespoons oil	½	cup cooking sherry
2	onions, coarsely chopped	2	tomatoes, cut into wedges
2	scallions, chopped	2	green bell peppers, cut into strips
2	pounds skirt steak		
	Black pepper to taste	2	pounds fresh mushrooms, sliced
	Garlic to taste		
1	heaping teaspoon sugar	1	cup beef bouillon
⅓	cup soy sauce	1	tablespoon cornstarch

- Heat oil in a large skillet. Add onion and scallions and sauté. Season beef with pepper and garlic. Add beef to skillet and brown on all sides.
- Mix sugar with soy sauce. Add mixture to beef in skillet. Add sherry and cover skillet tightly. Cook over low heat for 5 minutes.
- Add tomatoes, bell peppers and mushrooms and bring to a boil. Cook briskly for 5 minutes.
- Combine bouillon and cornstarch to make a smooth paste. Add mixture to skillet. Cook, stirring occasionally, until thick and smooth.

Grandma Sara was my mom. She tiptoed into her twenties just as the Germans stormed into Poland, and I always marveled that somewhere along the line, she became a glorious cook. And, even though her Auschwitz tattoo peeked over the wooden stirring spoon, my mom always cooked with a smile. The recipes she has left us to enjoy are simple to make and beautiful on the plate. I have made two changes. Since my mom never felt a need for written recipes, the measurements have been added by me. And, I have omitted the oil in the browning step, to lighten the recipe a bit. It's likely there was no Teflon around when my mom began cooking and omitting the oil doesn't impact the flavor at all. Please smile while you make this tsimmis.

Short Ribs with Tsimmis

MEAT

3	pounds short ribs, cut on the long side (the opposite way you would cut for grilling)	⅓	cup light brown sugar
		½	teaspoon cinnamon
		1	teaspoon salt
2	medium onions, cut into chunks	3	medium-size sweet potatoes, cut into 1-inch slices
1	cup water	1	cup yellow raisins

- Brown short ribs well in a nonstick pan. Add onion until they glisten a bit. Transfer meat and onion to a clay or ceramic casserole dish with a tight-fitting cover.
- Add water, brown sugar, cinnamon and salt to same nonstick pan. Heat and stir. Pour mixture over ribs and cover casserole dish.
- Place covered casserole dish in cold oven and turn heat to 350 degrees. Bake 1½ hours; no need to check while baking.
- After 1½ hours, add potato slices and raisins. Bake, covered, for 45 minutes longer.
- 4 servings

Recipe can be prepared up to 4 days ahead. Prepare through the 1¼ hours of baking. When ready to serve, add potatoes and raisins and bake at 350 degrees for 1 hour.

If you like to serve your tsimmis the way my mom did, serve with white rice or noodles to soak up all the delectable sauce, and fresh, slightly crunchy green beans on the side.

BEEF CHILI
MEAT

2   tablespoons oil
2   pounds ground beef
3   medium onions, chopped
1   green bell pepper, chopped
2   cloves garlic, minced
3   cups stewed tomatoes
2   (15-ounce) cans kidney beans, rinsed and drained
1½ tablespoons chili powder, or to taste
1   teaspoon cayenne pepper or hot pepper sauce

2   cubes bouillon, mixed with 1 cup water (optional)
1   teaspoon ground cumin
½   teaspoon chipotle powder (optional)
1   (4-ounce) can diced green chiles
2   (15-ounce) cans tomato sauce (optional)
    Salt and pepper to taste

- Heat oil in a saucepan. Add beef, onion, bell pepper and garlic and sauté until beef is browned; drain fat and return beef mixture to saucepan.
- Add tomatoes, beans, chili powder, cayenne pepper, bouillon, cumin, chipotle powder, chiles and tomato sauce. Season with salt and pepper.
- Simmer 1 hour or until chili starts to thicken.

Vegetarian option: Replace beef with a 15-ounce can each of corn, black beans and cannellini beans.

Quick Sauerbraten

MEAT

Fast and simple beyond belief ... and you can't imagine how delicious this is for so little effort. Some advanced preparation needed.

1   (4-pound) boneless pot roast (chuck or brisket works well)
    Salt and pepper to taste
1   quart commercial beet borscht

¼   cup distilled vinegar
¼   cup vegetable oil
2   large onions, sliced
8-10 ginger snaps, crushed

- Season pot roast on all sides with salt and pepper and place in a large glass bowl. Pour borscht and vinegar over beef. Cover and refrigerate 2 days.
- Drain beef, reserving marinade. Heat vegetable oil in a large pot or Dutch oven. Brown beef on all sides in hot oil. Add onion and reserved marinade. Cover tightly and simmer 1½ to 2 hours or until meat is tender.
- Remove beef and cut into thick slices.
- Skim fat from pan juices and stir in enough ginger snaps until juices thicken slightly. Season with salt and pepper. Spoon some pan juices over beef and serve remainder on the side.

Serve with plenty of wide noodles and red cabbage cooked with apples.

STIR-FRIED BEEF AND VEGETABLES
MEAT

1	pound beef skirt steak, well trimmed	3	teaspoons oil, divided
2	tablespoons lite teriyaki sauce	2	medium onions, cut into wedges
2	tablespoons dry vermouth	1	bunch broccoli, cut into ½-inch chunks
2-3	cloves garlic, crushed	1	green or red bell pepper, cut into chunks
⅛-¼	teaspoon dried red pepper flakes	½	pint cherry tomatoes, halved
1¾	cups beef broth		
2	teaspoons cornstarch		

- Cut beef into 1½-inch strips. Cut strips diagonally across the grain into ⅛-inch thick pieces.
- In a small bowl, combine teriyaki sauce, vermouth, garlic and pepper flakes. Add beef strips and toss to coat well.
- In a separate bowl, combine beef broth and cornstarch; set aside.
- Heat 2 teaspoons oil until very hot in a medium skillet over high heat. Add beef strips and cook quickly for 3 to 5 minutes, stirring frequently. Remove beef with a slotted spoon to a bowl; set aside.
- In same skillet, heat remaining 1 teaspoon oil. Add onion, broccoli and bell pepper and stir-fry 3 to 4 minutes.
- Stir in broth mixture, cover and reduce heat. Cook 5 minutes or until vegetables are crisp-tender. Add cherry tomatoes and beef strips and cook, stirring gently, until sauce thickens.

MARTHA'S MOM'S FILLET OF BEEF
MEAT

1	whole fillet of beef	Worcestershire sauce
1½	(10-ounce) bottles chili sauce	Margarine

- Preheat oven to 300 degrees.
- Place beef fillet in a baking pan. Pour chili sauce liberally over beef. Sprinkle Worcestershire sauce along the top of the fillet. Dot fillet every 1½-inches with thin slices of margarine.
- Bake 25 to 30 minutes, testing for doneness in the thickest part; do not overcook.

The more Worcestershire sauce used, the more tang you get.

THAI PEANUT SAUCE
PAREVE

1 cup coconut milk	1 tablespoon lime juice
1 tablespoon curry paste or curry powder	½ teaspoon salt
1 tablespoon satay or chili paste	1 tablespoon chopped fresh tarragon, or 1 teaspoon dried, plus extra for garnish
2 tablespoons chunky peanut butter	1 green onion, chopped
2 tablespoons sugar	

- Bring coconut milk to a boil in a skillet. Reduce heat to medium and stir in curry and satay paste. Stir in peanut butter, sugar, lime juice and salt.
- Simmer 10 minutes or until slightly thickened. Remove from heat and cool to room temperature.
- As mixture cools, stir in tarragon. If sauce is too thick, thin with white wine. Garnish with extra tarragon and green onion.

Excellent as a dipping sauce with beef or chicken.

STIR-FRY GARLIC SAUCE
PAREVE

¼ cup soy sauce	2 tablespoons molasses
½ cup water	3 cloves garlic, crushed
½ cup brown sugar	

- Combine all ingredients and mix well.
- 1 cup sauce

To thicken sauce, bring to a boil in a saucepan.
Dissolve 1 tablespoon cornstarch in 2 tablespoons water or orange juice and add to sauce. Simmer 2 to 3 minutes or until thickened, stirring often.

Honey Garlic Sauce: Prepare sauce as above, using only ¼ cup brown sugar and adding 2 tablespoons honey.

This sauce is excellent for chicken, meatballs, fish, tofu, beef ribs or vegetables.

ROPA VIEJAS
(Shredded Beef - "Old Clothes")

MEAT

4	skirt steaks		Salt to taste
3	medium-size yellow onions, 1 whole, 2 thinly sliced, divided	¼	cup olive oil
		2	red bell peppers, thinly sliced
4	cloves garlic, smashed, divided	1	yellow bell pepper, thinly sliced
1	teaspoon black peppercorns	2	teaspoons ground cumin
1	tomato, quartered	2	tablespoons tomato paste
3	green bell peppers, thinly sliced	1	teaspoon vinegar
	Juice of 2 limes		Black pepper to taste
		3	tablespoons chopped fresh cilantro

- Combine skirt steaks with whole onion, 2 cloves garlic, peppercorns, tomato and green bell pepper. Add water to cover and bring to a simmer. Cook about 1½ hours.
- Cool in pan. Remove cooled meat and discard other pan ingredients. Shred beef with fingers.
- Place shredded beef, lime juice and a little salt in a bowl. Marinate in refrigerator overnight.
- Sauté meat in olive oil in a skillet until brown. Remove meat and set aside.
- Add red and yellow bell peppers, remaining 2 cloves garlic and cumin to skillet. Sauté over medium heat until softened.
- Add meat and tomato paste to vegetables. Stir in vinegar and season with salt and pepper. Garnish with cilantro.
- 8 servings

Serve with rice, rice and beans, black beans, fried plantains, sliced tomatoes, sliced avocado or guacamole and/or warmed tortillas.

Plantains: Select ripe plantains from the produce department. Slice into large diagonal pieces and fry in vegetable or peanut oil until golden and caramelized.

Shepherd's Pie

MEAT

1 pound ground beef
1 large onion, chopped
2 large carrots, diced
1 cube beef bouillon
1½ cups boiling water
3-4 teaspoons nondairy powdered gravy mix
½ cup cold water
Salt and pepper to taste
¼ teaspoon garlic powder (optional)

1 teaspoon nutmeg (optional)
Worcestershire sauce to taste (optional)
Dash of soy sauce (optional)
8-10 medium potatoes, peeled and quartered
Kosher nondairy creamer
Margarine

- Preheat oven to 350 degrees.
- Brown beef in a skillet, breaking up lumps with a spatula. Drain fat and set beef aside on a plate.
- Add onion to same skillet and sauté until translucent. Return browned beef to skillet and continue cooking mixture.
- Meanwhile, boil carrot in a saucepan until tender; drain.
- Mix bouillon cube with 1½ cups boiling water. In a separate container, combine gravy mix and ½ cup cold water and mix well, adding more water if needed. Stir hot bouillon and gravy into beef mixture.
- Add salt and pepper, garlic powder, nutmeg and mix well. Add Worcestershire sauce and a dash of soy sauce. Stir in carrots and more water, if needed.
- Simmer mixture over low heat for 30 minutes.
- Meanwhile, cook potatoes in boiling water until soft. Drain potatoes and mash with nondairy creamer and margarine.
- Spoon meat mixture into a large casserole dish, reserving most of gravy in skillet. Spoon mashed potatoes around the edges of the dish. Gradually work potatoes into the center and seal on all sides.
- Bake 15 to 20 minutes or until potatoes start to brown. If potatoes are prepared ahead, bake 30 to 40 minutes. Serve gravy on the side.

Beef Wellington
MEAT

1	(3-pound) rib-eye roast, trimmed	6	chicken livers, broiled (optional)
1	pound mushrooms, minced	2	tablespoons brandy (optional)
6	scallions, minced		Simple Flaky Dough (see sidebar)
4	tablespoons margarine		
2	tablespoons chopped fresh parsley	1	egg yolk, beaten with 1 tablespoon water

- Preheat oven to 400 degrees.
- Bake roast for 1½ hours or until done; set aside to cool. Increase oven temperature to 450 degrees.
- Sauté mushrooms and scallions in margarine. Add parsley and cook 2 minutes; set aside to cool.
- Optional: process chicken livers in a blender. Mix in brandy and set aside.
- On a floured board, roll dough to ⅛-inch thick into a rectangle a little more than double the size of the rib-eye roast. Spread liver mixture over dough to within 1-inch of the edges. Scatter mushroom mixture over top. Place roast in center of dough on mushrooms.
- Bring a long side of the dough up over the roast. Brush edge with some beaten egg. Bring the other long side of dough up, overlapping the egg-brushed dough. Press to seal. Fold up both ends of the dough and brush with egg yolk to seal.
- Place wrapped roast, seam-side down, on a large baking sheet or pan. Brush top and sides with remaining egg yolk. Cut 2 to 3 slashes in dough to create vents.
- Bake 20 minutes or until pastry is golden brown. Slice and serve.

SIMPLE FLAKY DOUGH
PAREVE OR MEAT

2	cups flour
½	teaspoon salt
2	sticks margarine
	Sesame seeds (optional)
⅓	cup ice water
2	tablespoons vinegar
1	egg yolk
1	teaspoon water

- Mix flour with salt in a mixing bowl. Cut in margarine with a pastry blender. Mix in sesame seeds.
- In a separate bowl, mix ice water, vinegar and egg yolk. Add liquid mixture to flour mixture, a little at a time, until thoroughly combined; do not overmix, dough should be soft, not sticky.
- Refrigerate dough in a plastic bag for 2 hours or more before rolling.

This dough can be used to wrap around cocktail franks or large franks cut into thirds. Bake at 350 degrees for 15 to 20 minutes or until golden brown.

Meat mixture can also be formed into small, bite-size patties and served with toothpicks as an appetizer at an evening party.

ISRAELI KEBABS
(Ground Beef or Turkey)

MEAT

2	pounds ground beef or turkey	2	teaspoons Worcestershire sauce
1	bunch parsley, chopped	1-2	teaspoons baharat (available in Middle Eastern Israeli markets)
1	large onion, grated		
¼	cup bread crumbs	1	teaspoon ground cumin Salt and pepper to taste
2	eggs		

- Preheat oven to 375 degrees.
- Combine all ingredients and form into individual serving-size cylinder-shaped patties. Place in a greased baking dish.
- Bake 30 minutes.

Best served with "amba" - curried mango
(the yellow spice you see offered at falafel restaurants in Israel).

GLAZED CORNED BEEF

MEAT

1¾	pounds corned beef	2	tablespoons olive oil
⅔	cup brown sugar	2	tablespoons spicy mustard
1½	cups ketchup		
¾	cup vinegar		

- Cook corned beef in boiling water for 2 hours or until tender.
- Meanwhile, combine brown sugar, ketchup, vinegar, olive oil and mustard in a saucepan. Simmer sauce until well blended.
- When tender, transfer corned beef to a greased roasting pan. Pour sauce over beef.
- Preheat oven to 350 degrees.
- Bake, uncovered, for 30 minutes or until brightly glazed. Let rest for at least 30 minutes prior to slicing.

Veal Piccata
MEAT

6	veal cutlets, pounded thin	1	cup chicken broth, or more if needed
1	egg, beaten with 1 tablespoon water	2	tablespoons flour
½	cup bread crumbs	¼	cup lemon juice
	Salt and pepper to taste	2	(10-ounce) bags fresh spinach (optional)
2	tablespoons olive oil	¼	cup chopped fresh parsley

- Dip veal in egg mixture, then coat well with bread crumbs and season with salt and pepper.
- Heat olive oil in a large skillet. Brown veal on both sides in hot oil. Add broth and simmer 15 minutes or until veal is cooked through.
- Dissolve flour in lemon juice. Remove veal from skillet and stir in flour mixture. Cook and stir over low heat until thickened and smooth.
- Add spinach and place veal on top. Sprinkle with parsley. Serve over rice or pasta, if desired.
- 4 servings

This recipe may be adapted for chicken.
Use cutlets pounded thin just like the veal.

Roasted Rack of Veal
MEAT

1	(4½-pounds) rack of veal	¼	cup fresh basil leaves
6-8	cloves garlic, each cut into eighths		Zest of 1 orange
¼	cup fresh rosemary leaves	1	teaspoon kosher salt
¼	cup fresh thyme leaves	½	teaspoon black pepper
		½	cup olive oil

- Place veal on a platter. Poke holes all over veal about 1-inch apart by pushing a paring knife through the fat and turning. Insert a garlic slice into each hole.
- Combine any remaining garlic with rosemary, thyme, basil, zest, salt and pepper in a food processor fitted with a steel blade. Pulse until finely chopped. Add olive oil and process until mixture forms a chunky paste. Rub mixture all over veal. Cover and refrigerate at least 2 hours or overnight.
- When ready to cook, preheat oven to 425 degrees or preheat a grill.
- Roast or grill, uncovered, for 25 minutes. Let meat rest 15 to 20 minutes before carving. Serve 1 bone per person.

CHEF JEFFREY'S MARINATED LAMB WITH ROASTED POTATOES AND CARROTS

MEAT

2	racks of lamb, preferably organic		and cut into 1-inch cubes
1½	cups Miso-Shallot Marinade, divided *(see recipe below)*	1	(1-pound) package baby carrots
3	large potatoes, preferably Yukon Gold, unpeeled	1	cup sliced scallions, white and green parts
			Kosher salt and freshly ground pepper to taste

- Rub lamb all over with 1 cup marinade. Marinate racks in marinade for 4 hours.
- Preheat oven to 525 degrees with empty roasting pan in oven.
- Toss potato, carrots and scallions with remaining ½ cup marinade and salt and pepper to taste.
- Remove hot roasting pan from oven and add vegetable mixture to pan (it sizzles!) Place racks of lamb on vegetables.
- Roast 10 to 15 minutes or until lamb is brown. Reduce oven temperature to 250 degrees and roast 10 minutes longer or until a meat thermometer indicates roast is cooked to desired degree of doneness. Remove from oven and let rest on a carving board for 5 to 10 minutes before carving.
- Place roasted vegetables on a large platter. Top with carved lamb.
- 4 servings

This is a beautiful one-dish meal.

MISO-SHALLOT MARINADE

PAREVE

1	cup miso	1	teaspoon sesame oil
1	cup chopped shallots	3	cups canola oil
1	tablespoon sugar		Salt and pepper to taste
2	tablespoons freshly squeezed lemon juice		

- Combine miso, shallots, sugar, lemon juice and sesame oil in a food processor and purée. With motor running, slowly add canola oil to emulsify mixture.

Marinade can be stored in refrigerator for 2 to 3 weeks.

A wonderful marinade for beef, chicken or fish.

SAVORY CROWN LAMB ROAST
MEAT

2   crown lamb roasts, each with 14 chops (each consisting of two 7-rib racks tied together)

½   cup chopped fresh rosemary

1   head garlic, minced

2   tablespoons fresh thyme, or 2 teaspoons dried

1   tablespoon black pepper

1   tablespoon salt

¼   cup olive oil

Sprigs of rosemary for garnish

- Preheat oven to 450 degrees.
- Place roasts, spaced apart, in a large roasting pan.
- Combine rosemary, garlic, thyme, pepper, salt and olive oil. Rub mixture over roasts. Cover bones loosely with aluminum foil.
- Bake 20 minutes for rare (125-130 degrees), 30 minutes for medium-rare (130-135 degrees) or 35 minutes for medium (135 to 140 degrees).
- Transfer roasts to a serving platter and let rest 5 minutes. Remove foil and cut string between ribs. Garnish with sprigs of rosemary.

This recipe makes a festive presentation. Your butcher will prepare the meat for you - don't forget to order it ahead of time.

VEAL IN WINE SAUCE

MEAT

9 tablespoons margarine, divided
2½ pounds veal rump roast, or beef top round, cut into 1½-inch cubes
⅓ cup brandy
1 teaspoon tomato paste
1 tablespoon flour
1¾ cups chicken broth
½ cup dry white wine
1 teaspoon currant jelly
1½ teaspoons black pepper, divided
½ pound ground veal
2 egg whites
1 cup plus 1 tablespoon pareve soy milk or non-dairy creamer, divided

1 teaspoon salt, or to taste
½ teaspoon chopped garlic
2 teaspoons chopped shallots
2 teaspoons chopped chives
8 ounces button mushrooms, halved if large
2 teaspoons lemon juice
24 pitted olives, combination of black and green
3 slices white bread, crusts removed
Chopped parsley for garnish

- Preheat oven to 375 degrees.
- Melt 4 tablespoons margarine in a Dutch oven, using a wooden spoon to stir margarine until hot.
- Brown veal cubes quickly in margarine in batches until well browned on all sides. When finished with last batch, return all veal cubes to pan.
- Heat brandy in a saucepan, tilting pan until flame ignites brandy. Pour brandy over veal. When brandy has burned off, remove veal cubes with a slotted spoon; set veal aside.
- Add 2 tablespoons margarine to pan juices. Remove from heat and stir in tomato paste and flour and stir until smooth. Blend in chicken broth, wine, jelly and 1 teaspoon pepper.
- Return Dutch oven to heat and stir sauce with a wooden spoon until it comes to a boil. Add veal cubes back to pan and cover.
- Transfer to center rack of oven and bake 1¼ hours, basting occasionally.
- Meanwhile, combine ground veal and egg whites in a mixing bowl and mix well with an electric mixer. Add 1 tablespoon soy milk while mixing vigorously. Add remaining 1 cup soy milk, a little at a time, mixing well before each addition. While mixing on high speed, add remaining ½ teaspoon pepper, salt, garlic, shallots and chives and mix well.

- Form meat mixture into balls. After 1¼ hours in oven, remove Dutch oven. Drop meat balls into gravy in Dutch oven. Return to oven and bake 10 minutes.

- Heat remaining 3 tablespoons margarine in a skillet. Add mushrooms and cook and stir with a wooden stick. Add lemon juice and a pinch of salt and pepper and sauté 2 to 3 minutes longer. Mix in olives. Add mixture to Dutch oven and bake 5 minutes longer.

- Toast bread slices and cut each in half diagonally, forming 6 triangles total. Arrange triangles around the edge of the casserole dish. Sprinkle parsley on top.

BLACK PEPPER-CRUSTED STANDING RIB ROAST AU JUS

MEAT

Boning the roast makes slicing the meat much easier at serving time. Have your butcher remove the backbone, or chine, from the whole rack and cut the meat off the ribs in one piece, then tie the meat back onto the bones. The roast can be served on or off the bones.

To crack whole peppercorns, enclose them in a resealable plastic bag and crush slightly with a meat mallet, or grind them in a pepper or coffee grinder.

What to drink? A medium to full-bodied red wine with a peppery spice such as syrah.

1	(8½-pound) standing rib roast, top fat removed Vegetable oil
12	tablespoons margarine, softened
2	tablespoons cracked or coarsely ground black pepper, or to taste
4	large cloves garlic, minced
½	teaspoon salt, plus as needed, divided
2¼	cups low-sodium broth
½	cup dry red wine Roasted red onions
1	large bunch watercress for garnish

- Preheat oven to 350 degrees.
- Position oven rack in bottom third of oven.
- Place roast, fat-side up, in a roasting pan. Brush exposed ends of roast with vegetable oil. Sprinkle roast lightly all over with salt.
- Mix 8 tablespoons margarine, black pepper, garlic and ½ teaspoon salt in a small bowl. Reserve 2 tablespoons pepper margarine for sauce. Spread remaining pepper margarine all over top (fat side) of roast. (Preparation can be done to this point up to 1 day ahead. Cover and chill roast and reserved pepper margarine separately.)
- Roast about 2 hours, 45 minutes or until an instant-read thermometer inserted into the thickest part of meat registers 125 degrees for medium-rare. Transfer roast to a platter and cover loosely with foil; let rest 30 minutes (temperature will rise slightly as it stands.)
- Strain pan juices from roasting pan into a measuring cup. Skim off any fat from top of pan juices. Discard fat and return pan juices to roasting pan. Set pan over 2 burners over high heat. Add broth and wine and boil 6 minutes or until liquid is reduced to 1¼ cups, scraping up any browned bits from bottom of pan.
- Whisk in reserved pepper margarine and remaining 4 tablespoons margarine. Season sauce with more salt and margarine if desired.
- Surround roast with roasted red onions. Garnish with watercress. Slice and serve with sauce.
- 8 servings

To roast onions in a roasting pan, drizzle sliced onions with extra virgin olive oil and a small amount of balsamic vinegar. Roast at 400 degrees for 15 to 20 minutes or until soft and caramel in color.

BEEF BOURGUIGNONNE
MEAT

3	cups red wine	4	tablespoons olive oil, divided	
2	tablespoons brandy			
2	onions, thinly sliced	2	onions, chopped	
2	carrots, chopped	1	tablespoon tomato paste	
2	tablespoons chopped fresh parsley	1	(10½-ounce) can vegetable broth	
1	bay leaf		Salt and pepper to taste	
4	cloves garlic, crushed, divided	3	tablespoons flour	
12	whole black peppercorns	4	tablespoons margarine	
1	teaspoon salt	1	pound fresh mushrooms, sliced	
2	pounds beef chuck roast, cubed			

- In a large bowl, combine wine, brandy, sliced onions, carrots, parsley, bay leaf, 2 cloves garlic, peppercorns and salt. Add beef and marinate in refrigerator up to 2 days.
- Preheat oven to 300 degrees.
- Drain beef and pat dry, reserving marinade. Heat 2 tablespoons olive oil in a skillet. Add beef to skillet and cook 10 minutes or until brown on all sides. Transfer beef to a separate bowl and set aside.
- Add reserved marinade liquid to skillet and deglaze, scraping up the bits from the bottom; pour out marinade and set aside.
- Heat remaining 2 tablespoons olive oil in skillet. Add chopped onion and sliced onion and carrot from marinade and sauté 5 minutes. Add to beef in bowl. Return skillet to heat. Add tomato paste, broth, reserved marinade and salt and pepper. Bring to a boil. Whisk in flour until lumps disappear. Add meat and vegetable mixture. Transfer to an ovenproof baking dish.
- Bake 3 hours, stirring occasionally. Season as needed with salt and pepper. About 30 minutes before serving, sauté mushrooms until brown and add to meat when done. Let stand 15 minutes before serving.

Deglazing the pan: After roasting or sautéing, food drippings and particles are left in the pan. The French term for this is "fond". The fond is filled with flavor and is wonderful to add to sauces and gravies. To deglaze, add wine, water or stock to the pan and scrape with a wooden spoon with the heat on high until the sauce boils.

LEMONY CHICKEN WITH GREEN BEANS AND POTATO

MEAT

8	tablespoons extra virgin olive oil, divided	1	pound fresh green beans, trimmed
4	lemons, divided	10	small red potatoes, halved or quartered depending on size
5	cloves garlic, lightly mashed with the side of a knife		
1	teaspoon salt	4	chicken breasts with bone, or 1 whole chicken cut into 8 pieces
½	teaspoon freshly ground pepper		

- Preheat oven to 450 degrees.
- Grease a 9x13-inch casserole dish with 1 tablespoon olive oil. Slice 2 lemons and arrange on bottom of casserole dish.
- In a mixing bowl, combine remaining 7 tablespoons olive oil, juice of remaining 2 lemons, garlic, salt and pepper. Add green beans and potatoes and toss to coat vegetables.
- With a slotted spoon, remove beans, potatoes and garlic from bowl and place atop lemon slices.
- Add chicken to marinade in bowl and toss to coat. Arrange chicken over vegetables in dish and pour marinade over all.
- Bake 50 minutes or until chicken is done. Remove chicken and keep warm. Return casserole to oven and roast 10 minutes longer or until vegetables are tender.
- 6 servings

Sauce ingredients can be doubled so there is extra for serving on the side.

Rancho Chicken
MEAT

1	(3-pound) chicken, cut up	1	(16-ounce) can cream-style corn
½	cup flour		
	Salt and pepper to taste	½	cup sliced green olives
4	tablespoons oil, divided	1	(6-ounce) can tomato paste
1	cup chopped onion	1	cup water
1	cup chopped green bell pepper	1	teaspoon chili powder

- Preheat oven to 350 degrees.
- Dredge chicken in flour seasoned with salt and pepper. Brown floured chicken in 2 tablespoons oil in a skillet. Transfer chicken to a 9x13-inch dish.
- Sauté onion and bell pepper in remaining 2 tablespoons oil until tender. Scatter sautéed vegetables over chicken. Pour corn over top and sprinkle with olive slices.
- Blend tomato paste, water and chili powder and pour mixture over chicken.
- Bake 1½ hours.

Vinegar Chicken
MEAT

1	(3-pound) chicken, cut up	2	tablespoons oregano
3	tablespoons canola oil	1	teaspoon garlic powder
1	cup cider vinegar	1	cube chicken bouillon

- Brown chicken in oil in a skillet until well browned.
- Combine vinegar, oregano, garlic powder and chicken bouillon and pour over chicken.
- Simmer, loosely covered, over medium-low heat for 45 minutes. Serve with rice.

Use hummus as an accompaniment to chicken, meat or vegetable dishes. The chickpea and sesame mixture can be found in any supermarket or specialty food store. Also, spread on grilled pita drizzled with extra virgin olive oil and sliced ripe tomatoes.

CHICKEN VERONIQUE
MEAT

4	large or 6 small chicken breasts, with bone and skin, excess skin and fat removed	2-3	cloves garlic, finely chopped
	Salt and freshly ground pepper to taste	1/2	teaspoon dried oregano
2	(6-ounce) jars marinated artichoke hearts	1/4	cup chopped fresh parsley
12	ounces white mushrooms, sliced		Olive oil if needed
			Juice of 1½ lemons
		1	cup white wine

- Season chicken breasts with salt and pepper; set aside.
- Drain liquid from 1 jar of artichoke hearts into a large skillet. Add mushrooms, garlic, oregano, parsley and salt and pepper to taste. Cook until all liquid is evaporated and mushrooms start to brown. Remove mushrooms from pan; set aside.
- Drain liquid from second jar of artichoke hearts into same skillet and heat until liquid starts to boil off and oil remains in pan. If necessary, add a little olive oil to pan. Brown chicken in hot oil for a few minutes on each side or until rich brown in color and slightly cooked.
- Add artichokes, lemon juice and wine to skillet. Cover and simmer about 15 minutes or until chicken is just cooked through; overcooking will dry out the chicken.
- Add mushrooms during the last few minutes of cooking and heat through. Adjust seasoning as needed.

The delicious juice makes noodles or mashed potatoes an excellent accompaniment.

ROAST DUCK WITH CURRANT SAUCE

MEAT

Duck

1	(4½- to 5-pound) duck	1	clove garlic, crushed
	Salt to taste	½	teaspoon whole
2	oranges, quartered		peppercorns

Basting Sauce

1	stick margarine	½	teaspoon sage
½	cup white wine	½	teaspoon salt
2	cloves garlic, crushed		

Wine Sauce

⅔	cup pan drippings from duck	1	cup currant jelly
3	tablespoons flour	1	teaspoon Dijon mustard
1	cup white wine	1	teaspoon salt

- Preheat oven to 425 degrees.

- Clean and dry duck. Sprinkle cavity with salt and stuff with orange, garlic and peppercorns. Fold skin flap over cavity to close and tie legs together with string. Fold wings under body and place duck, breast-side up, on a rack in an open roasting pan.

- For basting sauce, melt margarine in a saucepan over low heat. Remove from heat and stir in wine, garlic, sage and salt. Pour sauce over duck.

- Roast duck, uncovered, for 30 minutes. Reduce temperature to 375 degrees and roast 1½ hours, basting often. Remove from oven and cover with foil.

- To make wine sauce, mix ⅔ cup pan drippings from roast duck with flour in a saucepan and whisk until smooth. Add wine, jelly, mustard and salt and bring to a boil. Cook and stir until sauce is smooth and thick.

- Brush duck with wine sauce before serving. Serve remaining wine sauce on the side.

- 4 servings

Gala glaze can be used instead of wine sauce. To prepare, mix ½ cup brown sugar, 1 tablespoon cornstarch, 1 teaspoon caraway seeds and ¼ teaspoon salt in a saucepan. Stir in a 7-ounce bottle of 7-Up soda. Cook over low heat, stirring continuously, until slightly thickened. Add 1 cup raisins and cook until thick. Spoon glaze over duck during final 30 minutes of baking time.

Chicken Honey Raisin

MEAT

4	boneless, skinless chicken breasts	2	tablespoons olive oil
1	cup flour	½	cup white wine vinegar
2	tablespoons poultry seasoning	¾	cup chicken broth
6	tablespoons margarine, divided	1	tablespoon honey mustard
		½	cup white raisins

- Slice chicken into thin fillets, yielding 2 to 3 slices from each breast half. Pound chicken between 2 sheets of wax paper until thin.
- Mix flour and poultry seasoning in a shallow dish. Dredge chicken in flour mixture.
- Heat 2 tablespoons margarine and olive oil in a skillet. Add chicken and brown until golden on both sides. Remove chicken to a plate and keep warm
- Add wine vinegar to hot skillet and let cook a few minutes. Stir in broth, remaining 4 tablespoons margarine and mustard. Cook until reduced to about half.
- Sprinkle raisins over chicken and pour sauce on top.
- 4 servings

Chicken Paprikash

MEAT

2	large onions, chopped	1	chicken, cut into 8 pieces
1	Italian frying pepper, chopped (optional)	1½	tablespoons paprika
2	tablespoons vegetable oil		Salt to taste
1	pound mushrooms, chopped (optional)	1	(14½-ounce) can diced tomatoes, or 2 fresh, minced

- Sauté onion and pepper in oil in a skillet until onion starts to soften but not brown. Add mushrooms and sauté.
- Add chicken to skillet and brown on both sides. Sprinkle paprika over chicken to coat. Add salt and tomatoes to skillet and cover.
- Cook over low heat until chicken is done; cooking should generate a lot of liquid. Serve with noodles.

Use a mixture of sweet and hot paprika,
or add cayenne pepper in place of hot paprika.

ORANGE CHICKEN
MEAT

3	large boneless, skinless chicken breasts	⅓	cup orange juice
	Salt and pepper to taste	⅓	cup orange marmalade
1	egg	1	teaspoon fresh lemon juice
2	tablespoons water	½	teaspoon Worcestershire sauce
¼	cup flour	½	teaspoon Dijon mustard
½	cup seasoned bread crumbs	¼	teaspoon garlic powder
2	tablespoons olive or salad oil		

- Pound chicken to ¼-inch thick. Season with salt and pepper.
- Beat together egg and water in a shallow dish. Place flour in a separate shallow dish and bread crumbs in a third.
- Heat oil in a 10-inch skillet.
- Dredge chicken in flour and shake off excess. Dip in egg mixture and then into bread crumbs.
- Cook chicken in hot oil for 1½ to 2 minutes on each side or until golden brown. Remove chicken from skillet and keep warm.
- Pour orange juice into skillet and bring to a boil, scraping up any brown bits from the bottom. Add marmalade, lemon juice, Worcestershire sauce, mustard and garlic powder.
- Return chicken to skillet, turning to coat both sides. Cook on low heat for 10 minutes.

Recipe can be made in advance. Place browned chicken in an 8-inch baking dish. Cover with orange sauce and refrigerate until ready to reheat.

Warm in a 350 degree oven for 15 to 20 minutes.

Recipe can be doubled or tripled.

Garnish your dishes not only to enhance presentation, but to give a clue of the ingredients and flavors — oranges, lemons, limes for citrus marinades or a bouquet of herbs for savory dishes.

CHICKEN IN A POT
MEAT

When I was in medical school, my children were very young. I found very little time to prepare healthy meals at dinner time. So, my "Chicken in a Pot" became a staple in our home. I could prepare it the night before, and it cooked while I studied. The dish could be cooked and placed in the refrigerator overnight, and then served at dinner the next day. It tastes even better when reheated slowly.

The vegetables in the dish can be varied according to what the cook finds in the refrigerator, and also according to what family members like. It is a very hearty dish for cold winter meals. Enjoy!

1	(3½-pound) chicken, cut up, or combination of thighs and breasts Salt and freshly ground pepper to taste	1	red bell pepper, chopped
		4	small zucchini, chopped
½	cup canola or olive oil, divided	4	small yellow summer squash, chopped
2	medium onions, coarsely chopped	1	(2¼-ounce) can sliced black olives, drained Fresh or dried oregano to taste
4	cloves garlic, chopped	2	(28-ounce) cans plum tomatoes in sauce, or tomatoes in purée
2	green bell peppers, chopped		

- Season chicken generously with salt and pepper.
- Heat 2 tablespoons oil in a large stock pot or pan. When oil is very hot, add chicken in batches, browning well on all sides. Remove chicken and set aside.
- If necessary, add ¼ cup oil to pan and heat. Add onion and garlic and cook until softened and golden. Push to edge of pot. Add chicken to center of pot, skin-side down.
- Spoon onion mixture over chicken. Add all bell peppers, zucchini, squash and olives. Season with salt and pepper and oregano. Pour tomatoes over all.
- Simmer, tightly covered, for 40 minutes or until vegetables and chicken are cooked through.
- Serve in large bowls with crusty bread to sop up the delicious juices.

This tastes even better when made a day in advance.

Other vegetables can be substituted.

Aunt Lillian's Oven-Fried Chicken Breasts

MEAT

2	tablespoons olive oil	1	cup dry bread crumbs
2	tablespoons lemon juice	1	package boneless,
1	teaspoon garlic powder		skinless chicken breasts
¼	teaspoon salt		

- Preheat oven to 375 degrees.
- Mix olive oil, lemon juice, garlic powder and salt in a bowl. Pour bread crumbs on a plate.
- Dip chicken in oil mixture, then dredge in bread crumbs. Place in an ungreased baking dish and cover with foil.
- Bake 30 minutes. Remove foil and bake 20 minutes longer or until chicken is brown.

Chicken thighs can be substituted for the breasts; cooking time will be slightly longer.

Pineapple Coffee Chicken

MEAT

1	(8-ounce) can crushed pineapple, undrained	½	teaspoon ground ginger
2	cups ketchup	1	teaspoon salt
¼	cup brown sugar	½	cup strong coffee
2	cloves garlic, minced, or ½ teaspoon garlic powder	2	whole frying chickens, quartered

- Mix pineapple with juice, ketchup, brown sugar, garlic, ginger, salt and coffee to make a marinade.
- Arrange chicken in a 9x13-inch baking pan. Pour marinade over chicken. Cover pan with foil.
- Refrigerate at least 3 hours or overnight, turning chicken several times.
- When ready to bake, preheat oven to 350 degrees.
- Bake 1 to 1½ hours.

TURKEY CHILI
MEAT

This chili can be prepared a day in advance, cooled, covered and refrigerated. To serve, rewarm gently, covered. The flavor improves if made in advance. Freezes well, too.

1 tablespoon vegetable oil
2 medium onions, chopped
1½ teaspoons dried oregano
1½ teaspoons ground cumin
1½ pounds extra lean ground turkey
¼ cup chili powder
2 bay leaves
1 tablespoon unsweetened cocoa powder
1½ teaspoons salt
¼ teaspoon cinnamon
1 (28-ounce) can tomatoes, undrained

24 ounces canned chicken or beef broth
1 (8-ounce) can tomato sauce
1 tablespoon seeded and minced jalapeño pepper
2 (15-ounce) cans beans, rinsed and drained, such as kidney or cannellini beans
Toppings: chopped fresh cilantro, sliced black olives, chopped red onion and chopped avocado

- Heat vegetable oil over medium heat in a large heavy pot. Add onion and cook, stirring occasionally, until golden and softened. Mix in oregano and cumin and cook and stir 1 minute.

- Increase to medium-high heat and add turkey. Cook and stir until no longer pink, breaking up lumps with the back of a spoon.

- Mix in chili powder, bay leaves, cocoa powder, salt and cinnamon. Add tomatoes with juice. If tomatoes are whole, break up with spoon. Stir in broth, tomato sauce and jalapeño pepper.

- Bring to a boil. Reduce heat and simmer 45 minutes, stirring occasionally to prevent bottom from sticking or burning.

- Add beans and simmer 10 minutes longer. Remove and discard bay leaves before serving.

- Serve in bowls with toppings sprinkled over individual servings or passed separately.

Serve with pareve cornbread or a crusty loaf of warmed bread. Ground chicken or beef can be substituted for the turkey.

IRAQI SWEET AND SPICY CHICKEN
MEAT

1   roasting chicken, cut into 8 pieces, excess skin and fat removed
     Salt and pepper to taste
     Olive oil

2   medium onions, chopped

2   cloves garlic, chopped

¾   cup dried, pitted dates

¾   cup dried apricots

2   teaspoons baharat (found in Middle Eastern Jewish markets)

1   (12-ounce) can frozen orange juice concentrate, thawed

¼   teaspoon cayenne pepper, or to taste

½   cup slivered almonds, lightly toasted

1½   tablespoons toasted sesame seeds

- Preheat oven to 350 degrees.
- Season chicken generously with salt and pepper.
- Heat a small amount of olive oil over medium-high heat in a large skillet. Add chicken and sauté in batches until nicely browned on both sides. Place chicken pieces in a 9x13-inch baking pan when they are cooked.
- Add more oil to skillet if needed. Add onion and garlic and sauté over medium heat until softened and golden. Spoon sautéed mixture over chicken. Sprinkle dates and apricots on top.
- Stir together baharat, juice concentrate and cayenne pepper in a bowl. Pour mixture over chicken, vegetables and fruit and cover pan tightly with foil.
- Bake about 1 hour, depending on size of chicken pieces. Check after 30 minutes; if mixture looks dry, add some water, broth or orange juice to prevent dish from drying out.
- During final 5 minutes of baking, remove foil and sprinkle with almonds and sesame seeds. Serve with couscous.

The following is a recipe for baharat in case it cannot be found in the store.

PAREVE

2   tablespoons freshly ground pepper

1   tablespoon ground coriander

1   tablespoon ground cloves

2   tablespoons ground cumin

½   teaspoon ground cardamom

2   teaspoons ground nutmeg

¼   teaspoon cinnamon

- Combine all ingredients. Store leftovers in a spice jar.

Chicken Sesame with Cumberland Sauce

MEAT

- ¾ cup flour
- 2 eggs, lightly beaten
- 2 tablespoons soy sauce
- 1 tablespoon paprika
- ½ teaspoon salt
- ½ teaspoon garlic powder
- ¼ teaspoon black pepper
- 1 cup dry unseasoned bread crumbs
- ½ cup sesame seeds, toasted
- 10 chicken breast cutlets, or 5 boneless, skinless breasts, pounded to an even thickness

Margarine or vegetable oil for sautéing

Sauce

- 1 (16-ounce) jar apricot preserves
- 1 clove garlic, crushed
- 1 teaspoon soy sauce
- ¼ cup water

- Set out 3 shallow bowls or rimmed dishes. Place flour in first bowl. In second bowl, mix together egg, soy sauce, paprika, salt, garlic powder and pepper. Combine bread crumbs and sesame seeds in third bowl.

- Dredge cutlets in flour, then dip in egg mixture and finally in bread crumb mixture. Place on a wax paper-lined baking sheet and, if time, refrigerate until chilled. The breading will adhere better if chilled.

- Heat margarine in a large skillet until sizzling. Add breaded cutlets and sauté until golden and cooked through.

- Meanwhile, combine all sauce ingredients in a small saucepan and bring to a boil.

- When ready to serve, pour half of sauce over chicken and serve remaining sauce on the side.

This dish can be prepared ahead and also freezes well.

FESTIVE CHICKEN
MEAT

2	pounds boneless, skinless chicken breast halves
½	cup red wine vinegar
½	cup olive oil
1	cup white wine
2	tablespoons finely chopped garlic
¼	cup dried oregano
½	cup capers, drained (optional)
3	bay leaves
1	cup pitted prunes
1	cup dried apricots
1	cup pitted green olives
½-1	cup brown sugar

- Arrange chicken in a single layer in a baking dish.
- Combine vinegar, olive oil, wine, garlic, oregano, capers, bay leaves, prunes, apricots and olives and pour over chicken. Cover dish and refrigerate overnight.
- Preheat oven to 350 degrees.
- Sprinkle brown sugar over chicken. Bake 45 to 60 minutes, basting often. Serve hot or at room temperature.

Cooking time may vary depending on thickness and size of chicken breasts.

CHICKEN MARENGO
MEAT

½	cup flour
1	teaspoon salt
½	teaspoon black pepper
1	teaspoon dried tarragon
2	pounds boneless, skinless chicken breasts
4	tablespoons margarine
¼	cup olive oil
1	(14½-ounce) can chopped tomatoes
1	(4-ounce) can mushrooms
1	clove garlic, minced
1	cup dry white wine

- Combine flour, salt, pepper and tarragon in a shallow dish. Dredge chicken in flour mixture and shake off excess.
- Melt margarine with olive oil in a large skillet. Brown chicken on both sides in oil mixture. Remove chicken and set aside.
- Add tomatoes, mushrooms, garlic and wine to skillet and stir to mix. Add chicken back into skillet and cover.
- Simmer 40 minutes, turning chicken halfway through. Serve chicken with sauce from skillet and with rice or pasta.

BALSAMIC CHICKEN WITH ROASTED VEGETABLES

MEAT

1	(2- to 3-pound) chicken		Balsamic reduction
2	large cloves garlic		*(see below)*
⅓	cup olive oil, plus extra for drizzling	8	medium boiling potatoes, peeled and halved or quartered
½	cup balsamic vinegar, plus extra for drizzling Salt and pepper to taste	8	small zucchini, trimmed or cut lengthwise

- Cut chicken down center to butterfly and spread open. Flatten chicken, skin-side up, by pressing down with the heel of your hand. Rub both sides of chicken with garlic. Arrange chicken, skin-side down, in a shallow dish. Drizzle olive oil and vinegar over chicken and season with salt and pepper. Marinate 3 to 4 hours.

- When ready to bake, preheat oven to 400 degrees.

- Remove chicken from marinade and place on a rack in a roasting pan.

- Parboil potatoes for about 15 minutes; drain. Mix potatoes with zucchini in a bowl. Drizzle with olive oil and vinegar and season with salt and pepper. Arrange vegetables with chicken on rack.

- Roast 20 minutes, turning chicken and vegetables and basting with balsamic reduction. Continue roasting and basting until chicken is done, approximately 20 minutes.

Balsamic Reduction: Pour 1 cup balsamic vinegar into a stainless steel saucepan. Bring to a boil. Cook over medium heat for 10 minutes or until reduced to ¼ cup and vinegar turns to a glaze.

Cool to room temperature. Pour reduction into a plastic squeeze bottle to use for decorating a serving plate or as a recipe indicates.

CHICKEN AND LOTS OF GARLIC

MEAT

4	pounds chicken, cut into 8 serving pieces
	Salt and pepper to taste
2-3	tablespoons olive oil
½	cup dry white wine or broth
1	cup low-sodium chicken broth
2	fresh parsley sprigs
1	fresh rosemary sprig
2	fresh thyme sprigs
3	heads garlic, unpeeled and separated into cloves
1	bay leaf
2	tablespoons chopped fresh parsley
	Crusty bread, sliced

- Preheat oven to 350 degrees.
- Sprinkle chicken with salt and pepper.
- Heat olive oil in a 6- to 8-quart wide, heavy, ovenproof pot over medium-high heat until oil is hot but not smoking. Add chicken and brown on all sides, turning carefully, for 10 minutes or until golden brown. Transfer chicken to a plate.
- Deglaze pot with wine, scraping up brown bits from bottom. Cook until reduced by half. Add broth and bring to a boil.
- Tie together sprigs of parsley, rosemary and thyme with a string to make a bouquet garni. Add bouquet to liquid in pot along with garlic and bay leaf. Place chicken on top and cover pot tightly.
- Transfer to center of oven and bake, basting twice, for 1 hour, 10 minutes or until cooked through. If garlic is not soft, bake 15 minutes longer. (Hard cloves will ruin the dish and soft cloves will make it divine.)
- Place chicken on a serving plate. Drizzle with some of pan juices and garnish with chopped parsley.
- Squeeze out the mellow garlic and spread over slices of crusty bread.

Dish can be made up to 1 day ahead and refrigerated.
Reheat in a 350 degree oven, garnish and serve.

Bouquet Garni: a small bundle of herbs, such as thyme, parsley, bay leaf and the like, often tied in a cheesecloth bag and used for flavoring soups, stews, etc.

STELLA'S CHICKEN AND EGGPLANT STEW
MEAT

2	tablespoons olive oil
1	large onion, chopped
5	cloves garlic, chopped
2	bay leaves
3½-4	pounds skinless chicken thighs and legs
1¼	teaspoons kosher salt, divided
¾	teaspoon black pepper
¾	cup dry red wine
2	tablespoons tomato paste
1	(15-ounce) can diced tomatoes, undrained
1½	tablespoons dried marjoram
1½	tablespoons Hungarian sweet paprika
1	tablespoon dried onion flakes
½	cup reduced-sodium chicken broth
1	medium eggplant, peeled and cut into 1½-inch chunks
1	(10-ounce) package fresh mushrooms, halved
1	small red bell pepper, cut into ¼-inch thick strips
2	(10-ounce) packages fresh spinach, tough stems discarded, coarsely chopped

- Heat olive oil in a Dutch oven over medium heat. Add onion, garlic and bay leaves and cook and stir 8 minutes or until golden. Add chicken and sprinkle with 1 teaspoon salt and pepper. Simmer 5 minutes.

- Add wine and simmer, scraping up brown bits, for 1 to 2 minutes or until liquid is reduced by half.

- Stir in tomato paste, tomatoes with juice, marjoram, paprika, onion flakes and broth and simmer 5 minutes, stirring occasionally. Nestle chicken pieces into sauce. Simmer, loosely covered, for 20 minutes.

- Stir in eggplant, mushrooms, bell pepper and remaining ¼ teaspoon salt. Simmer 25 to 30 minutes or until chicken is cooked through.

- Add spinach and stir into sauce. For thicker sauce, before adding spinach, transfer cooked chicken to a platter and keep warm. Bring sauce to a boil and cook until sauce reaches desired consistency, then stir in spinach. Serve with wide noodles.

- 6 servings

Even better reheated the next day.

Roasted Chicken with Garlic and Lemon

MEAT

1	(5- to 6-pound) roasting chicken, or two (3-pound) pullets	5	heads garlic, separated into cloves, some cloves left unpeeled
	Salt and pepper to taste	3-4	sprigs fresh rosemary
½	cup olive oil	4	lemons

- Preheat oven to 375 degrees.
- Wash and dry chicken and remove any visible clumps of fat from inside of cavity. Wash and dry fat clumps and set aside. Season inside cavity lightly with salt and pepper. Drizzle a spoonful of olive oil into cavity. Stuff in a handful of garlic and rosemary and squeeze in juice of 1 lemon, adding squeezed lemon halves to cavity. Truss chicken. Brush outside of chicken with olive oil and sprinkle with salt and pepper. Place chicken, breast-side up, in a casserole dish.
- Flatten reserved chicken fat clumps with your fist and place them over the breast. Smash remaining garlic cloves with a large knife and lay them over chicken along with remaining rosemary.
- Squeeze remaining lemons over chicken, tossing squeezed halves into the casserole dish. Cover casserole dish.
- Roast chicken 1 hour. After an hour, uncover and increase temperature to 400 degrees. Cook 30 minutes to brown. Remove chicken from casserole dish to a serving platter and allow to rest for a few minutes.

Serve with garlic roasted potatoes and a green vegetable, such as fiddlehead ferns.

MINDY'S DELICIOUS CHICKEN

MEAT

Margarine

2 whole chickens, cut into eighths, or equivalent of boneless breasts

1 egg, beaten

Crushed corn flakes (not corn flake crumbs)

¼ cup chopped onion

¼ cup chopped fresh parsley

1 teaspoon salt

½ teaspoon black pepper

1 teaspoon dry mustard

½ teaspoon marjoram

Cold Lemon Sauce

1 tablespoon soy sauce

½ teaspoon salt

½ teaspoon black pepper

¼ cup oil

½ cup lemon juice

2 tablespoons lemon zest

1 clove garlic, crushed

- Preheat oven to 400 degrees.
- Melt margarine in a shallow baking pan in oven.
- Dip chicken pieces in beaten egg and roll in crushed corn flakes. Arrange chicken, skin-side down, in pan.
- Sprinkle chicken with onion, parsley, salt, pepper, mustard and marjoram.
- Bake 20 minutes. Turn and bake 20 to 30 minutes longer.
- Meanwhile, combine all sauce ingredients. Drizzle some sauce over cooked chicken and serve remaining sauce in a gravy boat on the side.

CRANBERRY STUFFED CHICKEN BREASTS
MEAT

4	large boneless, skinless chicken breasts	1	(16-ounce) can whole berry cranberry sauce
1	cup dry unseasoned bread crumbs or crushed corn flakes	1	stick margarine, melted
1	cup shredded coconut	½	cup white wine

- Preheat oven to 350 degrees.
- Pound chicken breasts until thin enough to roll. Cut breasts in half if large.
- Mix bread crumbs and coconut in a shallow dish. Coat chicken pieces with crumb mixture. Place a dollop of cranberry sauce on each breast and roll up tightly, starting at short end. Place rolls in a greased casserole dish. Spoon another dollop of cranberry sauce atop each roll.
- Carefully drizzle melted margarine over rolls. Add wine to dish.
- Bake, uncovered, for 35 to 40 minutes or until golden brown and crisp.

Recipe is easily multiplied to serve a larger number.
Baked chicken can be frozen. Thaw and reheat covered,
then uncover and bake until crisp.

HONEY CHILI GLAZE FOR CHICKEN, STEAK OR FISH
PAREVE

1	jalapeño pepper	½	teaspoon salt
2	tablespoons brown sugar	1	cup honey
½	teaspoon cider or rice vinegar	⅓	cup finely chopped roasted peanuts

- Chop jalapeño with brown sugar, wearing gloves to protect hands. Combine jalapeño mixture with vinegar, salt and honey in a saucepan.
- Simmer 2 minutes. Stir in peanuts.

This sauce is great on roasted chicken, steak or fish.

My Favorite Shabbat Chicken
MEAT

¾ cup apple juice
¼ cup chopped fresh
   cilantro or parsley
6-8 onions, thinly sliced and
   separated into rings
2 carrots, cut diagonally
   into ½-inch thick slices
3 stalks celery, cut
   diagonally into ½-inch
   thick slices

1 whole roasting chicken
   Few cloves of garlic
   Juice of 2 lemons
   Kosher salt and freshly
   ground pepper to taste
   Paprika to taste

- Preheat oven to 400 degrees.
- Pour apple juice into a roasting pan. Add enough water so liquid in pan is ¼-inch in depth. Sprinkle cilantro, onion, carrot and celery into pan.
- Remove excess fat from chicken. Rub garlic over inside and out of chicken. Place chicken over vegetables in pan.
- Squeeze lemon juice over chicken and place lemon halves in chicken cavity. Season inside and out of chicken with salt and pepper and paprika.
- Bake, uncovered, for about 50 minutes, depending on size of chicken. If onion is not brown when chicken is done, remove chicken from pan and keep warm. Return pan to oven and roast vegetables 10 to 20 minutes longer.

CHICKEN WITH WINE SAUCE
MEAT

3	tablespoons flour	12	ounces fresh mushrooms, thinly sliced
½	teaspoon salt		
⅛	teaspoon white or black pepper	⅓	cup chopped onion
		2	tablespoons chopped fresh parsley, plus extra for garnish
4	large boneless, skinless chicken breast halves		
4	tablespoons margarine, divided	1	cup white wine
		2	cups hot cooked rice

- Combine flour, salt and pepper in a shallow dish. Dredge chicken in flour mixture, shaking off excess. Reserve remaining flour mixture.

- Melt 2 tablespoons margarine in a skillet over medium heat. Brown chicken on both sides and remove from skillet; set aside.

- Add remaining 2 tablespoons margarine to skillet. Add mushrooms, onion and 2 tablespoons parsley and sauté until onion is transparent. Remove from heat.

- Stir in reserved flour mixture. Blend in wine and bring to a boil, stirring frequently. Cook until thickened.

- Return chicken to skillet. Cover and reduce heat. Simmer 25 minutes or until chicken is tender.

- To serve, place a piece of chicken over ½ cup rice on individual plates. Spoon sauce over the top. Garnish with extra chopped parsley.

- 4 servings

Chicken Curry

MEAT

4	tablespoons margarine or olive oil	1	teaspoon salt
2	small onions, chopped	½	teaspoon dry mustard
1	clove garlic, minced	1	bay leaf
1	stalk celery, chopped	3	cups chicken broth
1	tart apple, peeled or unpeeled, diced	1	chicken, cut into pieces and skin removed, or equivalent chicken breasts, cut into chunks
¼	cup flour		
1	tablespoon curry powder, or more to taste		

- Heat margarine in a saucepan. Add onion, garlic, celery and apple and cook 8 minutes, stirring occasionally.
- Combine flour, curry powder, salt and mustard and stir into saucepan. Cook and stir 2 minutes. Add bay leaf. Gradually stir in broth and cook and stir until sauce thickens.
- Add chicken to saucepan and cook about 1 hour or until done, depending on type of chicken; chicken breast chunks may only take 30 minutes to cook.

Serve with rice and mango chutney. Recipe doubles easily.

Olympic Seoul Chicken

MEAT

¼	cup distilled vinegar	8	skinless chicken thighs
3	tablespoons soy sauce	½	teaspoon dried red pepper flakes
2	tablespoons honey		
¼	teaspoon ground ginger	10	cloves garlic, coarsely chopped
2	tablespoons peanut oil		

- Mix vinegar, soy sauce, honey and ginger in a small bowl; set aside.
- Heat peanut oil in a skillet. Add chicken and brown in hot oil on both sides. Add pepper flakes and garlic and cook 2 to 3 minutes.
- Stir vinegar mixture into skillet. Cover and cook 15 minutes.
- Uncover and cook 3 to 4 minutes longer to allow juices to thicken.

GRILLED PEANUT CHICKEN WITH FRUIT SALSA

MEAT

3 pounds boneless, skinless chicken thighs, or combination thighs and breasts

½ cup hot water

½ cup creamy peanut butter (commercial brand, not health-food style)

¼ cup tomato-based chili sauce

2 tablespoons vegetable oil

2 tablespoons unseasoned rice vinegar

4 cloves garlic, minced

2 teaspoons grated fresh ginger

¼ teaspoon cayenne pepper

Fruit Salsa

2 cups chopped fresh fruit, such as a combination of plums, peaches, nectarines, etc.

1 cup peeled and chopped cucumber

2 tablespoons thinly sliced scallion

2 tablespoons chopped fresh cilantro

2 tablespoons sugar

2 tablespoons vegetable oil

2 tablespoons rice vinegar

Chopped peanuts and lime wedges for garnish

- Remove any excess fat from chicken. Pound chicken lightly to an even thickness; place in a plastic zip-top bag and set aside.

- In a bowl, gradually add hot water to peanut butter and stir until smooth. Mix in chili sauce, vegetable oil, vinegar, garlic, ginger and cayenne pepper. Add about half of marinade mixture or enough to cover chicken well to zip-top bag. Marinate chicken in refrigerator for 12 to 24 hours. Refrigerate remaining marinade separately.

- One to 2 hours before serving, combine all salsa ingredients. Refrigerate until serving. Before serving, adjust seasoning of salsa as needed.

- When ready to cook, preheat grill or broiler on high heat.

- Remove chicken from marinade, discarding marinade in plastic bag. Grill or broil chicken for about 5 minutes per side; thighs take longer to cook than breasts. Check for doneness by making a small cut in chicken; meat should be moist, breasts should be barely pink and thighs may appear slightly pinkish.

- To serve, heat reserved marinade. Serve sauce drizzled over chicken with fruit salsa on the side. Garnish plates with chopped peanuts and lime wedges. Serve with jasmine or basmati rice.

If you prefer chicken with bones, increase cooking time slightly.
Recipe doubles easily.

Chicken Cacciatore

MEAT

2   whole chickens, quartered
2   chicken thighs
    Salt and pepper to taste
    Chopped fresh rosemary
    (optional)
    Chopped fresh oregano
    (optional)
    Chopped fresh thyme
    (optional)
3   tablespoons olive oil
2   cups chopped onion

2   cups chopped green or red
    bell pepper
4   cloves garlic, chopped
1   (14½-ounce) can crushed
    tomatoes
½   cup red wine (optional)
1   pound favorite pasta,
    preferable ziti-type,
    cooked al dente and
    drained

- Preheat oven to 375 degrees.
- Place chicken pieces on a baking pan. Season with salt and pepper, rosemary, oregano and thyme.
- Bake 30 minutes or until chicken is done enough to be torn off the bone. Remove chicken from oven and cool 5 to 10 minutes. Remove meat from bones; set aside.
- Meanwhile, heat olive oil in a Dutch oven over medium heat until hot. Add onion and cook 5 minutes or until translucent. Add bell pepper and garlic and more fresh herbs, if desired. Stir in tomatoes. Cook 20 minutes.
- Add chicken pieces to vegetable mixture. Simmer 30 to 45 minutes.
- Stir in wine. Mix in drained pasta.

Dried Italian seasonings can be substituted for the fresh herbs.
Use plenty of seasoning, at least ½ teaspoon of each herb,
to give cacciatore plenty of taste.

Honey Balsamic Chicken with Tomatoes, Mushrooms and Peppers

MEAT

1	medium-size red bell pepper, cut into 1-inch pieces	¼	cup balsamic vinegar
1	medium-size yellow bell pepper, cut into 1-inch pieces	1	tablespoon chopped fresh rosemary
1	onion, thinly sliced	1½	teaspoons kosher salt, divided
8	ounces fresh mushrooms, such as button, cremini, etc., sliced ¼-inch thick		Freshly ground pepper to taste
1	(14½-ounce) can diced tomatoes, drained	1	(3½- to 4-pound) chicken, quartered, rinsed and patted dry, or 3 pounds chicken breasts
3	tablespoons olive oil	2½	tablespoons honey

- Preheat oven to 425 degrees.
- In a shallow 10½x15-inch glass baking dish, toss together both bell peppers, onion, mushrooms and tomatoes. Drizzle with olive oil and vinegar and sprinkle with rosemary, ½ teaspoon salt and a generous amount of pepper. Toss until well coated.
- Trim any excess fat from chicken. Arrange chicken pieces, skin-side down, in vegetable mixture, turning so chicken gets coated with oil and vinegar. Sprinkle with remaining 1 teaspoon salt and more pepper. Drizzle honey over chicken skin.
- Bake 50 to 60 minutes or until chicken is well browned and cooked through.
- 4 servings

Ma Po's Quick and Easy Tofu and Ground Turkey

MEAT

1	cup chicken broth	2-6	teaspoons chili paste, depending on desired hotness
3	tablespoons soy sauce		
1	tablespoon dry sherry	1	(16-ounce) package soft or firm tofu (not silken), cut into ½-inch cubes
2	teaspoons sugar		
½	teaspoon salt		
1	tablespoon cornstarch Vegetable oil	2	scallions, chopped
1	pound ground turkey or chicken	1	teaspoon Asian toasted sesame oil
2	cloves garlic, minced		

- Combine broth, soy sauce, sherry, sugar and salt in a bowl. Mix 2 tablespoons of sauce mixture with cornstarch in a separate bowl. Set both bowls aside.
- Add a small amount of vegetable oil to a wok or skillet over medium-high heat. Add ground turkey, garlic and chili paste. Cook and stir, breaking up clumps of meat with the back of a spoon, for a few minutes or until no longer pink.
- Add sauce mixture and tofu to wok. Bring to a boil and braise for about 5 minutes.
- Stir in cornstarch mixture and cook 3 minutes or until slightly thickened.
- Add scallions and sesame oil and cook briefly until heated through.

Serve with white or brown rice accompanied by broccoli or snow peas.

CORNISH HENS - EASY AND DELICIOUS

MEAT

2	tablespoons chopped fresh cilantro	⅔	cup yellow cornmeal
2	tablespoons chopped scallions	⅓	cup flour
1	tablespoon chopped fresh ginger	1	teaspoon kosher salt
		½	teaspoon black pepper
2	eggs, lightly beaten	4	(14-ounce) Cornish game hens, butterflied with backbone removed
2	heaping tablespoons ground cumin	2	tablespoons olive oil

- Preheat oven to 375 degrees.
- Mix together cilantro, scallions and ginger on a large plate. Place egg in a shallow dish. In a separate large plate, combine cumin, cornmeal, flour, salt and pepper.
- Dip hens in cilantro mixture, then dip in egg and dredge in cornmeal mixture to coat.
- Place a large skillet over medium-high heat. When hot, add olive oil. Add hens to skillet, one at a time, and cook 4 minutes each or until golden brown. Transfer hens to a large baking pan.
- Bake 15 minutes or until hens are deep brown and cooked through.

POMEGRANATE CHICKEN

MEAT

¼	cup olive oil		Juice of 1 lemon
1	tablespoon minced garlic	1	tablespoon sugar
1	chicken, cut into 8 pieces	¼	teaspoon cinnamon
1	pomegranate, halved		Salt and pepper to taste
¼	cup dry white wine or ginger ale		

- Preheat oven to 375 degrees.
- Combine olive oil and garlic and brush over chicken. Place chicken in a roasting pan. Roast 45 minutes or until skin is browned.
- Meanwhile, remove 2 tablespoons pomegranate seeds. Squeeze remaining pomegranate into a sieve to collect juice in a small bowl. Heat pomegranate juice with wine, lemon juice, sugar and cinnamon in a small saucepan. Simmer over low heat for 5 minutes. Season with salt and pepper.
- Transfer roasted chicken to a serving platter. Pierce each chicken piece in a few places. Pour pomegranate sauce over chicken and garnish with pomegranate seeds. Serve hot or at room temperature.

SPICED CRANBERRY SAUCE
PAREVE

3	small oranges, Clementine if available, halved crosswise
1	(12-ounce) bag cranberries
1¾	cups sugar
1	cup unpeeled and diced McIntosh apple
½	cup raisins
½	cup orange juice
1	tablespoon vinegar
½	teaspoon ground ginger
½	teaspoon cinnamon

- Combine all ingredients in a saucepan and partially cover. Bring to a boil. Reduce heat and simmer 8 to 10 minutes or until cranberries pop. Remove orange halves.

4   cups cranberries
1   cup dried apricots, chopped
2   cups sugar
1   cup golden raisins
1   cup water
1   cup orange juice
1   tablespoon orange zest (optional)

- Combine all ingredients in a saucepan. Cook over medium heat until sugar dissolves.
- Increase heat and bring to a boil. Cook, covered, stirring occasionally, for 8 minutes or until cranberries pop. Transfer to a bowl, cover and refrigerate. Sauce thickens as it cools.
- 5 cups

Recipe doubles easily. Store in refrigerator for up to 1 month.

HERBED BAKED CHICKEN
MEAT

6   boneless, skinless chicken breasts
3   eggs, well beaten
    Pareve bread crumbs
2   tablespoons olive oil
1   cup sun-dried tomatoes in oil
1   cup green olives
1   cup green peas, drained if canned, or frozen

- Dip chicken breasts in egg, then dredge in bread crumbs to coat.
- Heat olive oil in a skillet over medium heat. Add chicken to hot oil and sauté until golden. After turning chicken once, add tomatoes, green olives and peas to skillet and cook about 30 minutes or until chicken is cooked through.

Serve with basmati rice. Onion or eggplant can be added.

KATZ'S TURKEY MEATLOAF
MEAT

½   large white onion, chopped
1   tablespoon margarine
3   pounds ground turkey
5   eggs
2   teaspoons salt
1   teaspoon black pepper
¾   cup ketchup
2   cups bread crumbs
2   tablespoons chopped fresh parsley
3   tablespoons Worcestershire sauce

- Preheat oven to 350 degrees.
- Sauté onion in margarine. Cool and transfer to a large mixing bowl.
- Add turkey, eggs, salt and pepper and mix. Add ketchup, bread crumbs, parsley and Worcestershire sauce and mix. Shape mixture into a loaf on a greased baking sheet.
- Bake 1 to 1½ hours or until a meat thermometer reaches 160 degrees.

For a sauce for over the meatloaf, mix a 15-ounce can tomato sauce, ½ cup brown sugar, ¼ cup vinegar and 1 teaspoon prepared mustard. Pour sauce over meatloaf during final 45 minutes of baking.

Roast Turkey
MEAT

1 (12- to 14-pound) fresh
   turkey
   Kosher salt and freshly
   ground pepper to taste
1 lemon, halved
1 large Spanish onion

   Herbs of choice
4 tablespoons margarine,
   softened
½ cup good olive oil
1½ teaspoons garlic powder
2 teaspoons paprika

Savory Flavor

2 cups low-sodium chicken
   broth
¾ cup white wine
¼ cup olive oil

   Lots of fresh or dried
   herbs, such as rosemary,
   thyme and herbes de
   Provence

Sweet Maple-Dijon Glaze

   Oranges and or apples
   (optional)
1 cup pure maple syrup
1 stick unsalted margarine

½ cup Dijon mustard
½ teaspoon salt
¼ teaspoon freshly ground
   pepper

- Preheat oven to 350 degrees.
- Remove giblets and wash turkey well inside and out. Remove any excess fat and feathers and pat outside of turkey dry. Place in a large roasting pan. Season inside cavity generously with salt and pepper.
- Stuff cavity with lemon halves, onion and herbs. Rub outside with softened margarine and olive oil. Sprinkle with garlic powder, paprika and more salt and pepper.
- For a savory flavor, pour broth, wine and olive oil over turkey in pan. Sprinkle with herbs.
- For a sweet flavor, stuff cavity with additional fruit, such as oranges and/or apples. Combine syrup, margarine, mustard, salt and pepper in a saucepan over medium heat. Simmer, stirring occasionally, for 10 minutes. Keep warm. Baste turkey with maple sauce every 30 minutes while baking.
- Tie legs together with string and tuck wing tips under the body of the turkey. (If desired, sliced onions that have been coated with olive oil can be scattered in bottom of pan.)
- Roast turkey about 20 minutes per pound or until the juices run clear when the leg or thigh is pierced.
- Remove turkey to a cutting board and cover with foil. Let rest 20 minutes before carving.

WALNUT STUFFING FOR TURKEY

MEAT

12	cups cubed day-old coarse bread, such as challah, white or wheat	½	teaspoon ground sage
2	sticks margarine	1	teaspoon salt
2	cups sliced celery	¼	teaspoon black pepper
1	cup sliced fresh mushrooms	½	cup giblet broth, or 1 chicken bouillon cube dissolved in ½ cup hot water
1	cup coarsely chopped onion	1	cup coarsely chopped walnuts
2	teaspoons crumbled fresh thyme	½	cup chopped fresh parsley

- Preheat oven to 350 degrees.
- Place bread cubes in a large baking pan. Bake 20 minutes or until lightly toasted, stirring once or twice.
- Melt margarine in a large skillet. Add celery, mushrooms and onion and sauté lightly. Stir in thyme, sage, salt, pepper and broth. Pour mixture over bread and toss to moisten evenly. Stir in walnuts and parsley.
- Pack stuffing into turkey, or spoon into a baking dish and cover. To bake separately, bake at 350 degrees for 30 minutes. Uncover and bake 10 to 15 minutes longer or until top is lightly toasted.
- 2½ quarts, enough for a 12-pound turkey.

Vegetables &
Potatoes

Vegetables & Potatoes

From artichokes to zucchini, Jewish cooking offers so many wonderful ways to prepare vegetables, defined as any part of a plant consumed by humans (for example, the root of the beet, the flower buds of cauliflower and broccoli, the leaves of lettuce and spinach.) Vegetables are *pareve* by nature, and become dairy or meat depending on the preparation. Our grandmothers relied on root vegetables, as well as lentils, dried beans and pickled vegetables during the winter months; however, many of our mothers relied on the "cans of the 50's" to enhance their main course preparation, but we know that "fresh is best". However, seasonal raw or cooked choices are the best, and today we have access to most vegetables year-round due to excellent shipping and storing innovations.

When choosing your vegetables, try to balance tastes and textures. If your entrée has a softer texture - meatloaf, brisket or chicken - choose colorful, crunchy or spicy vegetables to balance your plate.

Potatoes have also been used in Jewish cooking for stuffings, *kugels*, side dishes, salads and stews. Recently, mashed potato bars have been set up at elaborate events - with choices of toppings to include Gorgonzola cheese, pecans, arugula, roasted garlic, or just about any meat or vegetable combination. Today there are nearly fifty varieties of potatoes and they come in purple, gold, red, as well as white. Sweet potatoes are full of fiber and antioxidants, and white potatoes are high in iron. Enjoy the versatility!

Butternut Squash and Apples
PAREVE

2	pounds butternut squash	1	tablespoon flour
2	baking apples, peeled, cored and cut into circles	½	teaspoon cinnamon Orange marmalade (optional)
½	cup brown sugar		
4	tablespoons margarine, melted		

- Preheat oven to 350 degrees.
- Peel squash and cut into round, ½-inch thick slices. Remove seeds and arrange slices in an ungreased 8x12-inch baking dish. Layer apple slices over squash.
- Combine brown sugar, melted margarine, flour and cinnamon. Sprinkle mixture over apple slices. Cover dish with foil.
- Bake 50 to 60 minutes. If desired, dollop orange marmalade on top.

*If making a large amount,
you can make multiple layers of squash and apples.*

*Apples can be caramelized in 1 to 2 tablespoons margarine in a skillet
before adding to casserole. Cook slowly until brown and syrupy.*

Grilled Asparagus with Hard-Boiled Eggs
DAIRY

32	thick spears asparagus, trimmed	¼	teaspoon black pepper
6	tablespoons extra virgin olive oil, divided	¼	cup lemon juice
½	teaspoon kosher salt	3	tablespoons Parmesan cheese
		2	hard-boiled eggs, chopped

- Toss asparagus in 2 tablespoons olive oil with salt and pepper. Grill or broil asparagus over medium heat 5 to 7 minutes or until skin is charred all over and stalks feel soft in thickest part.
- Place asparagus on a platter and drizzle with remaining 4 tablespoons olive oil. Pour lemon juice on top and sprinkle with Parmesan cheese and chopped egg.

Be careful when slicing and dicing — always secure food to be sliced by halving and placing on its flat side.

This is a very nice presentation for a brunch or buffet table.

For a pareve dish, substitute ¼ cup toasted sesame seeds for the Parmesan cheese and egg.

How do you know how to trim asparagus? Hold a stalk at the thick end and below the tip. Snap as if it were a wishbone. Use this as a model and cut others in the same place.

BUTTERNUT SQUASH PUDDING

DAIRY OR PAREVE

1½ pounds butternut squash, peeled and cut

½ cup sugar

¼ teaspoon nutmeg (optional)

¾ cup flour

4 eggs, lightly beaten

1½ cups nondairy creamer, or ¾ cup milk and ¾ cup half-and-half

¼ teaspoon cinnamon (optional)

1 stick margarine or butter, melted

- Preheat oven to 350 degrees.
- Place squash in a saucepan and cover with water. Bring to a boil and cook 25 minutes or until softened. Drain and mash.
- Add sugar, nutmeg, flour, egg, creamer and cinnamon. Blend in margarine and pour mixture into an 8- or 9-inch square or round baking pan.
- Bake 1 hour or until firm to the touch.

Butternut squash is a "winter" squash which is in season from September to December, but can keep for months if stored in a cool, dry place.

Sometimes I cheat and buy it already cut and ready for boiling. I throw it in a pan and boil 20 to 30 minutes, mash it with a little butter and season it with salt, pepper and maple syrup to taste. It is like whipped potatoes.

Nanny Gabby's Spinach Bake
DAIRY

2 large onions, finely chopped	3-4 tablespoons cottage cheese
3-4 tablespoons olive oil	4 eggs
2 (10-ounce) packages frozen chopped spinach	1 teaspoon baking powder
1 cup Parmesan cheese	Salt and pepper to taste
	Dash of allspice

- Preheat oven to 350 degrees.
- Sauté onion in olive oil until golden. Add spinach and cook until liquid has evaporated and spinach starts to stick to bottom of pan.
- Add Parmesan and cottage cheeses, eggs, baking powder, salt and pepper and allspice. Mix well and transfer to a greased rectangular glass baking dish.
- Bake in center of oven for 40 to 45 minutes or until golden on top.
- Recipe can be frozen before baking.

Mushrooms with Garlic and Herbs
PAREVE

1 pound assorted mushrooms, such as baby bella, porcini or chanterelle	1 tablespoon finely chopped fresh thyme
3 tablespoons extra virgin olive oil	2 teaspoons lemon juice
	Salt and pepper to taste
2 cloves garlic, thinly sliced	1 tablespoon finely chopped fresh Italian parsley
3 tablespoons white wine	

- Wipe mushrooms gently, trim stems and ends. Leave mushrooms whole, or thickly slice if large.
- Heat olive oil in a large skillet. Add mushrooms, garlic, wine and thyme. Cook over medium to high heat, stirring often, for 15 to 20 minutes or until lightly browned; be careful that garlic does not brown.
- Add lemon juice and season with salt and pepper. Transfer to a heated serving dish and sprinkle with parsley.

For convenience, dried herbs can be substituted for fresh.

Serve with a grilled, juicy steak or plain grilled lamb or veal chops. Or for a vegetarian option, serve over grilled polenta.

Polenta is available prepared or uncooked in most supermarkets.

Ratio of fresh herbs to dried herbs: 3 to 1; for example, 3 tablespoons fresh is equivalent to 1 tablespoon dried.

THREE-VEGETABLE PATÉ

DAIRY

This recipe is one of the more challenging in our community collection, but well worth the effort involved. The compliments you will receive when serving will make you smile with satisfaction. It is both elegant and colorful when sliced on a plate with a meal or served as an appetizer to spread on crackers.

½	cup chopped scallions, white part only
1	stick unsalted butter, divided
1	(10-ounce) package frozen chopped spinach, thawed and squeezed dry
7	eggs, divided
¾	cup half-and-half, divided
½	cup dry whole wheat bread crumbs, divided
¼	cup freshly grated Parmesan cheese
1	pound fresh button mushrooms, trimmed and wiped clean

1	tablespoon lemon juice
1	small white onion, chopped
2	tablespoons dry sherry
	Salt and freshly ground black pepper to taste
3	large carrots, cooked until soft
2	tablespoons unbleached all-purpose flour
¼	teaspoon ground ginger
¼	teaspoon ground nutmeg

- Preheat oven to 350 degrees.
- Sauté scallions in 2 tablespoons butter until translucent. Add spinach and sauté 3 minutes longer. Remove from heat and set aside.
- Lightly beat 3 eggs in a medium bowl. Add ½ cup half-and-half, ¼ cup bread crumbs and Parmesan cheese. Mix in spinach mixture until well blended. Spoon mixture into a greased 9x5-inch loaf pan and smooth surface.
- Toss 6 perfect mushrooms with lemon juice; set aside. Chop remaining mushrooms.
- Melt 4 tablespoons butter in a saucepan. Add whole mushrooms and sauté 5 minutes, turning often. Arrange whole mushrooms in a row on top of spinach, leaving cooking juices in pan. Add chopped mushrooms and onion to same pan and sauté until onion is translucent. Stir in sherry and season with salt and pepper. Remove from heat. Lightly beat 2 eggs and add to sautéed vegetables in pan along with remaining ¼ cup bread crumbs. Spoon mixture over spinach layer.

- Purée cooked carrots in a blender or food processor until smooth. Melt remaining 2 tablespoons butter in a medium saucepan. Stir in remaining ¼ cup half-and-half, flour, ginger and nutmeg. Cook, stirring constantly, until mixture comes to a boil. Remove from heat and beat in remaining 2 eggs and carrot purée. Spoon carrot mixture over mushroom layer in pan. Cover with wax paper, then foil. Set in a larger deep pan. Pour boiling water into outer pan to a depth of 2 inches.

- Bake 2 hours or until the paté feels firm to the touch. Cool in pan on a wire rack for at least 1 hour. Refrigerate overnight.

- Allow paté to come to room temperature before serving. Run a thin knife around the paté and turn out onto a plate, then invert again onto a serving plate so paté ends up right-side up.

LENTILS AND TOMATOES
PAREVE OR MEAT

1½	cups dried lentils	3	medium tomatoes, chopped
2-3	cups vegetable or chicken broth	2	tablespoons tomato paste
2	medium onions, chopped		Salt and pepper to taste
2	cloves garlic, chopped	1	teaspoon dried dill
1	tablespoon olive oil		

- Combine lentils and enough broth to cover them in a saucepan. Bring to a boil. Reduce heat and simmer until tender. Pour off liquid so that lentils are just covered with broth.
- Meanwhile, sauté onion and garlic in olive oil in a skillet for 5 to 8 minutes. Add tomatoes and tomato paste and cook 5 minutes longer. Season with salt and pepper and dill. Add vegetable mixture to lentils.
- Simmer over low heat until liquid has evaporated, but mixture is not too dry.

Sliced mushrooms may be added and sautéed with the onion and garlic.

CARROT SOUFFLÉ
PAREVE

1½	pounds carrots	1½	teaspoons baking powder
1	stick margarine	1½	cups sugar
3	eggs	¼	teaspoon cinnamon
¼	cup flour		

- Preheat oven to 350 degrees.
- Boil carrots in water until soft. Drain and mash with a potato masher. Add margarine, eggs, flour, baking powder, sugar and cinnamon and mash until smooth. Transfer to a lightly greased 1½-quart casserole dish.
- Bake 1 hour, 10 minutes or until soufflé is set.
- 8 servings

The sugar can be cut to 1 cup and the margarine can be reduced to 4 tablespoons.

Recipe can be doubled or tripled easily; recipe freezes well.

Keep in mind if soufflé type recipes are not served immediately, they will fall, but still taste delicious.

ZESTY GREEN BEANS
PAREVE

2 pounds fresh green beans, trimmed

2 tablespoons extra virgin olive oil

3 tablespoons fresh lemon juice

2 tablespoons finely chopped fresh tarragon, or 1 tablespoon dried
Salt and pepper to taste

- Blanch beans 2 to 3 minutes in boiling water. Plunge into ice water to stop cooking; drain well.
- Before serving, toss beans with olive oil, lemon juice and tarragon. Season with salt and pepper.
- 6 servings

Beans may be cooked up to 1 day ahead and stored in an airtight container with a paper towel to absorb moisture that would make them soggy. Just before serving, toss with the dressing.

Steamed green beans are delicious plain, but for a change of pace, brown butter in a saucepan, add toasted pine nuts or any toasted nut of choice, then toss with steamed beans. Actually, this works with any simple steamed vegetable if you are not counting calories.

ASPARAGUS WITH PISTACHIO NUTS
DAIRY OR PAREVE

2½ pounds white or green asparagus, ends trimmed

½ cup shelled pistachio nuts

2 tablespoons unsalted butter or margarine
Salt and pepper to taste

2 hard-boiled eggs

1 tablespoon chopped fresh chives

1 tablespoon chopped fresh tarragon

1 tablespoon chopped fresh parsley

- Preheat oven to 400 degrees.
- Steam asparagus 5 to 8 minutes or until just tender; cooking time will depend on thickness of stalks.
- Toast pistachio nuts in oven until lightly browned. Cool, then chop nuts.
- In a large skillet, melt butter until lightly browned. Add cooked asparagus and season with salt and pepper. Transfer to a serving platter.
- Grate eggs over the top and sprinkle with toasted nuts, chives, tarragon and parsley.

White asparagus can also be used for a change. It is also nice to combine the 2 colors.

The topping for the asparagus is so crunchy, even if you don't like asparagus, you will enjoy this recipe.

TOMATO SAUCE STRING BEANS
PAREVE

1½	pounds string beans	1	tablespoon minced fresh basil, or 1 teaspoon dried
2-3	cloves garlic, minced	1	teaspoon salt
3	tablespoons olive oil	1	teaspoon white pepper
1	(28-ounce) can crushed tomatoes	⅛-¼	teaspoon cayenne pepper
1	tablespoon minced fresh parsley, or 1 teaspoon dried	¼	cup dry red wine (optional)
1	tablespoon minced fresh oregano, or 1 teaspoon dried		

- Steam beans 5 minutes. Run under cold water to stop cooking, drain and set aside.
- Sauté garlic in olive oil in a skillet. Mix in tomatoes, parsley, oregano, basil, salt, white pepper, cayenne pepper and red wine. Simmer 45 minutes.
- Add cooked beans to tomato sauce and cook 5 minutes longer. Can be made in advance and served hot or cold.

Recipe does not freeze well.

FRIED GREEN TOMATOES
DAIRY OR PAREVE

3	tablespoons cornmeal	3	tablespoons butter or margarine
3	tablespoons flour	3	tablespoons oil
	Herb salt and pepper to taste		
4	large green tomatoes, sliced ¼-inch thick		

- Combine cornmeal, flour and herb salt and pepper in a shallow dish. Dip tomato slices in mixture.
- Heat butter and oil in a skillet. Sauté tomatoes in butter and oil over medium-high heat, turning only once, until brown on both sides. Serve immediately.

Butternut Squash Purée with a Praline Crunch

DAIRY OR PAREVE

4 medium butternut squash, peeled and cubed

½ cup brown sugar

¼ cup extra virgin olive oil
   Salt and pepper to taste

Topping

4 tablespoons butter or margarine, melted

2 cups cornflakes, crushed

¾ cup walnuts, chopped

½ cup brown sugar

- Preheat oven to 400 degrees.
- Combine squash cubes, brown sugar and olive oil in a large bowl. Season with salt and pepper and toss to mix. Spread mixture on a baking sheet.
- Roast in oven 35 minutes or until soft. Reduce oven temperature to 350 degrees.
- Purée squash and transfer to a baking dish.
- Combine all topping ingredients and sprinkle over purée. Bake at 350 degrees for 30 minutes.
- 8-10 servings

A good side dish for chicken, turkey or fish.

Spinach Soufflé

DAIRY

1	(3-ounce) package cream cheese, softened	1	small onion, chopped (optional)
½	cup half-and-half	8	ounces mushrooms, sliced (optional)
½	cup Parmesan cheese		Salt and pepper to taste
1	egg		
2	(10-ounce) packages frozen chopped spinach, thawed and squeezed dry		

- Preheat oven to 375 degrees.
- Combine cream cheese, half-and-half, Parmesan cheese and egg until smooth. Mix in spinach.
- Sauté onion and mushrooms, if using, and add to spinach mixture. Season with salt and pepper and transfer to greased small soufflé dishes or a pie plate.
- Bake 40 minutes or until light brown.

Can be prepared a day ahead and baked the next day. Recipe doubles easily.

MASHED YELLOW TURNIPS WITH CRISPY SHALLOTS

DAIRY

1 cup canola oil

9 tablespoons butter, divided

6 shallots, peeled and thinly sliced into rings

2 large turnips (about 4 pounds), peeled and cut into 1-inch chunks

2 teaspoons coarse salt, divided

1 cup milk, warmed
  Freshly ground black pepper to taste

- Heat oil and 6 tablespoons butter in a skillet until mixture begins to bubble. Add shallots and sauté until brown and crispy. Remove shallots with a slotted spoon and drain on paper towels; set aside.

- Boil turnip chunks in water with 1 teaspoon salt for 40 minutes or until easily pierced by a knife; drain. Purée turnips in a food processor until smooth. Add remaining 3 tablespoons butter and milk and blend until combined. Season with remaining 1 teaspoon salt and pepper to taste.

- Reheat in microwave if necessary. Sprinkle shallots on top before serving.

White and yellow turnips are excellent in chicken stock. They add a sweetness as long as too many of them are not used. Be careful not to overcook them or they might taste bitter. Iraqi Jews stew white turnips in date syrup (dibis) which is available in Middle Eastern markets. You can use brown sugar instead. Peel 1 pound and cut turnips into bite-size pieces. Pour in a pot and cover with water. Add 2 tablespoons date syrup or brown sugar and simmer 30 minutes or until most of liquid is absorbed. They are tender and sweet to eat.

White Bean, Spinach and Potato Gratin with Herbed Garlic Butter

DAIRY

4	tablespoons butter, softened	1½	cups canned white beans, drained
4	cloves garlic, minced	¾	cup shredded Gruyère or other cheese
2	tablespoons chopped fresh parsley	1½	cups vegetable broth
½	teaspoon dried thyme	¼	teaspoon paprika
¼	teaspoon dried oregano	¼	teaspoon salt
1	pound fresh spinach		Black pepper to taste
1	onion, sliced		
4	baking potatoes, thinly sliced		

- Preheat oven to 350 degrees.
- Cream butter with garlic, parsley, thyme and oregano. Spread some of mixture on the bottom of a 14-inch casserole dish.
- Steam spinach, drain and chop.
- Sauté onion in some of remaining herb butter.
- Layer potato slices, beans, spinach, onion, cheese and broth, making 2 layers, in prepared casserole dish. Dot with remaining herb butter and sprinkle with paprika, salt and pepper.
- Bake 1 hour or until potatoes are tender and top is golden.
- 6 servings

PARSNIPS AND SWEET POTATOES
PAREVE

1-1½ pounds parsnips, peeled and cut into ½-inch diagonal pieces

1-1½ pounds sweet potatoes, quartered and cut into ½-inch diagonal slices

2 tablespoons olive oil

Salt and pepper to taste

2 tablespoons maple syrup

1 tablespoon Dijon mustard

Chopped fresh parsley (optional)

- Preheat oven to 450 degrees.
- Toss parsnips and sweet potatoes with olive oil on a rimmed baking sheet. Season generously with salt and pepper and spread in a single layer.
- Roast in oven, turning occasionally, for 30 minutes or until tender and golden. Transfer to a large bowl.
- In a small bowl, combine syrup and mustard. Pour mixture over vegetables and toss to coat. Sprinkle with parsley and serve.

Recipe can be made with other vegetables,
but adjust roasting times accordingly.

ROASTED POTATOES AND ARTICHOKES WITH FETA CHEESE
DAIRY

2 pounds small red potatoes, quartered

2 (14-ounce) cans artichoke hearts, drained and halved

2 teaspoons dried thyme

2 teaspoons dried oregano

1 teaspoon dried dill

2 tablespoons olive oil

½ teaspoon salt

¼ teaspoon black pepper

½ cup crumbled feta cheese

- Preheat oven to 425 degrees.
- Combine potatoes, artichoke hearts, thyme, oregano, dill, olive oil, salt and pepper in a large bowl and toss to coat. Arrange mixture in a greased 9x13-inch pan.
- Bake 40 minutes or until potatoes are tender, stirring occasionally.
- When done baking, mix potatoes with feta cheese.
- 4 servings

Recipe can be prepared ahead without the cheese.

This is not a common combination of vegetables, but is rather tasty for a change. The parsnip really needs to be scrubbed like a carrot and peeled like one as well, as the skin can be bitter. Parsnips look like giant white carrots.

Artichokes are another treasure of our Italian Jewish heritage in addition to pasta. We eat them steamed, stuffed or fried. If you really like them, you can include them in pea and spinach recipes or potato and rice salads or with main meals such as chicken or veal. Some say that when they are served at the Rosh Hashanah feast they symbolize renewal and happiness.

POTATO CHEESE CASSEROLE

DAIRY

5	pounds potatoes, peeled	1	cup sour cream
3	eggs		Salt and pepper to taste
1	cup milk	1	pound mozzarella cheese, shredded
1½	sticks butter		

Topping

¾	cup Parmesan cheese	1	teaspoon butter, melted
½	cup bread crumbs		Parsley for garnish

- Preheat oven to 350 degrees.
- Cook potatoes in boiling water until tender. Drain and transfer to the large bowl of an electric mixer. Add eggs, milk, butter and sour cream and beat until mashed and blended. Season with salt and pepper.
- Spoon half the potato mixture into a casserole dish. Sprinkle with mozzarella cheese. Spread remaining potato mixture over cheese.
- Combine all topping ingredients and sprinkle over potatoes.
- Bake 30 minutes. Garnish with parsley.

More flavorful cheeses, such as Gorgonzola, feta or sharp Cheddar, may be substituted for the mozzarella.

CAULIFLOWER CASSEROLE

PAREVE

2	pounds cauliflower, cut into pieces	¼	cup mayonnaise
6	eggs	1½	cups corn flakes, crushed
1	(1-ounce) package dry onion soup mix		

- Preheat oven to 350 degrees.
- Combine cauliflower, eggs, soup mix and mayonnaise in a bowl. Mix well and spoon into a greased 9x13-inch baking pan. Sprinkle corn flakes on top.
- Bake about 50 minutes.

Italian Potato Casserole

DAIRY OR PAREVE

3 (10-ounce) jars marinated artichoke heart, drained

3 (16-ounce) cans small sliced potatoes, drained

1 (16-ounce) can black olives, sliced, drained

1 (4-ounce) jar roasted red peppers, drained well and sliced

¾ cup salad oil

3-4 cloves garlic, minced

1½ cups plain bread crumbs

Handful of grated cheese (optional)

- Preheat oven to 400 degrees.
- Combine all ingredients except cheese and spoon into a 9x13-inch baking dish. Sprinkle cheese on top.
- Bake 15 to 20 minutes.
- 10-12 servings

If using only 2 cans potatoes, yields 6 to 8 servings.

Candied Sweet Potatoes

DAIRY OR PAREVE

4 medium sweet potatoes

⅔ cup dark brown sugar

¼ cup water

4 tablespoons butter or margarine

1 tablespoon lemon juice

½ cup maple syrup

¼ cup cognac or orange juice, or combination

- Preheat oven to 350 degrees.
- Cook potatoes in boiling water to cover for 15 minutes or until barely soft; drain and cool. Peel and slice potatoes and arrange in a greased casserole dish.
- Combine sugar, water, butter, lemon juice and maple syrup in a saucepan. Bring to a boil. Stir in cognac. Pour mixture over potatoes.
- Bake, uncovered, for 30 minutes, basting several times with syrup in casserole dish.

For extra flavor, make an extra batch of the syrup sauce.
Heat extra sauce and pour over sweet potatoes just before serving.

Good for Thanksgiving dinner.

DOUBLE CORN PUDDING
DAIRY OR PAREVE

2   eggs
2   (16-ounce) cans creamed corn
2   (16-ounce) cans corn, drained
2   (8½-ounce) packages corn muffin mix
1   stick butter or margarine, melted

- Preheat oven to 350 degrees.
- Beat eggs in a mixing bowl. Add all cans of corn, muffin mix and melted butter. Mix well and pour into a greased 2-quart casserole dish, or a 9x15-inch glass dish.
- Bake 45 minutes or until golden brown.

CORN PUDDING
DAIRY

1   stick butter, softened
½   cup sugar
5   eggs
½   cup flour
1   heaping teaspoon baking powder
2   (16-ounce) cans creamed corn

- Preheat oven to 375 degrees.
- Cream together butter and sugar. Beat in eggs one at a time. Add flour and baking powder. Mix in creamed corn.
- Pour mixture into a greased 2-quart casserole or soufflé dish. Bake 1 hour or until slightly puffed and golden brown on top.

BRAISED FENNEL
DAIRY, PAREVE OR MEAT

3-4	fennel bulbs, trimmed and vertically sliced	½	cup vegetable or chicken stock
2	tablespoons butter or margarine	¼	cup white wine
1	teaspoon dried oregano		Chopped fresh parsley for garnish
	Salt and pepper to taste		

- Arrange fennel in a large, heavy skillet. Dot with butter and sprinkle with oregano, salt and pepper.
- Add stock and wine to skillet. Cover and simmer 20 minutes or until tender. Garnish with parsley and serve hot.
- 6 servings

Leftover roasted potatoes can be added for variety.

Fennel roasts well, too. One large bulb per two people. Simply drizzle the trimmed and halved fennel bulbs with olive oil, salt and pepper to taste. Roast at 500 degrees for 15 minutes. If dairy - sprinkle grated Parmesan cheese on top near the end and let it bubble.

SMASHED POTATOES
DAIRY

3	pounds red potatoes, halved	½	cup chopped pecans
1½	teaspoons kosher salt, or to taste	½	pound blue cheese, crumbled
2	cups arugula		Salt and pepper to taste

- Bring 6 quarts of water to a boil. Add potatoes and kosher salt and cook until tender; drain.
- Smash potatoes, but do not mash until smooth. Add arugula and stir until wilted. Mix in pecans and blue cheese. Season with salt and pepper.

Squash, Potato and Onion Bake
DAIRY

4	medium potatoes, peeled and sliced	1¼	pounds yellow squash, sliced
	Salt and pepper to taste	1	cup Parmesan cheese
1	stick butter or margarine	1	cup sour cream
2	medium onions, sliced		

- Preheat oven to 350 degrees.
- Arrange a layer of potato slices over the bottom of a greased 9-inch square baking pan. Sprinkle with salt and pepper and dot with butter. Add a layer of onion slices and a layer of sliced squash. Repeat layers, ending with squash, seasoning between layers with salt and pepper and dotting with butter. Cover tightly with foil.
- Bake 1½ hours or until tender.
- Mix Parmesan cheese and sour cream and spread over top of casserole.
- Broil 3 to 5 minutes or until topping is browned.

Green Beans with Black Sesame Seeds
PAREVE

2-3	tablespoons olive oil	2	tablespoons soy sauce
2	cloves garlic, sliced	1	cup water
1	pound fresh green beans	2	tablespoons black sesame seeds
1	(16-ounce) package firm tofu, cubed	1	tablespoon sesame oil

- Heat olive oil in a wok or skillet. Add garlic and sauté 1 minute. Push garlic to the side and add beans, tofu, soy sauce and water to pan. Cover and cook 5 minutes or until beans are tender.
- Add sesame seeds and sesame oil to bean mixture and toss to coat. Transfer to a serving dish.

Spinach with Pine Nuts
PAREVE

2½ pounds spinach, rinsed and stemmed
2-3 tablespoons olive oil
2 small yellow onions, or 6 scallions, minced
¼ cup raisins, plumped in hot water and drained
¼ cup pine nuts, toasted
Salt and freshly ground black pepper to taste

- Place freshly rinsed spinach in a large skillet with only the rinsing water clinging to the leaves. Cook over medium heat, turning as needed, for just a few minutes or until wilted. Drain well and set aside.
- Add olive oil to empty skillet and place over medium heat. Add onion and sauté 8 minutes or until tender. Add spinach, raisins, and pine nuts. Sauté briefly to warm through. Season with salt and pepper. Serve warm or at room temperature.

Roasted Root Vegetables
PAREVE

3 pounds root vegetables, peeled and cut into 1-inch cubes (use potatoes, beets, rutabagas, parsnips, carrots or turnips)
2 medium onions, quartered
2 tablespoons olive oil
1 teaspoon salt
1 head garlic, cloves separated and peeled
½ cup fresh herbs (combination of rosemary, thyme, sage or parsley)
2 tablespoons balsamic vinegar

- Preheat oven to 400 degrees.
- Place root vegetables and onion in a roasting pan. Drizzle with olive oil and sprinkle with salt. Toss to coat vegetables; do not crowd vegetables in pan.
- Roast 30 minutes, tossing every 10 minutes. Add garlic and continue roasting 15 to 20 minutes longer or until all vegetables and garlic are tender.
- Sprinkle with herbs and drizzle with balsamic vinegar before serving.

HERB BUTTER
DAIRY

2 sticks unsalted butter, softened
2 tablespoons minced flat-leaf parsley
1 tablespoon chopped fresh sage
1 tablespoon lemon juice
2 teaspoons chopped fresh basil
½ teaspoon chopped fresh oregano
1 small clove garlic, chopped
Salt and freshly ground black pepper to taste

- Combine all ingredients and beat until mixed. Use immediately or roll into a log, wrap in plastic and freeze for a future use.

Great on vegetables, potatoes, fish and bread.

Mashed Cauliflower with Goat Cheese

DAIRY

1	large head cauliflower, cut into small pieces	½	teaspoon salt
¾	cup soft goat cheese	½	teaspoon black pepper
3	tablespoons sour cream	3	tablespoons chopped fresh chives and or parsley

- Steam cauliflower about 10 minutes or until tender. Transfer to a large bowl. With an immersion blender or a potato masher, purée cauliflower to desired texture.
- Add goat cheese, sour cream, salt and pepper and purée until combined. Stir in fresh herbs.

Neil and Stanley's Potato Kugel for a Crowd

PAREVE

7½	pounds potatoes	1	dozen eggs
2½	pounds onions, chopped	2	cups vegetable oil
2½	cups matzoh meal		Salt and pepper to taste

- Preheat oven to 350 degrees.
- Peel potatoes. Grate half the potatoes. Purée remaining half of potatoes.
- Combine grated potatoes, puréed potatoes, onion, matzoh meal, eggs and oil in a large bowl. Season with salt and pepper and mix well.
- Divide mixture between 2 greased 9x13-inch baking dishes, or for a more festive presentation, use 2 to 3 greased 10-inch springform pans.
- Bake 1 to 1½ hours or until golden and top is crispy.

Kugels, Pasta,
Rice & Grains

KUGELS, PASTA, RICE & GRAINS

Festive holiday meals would not be the same without *kugel*! As a traditional Jewish side dish, *kugel* - our version of crusty baked pudding or casserole - can be made in an infinite number of varieties: sweet or savory, dairy or *pareve*.

Pasta can be served in so many ways. How fortunate we are that the rabbis and businessmen, who had connections in Old Italy, brought back to their communities the idea of boiling dough! Pasta, displayed in a variety of shapes or colors, can be the main attraction at any meal by adding small amounts of vegetables and protein.

An ancient grain, rice is the main source of nourishment for a large part of the world population - 535 million tons are consumed annually. Long grain, wild, basmati, jasmine and Arborio, to name a few, are types of rice that can be used as either a first course, main course or side dish.

Experiment with buckwheat (kasha), barley, cornmeal polenta and other grains to add texture and versatility to any meal.

Browned Onion Kugels
DAIRY

6	ounces medium egg noodles	1¼	cups small curd cottage cheese
1	stick unsalted butter	1	tablespoon poppy seeds
3	cups chopped onion	4	eggs
1¼	cups sour cream	1	teaspoon salt
		¼	teaspoon black pepper

- Preheat oven to 425 degrees.
- Cook noodles in a 6- to 8-quart pot of boiling salted water. Drain in a colander and rinse under cold water; drain well.
- Melt butter in a 12-inch heavy skillet over medium heat. Use some of melted butter to brush 12 muffin tins.
- Add onion to skillet and cook, stirring occasionally, for 20 minutes or until well browned. Transfer onion to a large bowl and stir in drained noodles, sour cream, cottage cheese and poppy seeds.
- Lightly beat eggs with salt and pepper. Add to noodle mixture and stir until well combined. Divide mixture among buttered muffin tins.
- Bake in center of oven for 20 to 25 minutes or until puffed and golden. Loosen edges of kugels with a thin knife and cool in pan 5 minutes before serving.
- 12 kugels

Greek Rice with Chickpeas
PAREVE

1	cup brown rice	¼	cup finely chopped fresh parsley
1	onion, finely chopped		
3½	cups water	2	tablespoons lemon juice
1½	cups cooked chickpeas, or one (15-ounce) can garbanzo beans, drained		Salt to taste

- Cook rice and onion in water in a large covered pot over medium heat for 45 minutes. Add chickpeas, parsley, lemon juice and salt.
- Cook 10 minutes longer, stirring occasionally. Serve warm.
- 6 servings

Other beans, such as navy or kidney beans, may be used instead of chickpeas.

Substitute Israeli couscous for rice dishes, including risotto.

PECAN CRUSTED NOODLE KUGEL
DAIRY OR PAREVE

Crust

4	tablespoons butter or margarine, melted	½	cup brown sugar
		1	cup chopped pecans

Filling

1	(12-ounce) package medium noodles	16	dried apricots
		2	apples, peeled and sliced
2	tablespoons butter or margarine, melted	¼	cup sugar
		1	teaspoon salt
2	eggs, lightly beaten	½	teaspoon cinnamon

- Preheat oven to 350 degrees.
- For crust, pour melted butter into a Bundt pan. Sprinkle with brown sugar and spread pecans on top; set aside.
- To make filling, cook noodles according to package directions, drain. Mix noodles and butter. Add eggs, apricots, apple, sugar, salt and cinnamon. Pour filling over crust and refrigerate at least 1 hour.
- Bake 1 hour. Cool and invert.

ROASTED RED PEPPER AND RICOTTA PASTA SAUCE
DAIRY

1	clove garlic, crushed	2	tablespoons chopped fresh flat-leaf parsley
1	(15-ounce) container whole milk ricotta cheese, room temperature	1	tablespoon Parmesan cheese
1	(7-ounce) jar roasted red peppers, drained and rinsed	1	teaspoon chopped fresh oregano
¼	cup olive oil	1	pound pasta, cooked and drained

- Combine garlic, ricotta cheese, red peppers, olive oil, parsley, Parmesan cheese and oregano.
- Pour cheese sauce over hot pasta and toss. Serve immediately.

Try some of these sauces on grilled or baked polenta or any grain of your choice.

Polenta or Cornmeal — are they the same?

Polenta is a medium or coarse ground cornmeal. It is served soft, or porridge-style with olive oil, butter and a variety of cheeses. Polenta can also be chilled until firm and cut into squares to be grilled, baked or sautéed. It is a hearty side dish.

Spinach Noodle Pudding

DAIRY OR PAREVE

1	(8-ounce) package kluski (Polish) noodles	1	(1-ounce) package dry onion soup mix
1	(10-ounce) package frozen chopped spinach, thawed and squeezed dry	1	stick butter or margarine
		1/4	teaspoon garlic powder (optional)
1	cup non-dairy coffee creamer or milk	3	eggs, beaten

- Preheat oven to 350 degrees.
- Cook noodles according to package directions; drain well. Add spinach, creamer, soup mix, butter and garlic powder to noodles and stir well. Mix in eggs and pour into a greased 8- or 9-inch square pan.
- Bake 45 to 60 minutes. Cool slightly and cut into squares.
- 8-10 servings

This is a favorite family dish.

Fettucine or fettucine regatta may be substituted for the kluski noodles.

Meat Sauce for Pasta

MEAT

1	pound ground beef	1/8	teaspoon black pepper
1	tablespoon olive oil	1/2	teaspoon dried basil, or 2 tablespoons fresh
1	clove garlic, crushed		
1/2	medium onion, chopped	1	teaspoon dried oregano
1	teaspoon dried parsley	1	tablespoon margarine
1	(16-ounce) can tomatoes	1½	teaspoons sugar (optional)
1	(6-ounce) can tomato paste		

- Brown ground beef slowly with olive oil, garlic, onion and parsley; drain fat.
- Add tomatoes, tomato paste, pepper, basil and oregano. Cover and simmer 1 hour.
- Add margarine. If sauce is too acidic, add sugar.
- When ready to serve, reheat sauce and serve hot over 1 pound cooked and drained pasta.

NOODLE KUGEL

DAIRY

Filling

8	ounces medium or wide noodles	1	pint sour cream
6	eggs, divided	1	pound cottage cheese
1	stick butter, melted	½	cup sugar
		1½	cups milk, divided

Topping

1½	cups corn flakes	2	tablespoons sugar
1	teaspoon cinnamon	2	tablespoons butter, melted

- Preheat oven to 350 degrees.
- Cook noodles with a dash of salt until tender in a pot of boiling water; drain.
- Using a hand mixer, beat 4 eggs, melted butter, sour cream, cottage cheese, sugar and ½ cup milk until smooth. Add drained noodles. Pour mixture into a greased 9x13-inch glass dish.
- Beat remaining 2 eggs with remaining 1 cup milk and pour over noodle mixture.
- Bake 45 minutes. Remove from oven and cool slightly.
- Combine all topping ingredients and spread evenly over baked kugel.
- Bake 30 minutes longer.

Graham cracker crumbs may be substituted for the corn flakes and other topping ingredients.

Kasha and Orzo Pilaf
PAREVE OR MEAT

¾   **cup orzo**
1   **teaspoon salt, divided**
1½   **cups chicken or vegetable stock**
¾   **cup whole grain kasha (coarse grain)**
¾   **cup grated carrot**
2   **teaspoons margarine**

1½   **teaspoons chopped fresh thyme**
½   **teaspoon freshly ground black pepper**
¼   **cup finely chopped fresh parsley**
2   **scallions, chopped**

- Bring 4 cups water to a boil. Add orzo and ½ teaspoon salt. Cook 7 to 10 minutes or until orzo is tender. Drain and rinse with cold water; set aside.
- Bring stock to a simmer over low heat.
- In a large skillet, stir kasha over medium-high heat for 3 minutes or until lightly toasted. Reduce heat to low and slowly stir in hot stock. Add carrot, margarine, thyme, pepper and remaining ½ teaspoon salt. Cover and cook 10 to 12 minutes or until kasha is tender and all stock has been absorbed.
- Stir in drained orzo, parsley and scallions.

Recipe can be prepared in advance and reheated in oven at 350 degrees.

For a more traditional kasha recipe, substitute bow tie pasta for the orzo and substitute onions and mushrooms for the carrots and scallions.

Rice Pilaf
PAREVE OR MEAT

1   **tablespoon margarine**
¾   **cup fine egg noodles**
1   **cup long grain rice**

2   **cups water**
4   **chicken or vegetable bouillon cubes**

- Melt margarine in a skillet. Add noodles and cook and stir until lightly browned. Add rice, water and bouillon cubes.
- Cover and simmer 30 minutes or until rice is soft.

Tuna Tomato Sauce for Pasta

DAIRY OR PAREVE

½   cup olive oil
3-4   cloves garlic, finely chopped
1   large onion, finely diced
2-3   zucchini, diced
2   (28-ounce) cans crushed tomatoes in purée
1-2   (6-ounce) cans tuna packed in olive oil
1   cup sliced olives
2-3   tablespoons capers (optional)
5-6   anchovy fillets, crushed (optional)
½   teaspoon dried oregano
½   cup chopped fresh parsley
Salt to taste
1   pound linguini
Grated Parmesan or other strong-flavored hard-type cheese (optional)

- Heat olive oil in a heavy saucepan. Add garlic and onion and sauté until onion is translucent and starting to caramelize. Add zucchini and cook and stir over medium heat for 1 minute or until zucchini starts to soften.
- Stir in tomatoes. Add tuna, olives, capers, anchovies and oregano and mix well. Cover and simmer over medium heat for 10 to 15 minutes. Add parsley during last minute of cooking. Taste sauce and add salt as needed.
- Meanwhile, cook linguini according to package directions; drain. Serve sauce over drained linguini with generous amounts of grated cheese on the side.
- 4 servings

RICE, LENTILS AND FETA CASSEROLE
DAIRY

2	(14-ounce) cans vegetable broth	½	teaspoon garlic	
¾	cup dry lentils	½	teaspoon dried basil	
1	(14½-ounce) can stewed tomatoes	½	teaspoon dried oregano	
2	ounces crumbled feta cheese, or more to taste		Olives (optional)	
1	(10-ounce) package frozen spinach		Pine nuts (optional)	
			Salt and pepper to taste	

- Preheat oven to 350 degrees.
- Combine all ingredients in a casserole dish.
- Bake 1½ hours or until beans and rice are tender. If casserole becomes too dry while cooking, add extra liquid.

RICE AND BROCCOLI
PAREVE

1	cup white rice (not instant)	1	(16-ounce) package frozen chopped broccoli
2	cups water	1	(1-ounce) package dry onion soup mix
1	cup raisins	1	cup cashews
4	tablespoons margarine		

- Preheat oven to 350 degrees.
- Combine all ingredients except cashews and pour into a 9x13-inch glass baking dish.
- Bake, covered, for 45 minutes.
- Uncover and sprinkle cashews on top. Bake, uncovered, for 20 minutes longer or until water has evaporated.
- 4 servings

If doubling recipe, increase baking time.
Other types of rice can be used.
Try adding cranberries, raisins or currants for variety.

Long grain, wild, basmati, jasmine, Arborio, brown or white rice ... take your choice of one for salads and sides, with a sauce or simply steamed.

APPLESAUCE APRICOT KUGEL

DAIRY OR PAREVE

1	pound medium yolkless noodles, cooked and drained	1	cup white raisins
1	stick margarine or butter	1	tablespoon lemon zest
6	eggs, or equivalent substitute	1	tablespoon lemon juice
1	cup sugar	2	teaspoons vanilla
1	pound chunky applesauce	1	teaspoon cinnamon
1	(16-ounce) can apricots in water or juice, sliced, drained	1	teaspoon allspice (optional)
			Cinnamon sugar

- Preheat oven to 350 degrees.
- Combine drained noodles, margarine, eggs and sugar in a large bowl. Add applesauce, apricots, raisins, lemon zest and juice, vanilla, cinnamon and allspice. Mix well and transfer to a greased large glass baking dish.
- Bake 45 to 60 minutes. Sprinkle cinnamon sugar on top before serving.

RICE KUGEL

PAREVE

¾	cup sugar	4	eggs, beaten
½	tablespoon cinnamon	1	stick unsalted margarine, melted
1	cup dry rice, cooked		
1-1½	cups orange juice (depending on dryness of cooked rice)		Topping: cinnamon sugar, crushed graham crackers or corn flakes
½	cup white raisins		

- Preheat oven to 350 degrees.
- Sprinkle sugar and cinnamon in the bottom of a greased 9x13-inch pan.
- Combine cooked rice, orange juice, raisins, eggs and margarine in a large bowl. Pour mixture into prepared pan. Sprinkle topping of choice on top.
- Bake 1 hour.

Use brandy or other liqueur for some of the orange juice.

Ground Turkey with Peppers and Olives Pasta Sauce

MEAT

A quick and easy meal.

2	tablespoons olive oil	¾	cup sliced black olives
1	medium green bell pepper, coarsely chopped	1	tablespoon double concentrated tomato paste, or 2 tablespoons regular tomato paste
1	medium red bell pepper, coarsely chopped		
1	medium onion, finely chopped	2	tablespoons sugar
		½	teaspoon salt
1	medium clove garlic, finely chopped	½	teaspoon dried basil
		½	teaspoon dried oregano
1	pound ground turkey	¼	teaspoon dried rosemary
1	(28-ounce) can whole tomatoes	¼	teaspoon crushed red pepper flakes (optional)

- In a large skillet or saucepan, heat oil over medium heat. Add bell peppers, onion and garlic and sauté 2 to 3 minutes or until tender.
- Increase heat slightly. Add turkey and sauté 10 minutes or until turkey has lost its pink color and has left a brown glaze on the pan.
- Add tomatoes, breaking them up with a wooden spoon to dissolve browned bits in pan. Stir in olives, tomato paste, sugar, salt, basil, oregano, rosemary and pepper flakes.
- Gently boil 15 to 20 minutes or until thick. Serve over cooked spaghetti or other pasta.

Roasted Eggplant Pasta Sauce
DAIRY OR PAREVE

3   medium eggplants, unpeeled and cut into ½-inch cubes

9   tablespoons extra virgin olive oil, divided

1   large onion, chopped

3   cloves garlic, minced

3   (16-ounce) cans stewed tomatoes in juice

1   teaspoon dried oregano

2   tablespoons chopped fresh basil

½   teaspoon crushed red pepper flakes

Salt and pepper to taste

- Preheat oven to 400 degrees.
- Spread cubed eggplant on a baking sheet and drizzle with 6 tablespoons olive oil. Roast 20 to 25 minutes or until golden and tender, stirring halfway through.
- Meanwhile, sauté onion and garlic in remaining 3 tablespoons olive oil until onion is soft. Add undrained tomatoes and simmer 15 minutes or until thick.
- Stir eggplant into tomato sauce. Season with oregano, basil, pepper flakes and salt and pepper. Cook until heated through. Serve over pasta.

Parmesan cheese can be added to the sauce.

Spaghetti with Lemon
DAIRY

1   pound spaghetti

Juice of 4 lemons

⅔   cup olive oil

1¼   cups freshly grated Parmesan cheese

Sea salt and freshly ground black pepper

1   cup chopped fresh basil

Lemon zest (optional)

- Cook spaghetti in boiling salted water. Drain well and return to saucepan.
- Beat lemon juice with olive oil. Stir in Parmesan cheese until thick and creamy. Season with salt and pepper, and add more lemon juice if needed.
- Add lemon sauce to drained spaghetti along with basil and lemon zest and toss to mix. Delicious served at room temperature.

LEMON PASTA

Another version, this time with artichokes. Quick and easy.

DAIRY

1	pound spaghetti or fettucine	1	cup vegetable broth
1	cup sliced scallions	½	cup dry white wine
½	cup chopped fresh rosemary	¼	cup heavy cream
1	tablespoon olive oil	1	teaspoon lemon zest
1	(10-ounce) package frozen artichoke hearts, thawed and chopped	¼	cup chopped fresh parsley
			Salt and pepper to taste
			Lemon wedges for garnish

- Prepare pasta according to package directions; drain and return to pan.

- While pasta cooks, sauté scallions and rosemary in olive oil in a 12-inch skillet over medium to high heat until scallions are softened and clear. Add artichoke hearts, broth, wine, cream and lemon zest and bring to a boil.

- Add sauce and parsley to drained pasta. Season with salt and pepper. Toss in pot to mix. Portion onto plates or into bowls and garnish with lemon wedges.

*Red or yellow bell pepper or mushrooms may be
substituted for the artichokes.*

Cavatelli with Pine Nuts and Spinach

DAIRY

1	cup pine nuts	¾	cup vegetable stock
2	tablespoons olive oil	1½	pounds cavatelli or other small hearty pasta, cooked al dente
3	cloves garlic, minced		
½	teaspoon crushed red pepper flakes	¾	cup good quality Parmesan cheese
1½	pounds spinach or baby spinach, sliced into ½-inch strips		Salt and pepper to taste
3	tablespoons butter or margarine		

- Toast pine nuts in a dry skillet, being careful not to burn.
- Heat 2 tablespoons olive oil in a skillet. Add garlic and pepper flakes and sauté 1 to 2 minutes. Add spinach and stir just until wilted. Reduce heat to low. Add butter and stir until melted. Remove from heat and add stock.
- Toss spinach mixture with drained pasta, Parmesan cheese and pine nuts. Season with salt and pepper.
- 6-8 servings

Lentils and Rice

DAIRY

1	tablespoon vegetable oil	½	teaspoon black pepper
2	cups thinly sliced onion	4	cups water
1	cup dry long-grain brown rice	1	cup dried lentils
1	tablespoon curry powder	1	cup chopped fresh cilantro
1	teaspoon salt	½	cup low-fat sour cream

- Heat oil in a large Dutch oven over medium-high heat. Add onion and sauté 8 minutes or until golden brown, stirring occasionally. Add rice, curry powder, salt and pepper. Sauté 1 minute.
- Add water and lentils and bring to a boil. Cover, reduce heat and simmer 1 hour.
- Remove from heat and stir in cilantro and sour cream.

LIL'S NOODLE KUGEL
DAIRY OR PAREVE

Filling

1	pound wide flat noodles, cooked and drained	½	cup sugar
4	eggs, beaten	1½	cups chunky applesauce
1	(12-ounce) jar apricot preserves	1	stick butter or margarine, melted, or less if desired

Topping

1	cup graham cracker crumbs	1	teaspoon cinnamon
1½	tablespoons sugar	2	tablespoons butter or margarine, melted

- Preheat oven to 350 degrees.
- Combine noodles, egg, preserves, sugar and applesauce and pour into a greased 9x13-inch pan. Pour melted butter over the top.
- Mix all topping ingredients until crumbly and sprinkle over filling.
- Bake 1 hour to 1 hour, 15 minutes or until firm.

FETTUCCINE ALFREDO
DAIRY

8	ounces dry fettuccine pasta	3	tablespoons light cream or half-and-half
4	tablespoons butter, melted		Salt and white pepper to taste
¼	cup freshly grated Parmesan cheese, plus extra for serving		Chopped fresh parsley for garnish

- Prepare pasta according to directions on package. Drain pasta and transfer immediately to a warmed serving bowl. Add butter, Parmesan cheese, cream and salt and pepper to hot pasta and toss to coat pasta well.
- Garnish with parsley and serve with extra Parmesan cheese on the side.

NUTTED WILD RICE
PAREVE OR MEAT

1	cup dry wild rice	¼	cup chopped fresh mint, or to taste
4½	cups fat-free chicken stock or water	4	scallions, thinly sliced
1	cup pecan halves or almonds	2	tablespoons olive oil
1	cup yellow raisins or dried cranberries	⅓	cup fresh orange juice
	Zest of 1 large orange	1½	teaspoons salt, or to taste
			Freshly ground black pepper to taste

- Place rice in a strainer and run under cold water to rinse thoroughly. Transfer to a bowl and cover with double the amount of cold water; soak overnight. Drain.
- Bring stock to a boil. Add drained rice and gently simmer, covered, for about 45 minutes or until tender.
- Stir in pecans, raisins, orange zest, mint, scallions, olive oil, orange juice, salt and pepper. Adjust seasoning as needed. Let stand at least 2 hours or up to 1 day to allow flavors to develop.

CARROT RICE
DAIRY OR PAREVE

1	small onion, chopped	½	teaspoon cinnamon
2	tablespoons vegetable or canola oil, or 1 tablespoon oil plus 1 tablespoon butter		Pinch of salt
		¾	cup finely grated carrot
		½	cup dried cranberries or cherries
1	cup basmati rice	½	cup slivered almonds, toasted (see note below)
1	tablespoon orange zest		
¼	teaspoon cayenne pepper		

- Cook onion in vegetable oil until soft and translucent. Add rice and cook according to package directions, adding orange zest, cayenne pepper, cinnamon, salt and carrot before cooking.
- When rice reaches desired tenderness, remove from heat and stir in cranberries and almonds.

Almonds can be toasted while rice cooks by placing them in a shallow pan over low heat until golden brown and fragrant.

Basmati rice works well for this recipe because it does not become mushy.

Not Your Typical High-Fat Kugel
DAIRY

1	pound egg noodles, cooked and drained	¼	cup white or dark raisins
1	stick butter, cut into small pieces	8	ounces applesauce
		1	(16-ounce) can crushed pineapple
4	eggs, or 8 egg whites	4	teaspoons apricot preserves (optional)
½	cup sugar		

- Preheat oven to 350 degrees.
- Combine drained noodles and butter and mix thoroughly. Add eggs, sugar, raisins, applesauce and pineapple and stir to mix. Spoon mixture into a greased casserole dish. Top with 4 dollops of apricot preserves.
- Bake about 45 minutes. Cool before cutting. Reheat when ready to serve.

Shredded raw carrot or zucchini,
or a combination of the two can be used in place of the noodles.

Rice Cooked with Tea
DAIRY OR PAREVE

1½	cups long grain rice	¼	teaspoon ground cloves
1	tablespoon butter or margarine	¼	teaspoon black pepper
3½	cups hot jasmine tea	¼	teaspoon cinnamon
¼	teaspoon ground ginger	¼	teaspoon salt

- Sauté rice in butter in a large saucepan, stirring frequently. When rice is transparent, add tea, ginger, cloves, pepper, cinnamon and salt and cook until liquid is absorbed, being careful to not burn rice.
- Remove from burner and cover pot. Let stand 15 minutes.

Eating at my Aunt Helen's table was always an adventure because her cooking seemed more exotic than mom's. She would proudly share her recipes. To my surprise, many of them came off the side of a box. Once I thought this was the best rice I ever tasted, only to learn that the recipe came from the side of an Israeli tea box.

FALAFEL
PAREVE

2	(15-ounce) cans chickpeas, drained	2	teaspoons salt
2	onions, chopped	1/2	teaspoon black pepper
1	cup chopped fresh parsley	1/2	teaspoon cayenne pepper
4	cloves garlic, minced	2	teaspoons lemon juice
2	eggs	2	teaspoons baking powder
1/4	cup ground cumin	2	tablespoons olive oil
2	teaspoons ground coriander	2	cups plain soft bread crumbs
			Vegetable oil for frying

- Combine all ingredients except frying oil in a food processor. Process until smooth. With wet hands, form mixture into balls or patties; set aside.
- Fill a large skillet halfway with vegetable oil. Heat until hot.
- Drop balls or patties into hot oil and fry 2 to 3 minutes on each side, depending on size.

Enjoy falafel in pita bread with hummus, lettuce,
chopped tomato, sliced pickles or whatever you choose;
or try the following sauce instead of hummus.

CUCUMBER SAUCE
DAIRY

12	ounces plain yogurt or sour cream	2	teaspoons dried dill
2	tablespoons mayonnaise		Salt and pepper to taste
1	whole cucumber, peeled, seeded and finely diced		

- Combine all ingredients and mix well.

MUSHROOM RISOTTO
DAIRY

6	cups vegetable broth	1½	cups dry Arborio rice
3	tablespoons olive oil, divided	1½	cups dry white wine
		4	tablespoons butter
1	pound portobello mushrooms, thinly sliced	½	cup freshly grated Parmesan cheese
1	pound white mushrooms, thinly sliced		Salt and pepper to taste
2	shallots, chopped	3	tablespoons minced fresh chives or green onions

- Keep broth warm on the stovetop. Heat 2 tablespoons olive oil in a large skillet. Add all mushrooms and sauté until softened. Transfer mushrooms and their liquid to a bowl; set aside.

- Add remaining 1 tablespoon oil to same skillet and sauté shallots for 1 minute. Add rice and stir 2 minutes or until rice is golden. Add wine and cook and stir constantly until liquid is absorbed. Add warm broth, ½ cup at a time, stirring constantly until liquid is absorbed before adding more broth. This process will take about 20 minutes.

- Remove from heat. Stir in butter and sautéed mushrooms with liquid. Mix in Parmesan cheese and season with salt and pepper. Garnish with chives or green onions.

MOROCCAN COUSCOUS
DAIRY OR PAREVE

2	cups vegetable broth	⅓	cup golden raisins
5	tablespoons butter or margarine	2	cups dry couscous
⅓	cup chopped dried dates	2-3	teaspoons cinnamon, depending on taste
⅓	cup chopped dried apricots	½	cup slivered almonds, toasted

- Bring broth to a boil in a large saucepan. Add butter, dates, apricots and raisins. Cook 3 minutes.

- Remove from heat and stir in couscous. Cover and let stand 5 minutes. Stir in cinnamon and almonds and serve.

POLENTA WITH WILD MUSHROOMS

DAIRY

2	medium onions, chopped	8	cups vegetable broth
2	cloves garlic, minced	1½	cups coarse polenta or yellow cornmeal
¾	cup chopped white mushrooms		Salt and pepper to taste
¾	cup dried porcini mushrooms, chopped and soaked in warm water for 15 minutes	2	cups heavy cream
		½	cup grated Asiago or Parmesan cheese
½	cup olive oil, divided	¾	cup assorted fresh wild mushrooms, such as Portobello, oyster, chanterelle, etc.
4	tablespoons chopped fresh basil		
¼	teaspoon dried oregano		Fresh parsley or basil sprigs for garnish

- Sauté onion, garlic, white mushrooms and porcini mushrooms in 3 tablespoons olive oil until golden. Add basil, oregano and broth and bring to a boil.

- Slowly stir in polenta and simmer 10 minutes, stirring often. Mixture should be creamy and thick; add more broth if needed. Season with salt and pepper.

- Before serving, stir in cream and cheese. Sauté wild mushrooms in remaining olive oil until tender. Use wild mushrooms as a garnish along with fresh parsley or basil.

Passover &
Holidays

PASSOVER AND HOLIDAYS

The celebration of holidays and festivals is a reminder that as a Jewish culture, we are strongly connected to our sophisticated palates. Passover is the time to leave winter behind and welcome spring. Spring cleaning must have had its origins in Passover ritual. Everything, every can, every package of crackers, every pot and pan, every glass was removed from cabinets and sold to our non-Jewish neighbors. Eight days later, we bought it back.

Whether one cleaned with a candle and feather, or flashlight and dustbuster, Passover offered a fresh start. Glass plates instead of china, enameled pots and pans instead of the regular stainless steel ones, were used for Passover meals. Family members arrived. Even though we could not eat our regular tuna salad or peanut butter and jelly on bread, we never felt deprived by substituting *matzoh*-based products.

Seders can be noisy and rambunctious. Families and friends come together to sing, drink and eat a lively meal that lasts long into the night. We read over and over how we were strangers in the land of Egypt and how Moses pleaded repeatedly for our freedom. There is the reciting of the four questions by the youngest child, the listing of the ten plagues and finally the recounting of the exodus from Egypt.

One thing is most assuring - the food served is the same year after year, accompanied by the symbols and tradition of the *Seder* plate.

Nanny Gabby's Date Charoset
PAREVE

2	(10-ounce) packages pitted dates	4	teaspoons sweet Passover wine
1½	cups water	2	pieces matzoh, crushed

- Cook dates in water, stirring occasionally, over low heat. When soft and dry, remove from heat and cool. Purée cooled dates in a food processor.
- Transfer purée to a mixing bowl. Add wine and matzoh. Refrigerate until ready to serve. If charoset gets too hard in refrigerator, add more wine.

Fancy Charoset
PAREVE

1⅓	cups shredded coconut	1	cup coarsely chopped dried pear
1	cup coarsely chopped walnuts	2	tablespoons sugar
¾	cup raisins	1½	teaspoons cinnamon
1¾	cups coarsely chopped dried apple	2	tablespoons jam, cherry or other kosher for Passover flavor
¾	cup coarsely chopped prunes	¼	cup sweet wine

- Combine coconut, walnuts, raisins, apple, prunes, pear, sugar and cinnamon in a saucepan. Add water to cover, about 6 cups.
- Bring to a boil. Reduce heat to a simmer. Cook, stirring occasionally, for 1½ hours or until thick. Add water if mixture gets too sticky. Add jam and wine. Refrigerate or freeze until needed.

Ashkenazi Charoset
PAREVE

5	large apples, peeled and cut into large chunks	½	cup sweet wine
⅔	cup walnuts	1	tablespoon cinnamon
		2	tablespoons sugar

- Combine all ingredients and mix well. Pulse mixture in a food processor to desired consistency. Adjust seasoning and chill.

*Charoset can be prepared ahead as it
will keep in refrigerator for several days.*

I remember seders being very noisy with rambunctious cousins and all my aunts and uncles drinking wine and chatting through what was a seemingly endless meal that lasted long into the night. Someone younger than I was always asleep under the table by the end. Actually, now that I make the seder, I realize how much work the seders were for my mom and aunts, but I want my children and grandchildren to have their memories, too.

FOOLPROOF MATZOH BALLS

PAREVE

2	eggs	1	teaspoon salt
½	cup water		Dash of black pepper
⅓	cup oil	1	cup matzoh meal

- Beat together eggs and water in a bowl. Add oil, salt and pepper. Mix in matzoh meal. Cover bowl and refrigerate overnight.
- Roll chilled mixture into large marble-size balls. Drop balls into rapidly boiling salted water; pot of water should be kept covered and opened only enough to add balls.
- Cook 45 minutes, adjusting heat to keep water boiling. After cooked, cover pot tightly and keep covered until cool. Store in a sealed container of water.
- 10-12 matzoh balls

We serve these on Passover with our gefilte fish.

GRANDMA ROSIE'S BABULA BILKES FOR PASSOVER
(Potato Knishes)

PAREVE

6	large onions, chopped	2	eggs
	Vegetable oil	¼	cup matzoh meal
6-8	pounds potatoes, peeled and cubed		Salt and pepper to taste
		1	egg yolk

- Preheat oven to 350-375 degrees.
- Sauté onion in a little vegetable oil.
- Cook potatoes in boiling salted water; drain. Mash potatoes with sautéed onion. Cool. Mix in eggs and matzoh meal and season with salt and pepper.
- Shape mixture into elongated knishes. If mixture is too sticky, add extra matzoh meal. Place knishes on a greased baking sheet or dish. Smear a little egg yolk on top of each knish.
- Bake until browned.
- 20-30 knishes

GEFILTE FISH
PAREVE

Broth

6	pounds whitefish	1	pound carrots, thickly sliced
3	pounds pike	⅓	cup salt
2	large onions, coarsely diced	1	tablespoon white pepper

Fish

2	large onions, cut into chunks	1¼	cups matzoh meal
6	jumbo eggs	2-3	teaspoons white pepper
½	cup water, or enough to moisten	3	tablespoons salt

- Ask a fishmonger or your supermarket to fillet the whitefish and pike and give you the head, bones and skin.

- Use an aluminum or stainless steel 12-quart pot for broth. Clean fish heads, bones and skin thoroughly, removing all blood. Place heads, bones and skin on a square of cheesecloth. Bring sides of cheesecloth together and tie shut. Place cheesecloth in pot. Add onion, carrot, salt and pepper. Fill pot two-thirds full with cold water. Bring to a boil. Reduce heat and simmer, partially covered, for 1 hour.

- Place fish fillets in a food processor and pulse with onions in batches until pasty. Remove mixture and place in a large bowl. Add eggs, one at a time, with water alternately with matzoh. If mixture seems too wet, add more matzoh meal. Season with pepper and salt.

- With wet hands, form mixture into tennis ball size balls. Add balls to broth in pot. Cover and gently boil for 1 hour. Cool and transfer to a bowl or large casserole dish. Remove cheesecloth and discard its contents. Remove carrot and store in a container with some broth. Refrigerate overnight.

- To serve, garnish fish balls with reserved sliced carrot.

I was taught to make gefilte fish by my Aunt Sylvia, my mother's sister. As my mother and her sisters got older, I assumed the preparation of holiday meals. Aunt Sylvia had no real recipe, so we measured everything as best we could. The results met with her approval and I've been making it ever since.

CARROT PUDDING
DAIRY OR PAREVE

4	(16-ounce) cans sliced carrots, drained	1	teaspoon salt
8	eggs	1	stick butter or margarine, softened and cubed
4	teaspoons Passover baking powder	1	cup brown sugar
1½	cups matzoh meal (or flour for a non-Passover dish)	1	cup granulated sugar
		2	teaspoons hot water

- Preheat oven to 350 degrees.
- Beat carrots and eggs with an electric mixer. Add baking powder, matzoh meal, salt, butter, both sugars and hot water and blend well. Pour mixture into a 2-quart casserole dish.
- Bake about 1 hour. Serve hot.

MATZOH FARFEL KUGEL
PAREVE

3	cups matzoh farfel	1	teaspoon cinnamon
5	eggs, separated	2	cups applesauce
1	teaspoon salt	1	(8-ounce) can crushed pineapple, drained
¼	cup sugar		Cinnamon sugar
1	stick margarine, melted		

- Preheat oven to 350 degrees.
- Place farfel in a colander and pour hot water over the top.
- Beat egg yolks, salt, sugar and margarine in a bowl. Mix in farfel. Add cinnamon, applesauce and pineapple.
- Beat egg whites until stiff. Fold stiff egg whites into farfel mixture. Pour mixture into a greased 9x13-inch pan. Sprinkle cinnamon sugar on top.
- Bake 30 to 45 minutes or until firm and golden brown.

SAVORY PASSOVER KUGEL
PAREVE OR MEAT

10	sheets matzoh	1½	tablespoons paprika
5	cups chicken or vegetable broth	1	teaspoon garlic powder
2	cups hot water	½	teaspoon black pepper
½	cup vegetable oil	6	cloves garlic, minced
6	cups diced onion	2	pounds mushrooms
1	cup grated carrot	¼	cup chopped fresh parsley
1½	tablespoons salt	4	eggs
		8	egg whites

- Preheat oven to 375 degrees.
- Crack sheets of matzoh into a large bowl. Cover with chicken broth and hot water and let stand 10 minutes, stirring occasionally.
- In a large skillet, heat vegetable oil. Add onion and carrot and cook 5 minutes, stirring occasionally. Add salt, paprika, garlic powder, pepper, garlic and mushrooms and cook 5 minutes longer. Pour mixture into bowl with matzoh. Stir in parsley.
- Combine eggs and egg whites and add to matzoh mixture. Pour mixture into a greased 9x13-inch glass dish. Cover with foil.
- Bake 30 minutes. Uncover and bake 20 minutes longer. Cool 10 minutes before cutting.

This Passover kugel is made every year by Fran Lebowitz's mom, Ruth. Fran, a New York writer, who spent her first ten seders in Derby, Connecticut at her grandparents' house, was interviewed by a New York Times writer in the late 90's. The purpose was to ask about new trends in seders. Four questions from that interview give us food for thought.

Q: It's a contradiction in terms, but what modern traditions are people introducing to their seders this year?

A: I have no idea. I've gone to the same family seder for 47 years and I haven't been seated at the adult table yet. My little cousins have to fight me for the afikomen.

Q: Any interesting new food?

A: No. It's entirely possible that in the early 50's, a very large brisket was delivered to our family and we are still eating it. We not only have the same food but the same conversation.

Q: Where do you go for Passover?

A: I don't go anywhere else for the holidays but to my family. I went to London for one holiday when I was in my twenties and now it is mentioned each Passover as a new plague - "The year Fran went to London" - the one between locusts and blood.

Q: So nothing changes at your family seder? Is there anything liberating for you about the seder?

A: How freeing can it be to get to Poughkeepsie or New Haven by 6PM?

POTATO KUGEL FOR PASSOVER
PAREVE

5	pounds potatoes, peeled and grated	4	eggs
2	medium onions, grated	½	cup matzoh meal
6	tablespoons oil, divided		Salt and pepper to taste

- Preheat oven to 375 degrees.
- Combine potatoes and onion in a bowl. Add 3 tablespoons oil, eggs, matzoh meal and salt and pepper and mix well.
- Heat remaining 3 tablespoons oil in a 9x13-inch baking pan. While still hot, pour potato mixture into oil in pan.
- Bake 45 minutes or until brown.

SWEET MATZOH FRUIT KUGEL
PAREVE

1	cup dried apricots	1½	cups matzoh meal
1	cup dried prunes	⅓	cup sugar
5	eggs	3	apples, thinly sliced
1	teaspoon salt	4	tablespoons margarine
2	cups water		Cinnamon sugar

- Preheat oven to 350 degrees.
- Soak apricots and prunes in warm water. When soft, drain and cut fruit into small pieces.
- Beat eggs. Mix in salt, 2 cups water, matzoh meal and sugar. Add apricots, prunes and apples slices.
- Melt margarine in a 9x9-inch pan. Tilt pan to coat bottom and sides of pan and pour remainder of margarine into fruit batter. Pour batter into pan; batter will be thin. Sprinkle top with cinnamon sugar to taste.
- Bake 1 hour.

Farfel "Bombs"
PAREVE

¼	cup vegetable oil	2	eggs, beaten, or 1 egg plus 2 whites
1	medium onion, diced (2 cups)	¾	teaspoon kosher salt
2	cups matzoh farfel	¼	teaspoon black pepper

- Preheat oven to 375 degrees.
- Heat oil in a 2-quart saucepan over medium-high heat. Add onion and fry until well browned. Remove from heat and cool.
- Place farfel in a colander and run water over top, mixing thoroughly; drain well. Mix moist farfel with egg, fried onion, salt and pepper. Spoon batter into greased muffin tins.
- Bake 20 minutes or until cooked through and to desired crispness.

These can be made in advance and frozen. Reheat in 300 degree oven for 2 to 3 minutes to crisp.

Vegetable Kugel
PAREVE

6	tablespoons margarine	1½	cups grated carrot
¼	cup chopped green bell pepper	2	(10-ounce) packages frozen chopped spinach, cooked and drained
1	cup chopped onion	3	eggs, beaten
½	cup chopped celery	1½	teaspoons salt
1	(4-ounce) can mushrooms, or 4 ounces fresh mushrooms (optional)	⅛	teaspoon black pepper
		¾	cup matzoh meal

- Preheat oven to 350 degrees.
- Melt margarine in a skillet. Add bell pepper, onion, celery, mushrooms and carrot and sauté 10 minutes. Mix in spinach. Blend in egg, salt, pepper and matzoh meal. Spoon mixture into a 9x13-inch glass baking dish.
- Bake 45 minutes.

Kugel can be made ahead and frozen. Take out morning of use and cut into squares when partially thawed.

Roasted Asparagus Bruschetta for Passover

PAREVE

12	spears green asparagus		Salt and pepper to taste
12	spears white asparagus		Matzoh
	Balsamic vinegar	1	jar bruschetta mix
	Canola oil		

- Marinate asparagus in a mixture of vinegar, oil and salt and pepper for 1 hour. Drain and place asparagus on a quick-release foil-lined baking sheet.
- When ready to bake, preheat oven to 350 degrees.
- Bake 20 minutes or to desired doneness.
- Break each sheet of matzoh into 4 rectangular pieces. On each piece, place 2 spears of green asparagus facing in one direction and 2 spears of white asparagus facing in opposite direction. Top each piece with 2 tablespoons bruschetta mix. Serve as an appetizer.

Bagels for Passover

PAREVE

1/3	cup oil	1/4	teaspoon salt
2/3	cup water	1	cup matzoh meal
2	tablespoons sugar	3	eggs

- Preheat oven to 350 degrees.
- Combine oil, water, sugar and salt in a saucepan and bring to a boil. Stir in matzoh meal until mixture falls from the side of the pot. Cool 5 minutes. Add eggs one at a time and mix well.
- Drop dough by rounded tablespoonfuls onto a greased baking sheet. Wet finger and make a hole in center of each with wet finger.
- Bake 45 minutes.

Fried Matzoh
(Matzoh Brei)
DAIRY OR PAREVE

8	sheets matzoh			Salt and pepper to taste
3-4	cups boiling water		½	cup margarine or butter
4-5	eggs			

- Break matzoh into 1½- to 2-inch squares. Place matzoh in a colander. Pour boiling water over matzoh and drain immediately, leaving matzoh slightly moist. Transfer matzoh to a bowl.
- Beat eggs with salt and pepper and pour over matzoh. Toss matzoh until coated, but leave in large chunks.
- Heat butter in a 10- to 12-inch skillet. Add matzoh to skillet and cook, turning frequently, until golden brown. Serve warm.
- 4 servings

Breakfast is my favorite meal during Passover because of matzoh brei. A lower fat version is made with liquid egg whites, butter spray in the pan and butter substitute sprinkled in the moist mixture. Less water is needed when using egg whites. Some like it moist, some like it dry. We all like it hot! It's your taste and tradition.

Farmer Cheese Soufflé
DAIRY

1½	pounds farmer cheese		½	cup sugar
¼	cup peanut oil		1	teaspoon lemon juice
4	eggs, separated		1	teaspoon lemon zest

- Preheat oven to 350 degrees.
- Mash cheese in a bowl. Blend in peanut oil, egg yolks, sugar, lemon juice and zest.
- In a separate bowl, beat egg whites until soft peaks form. Fold whites into cheese mixture. Pour batter into a greased 1½-quart casserole dish.
- Bake 1 hour.

Splenda may be substituted for sugar.
If doing so, also eliminate lemon zest.

Passover Eggplant Casserole

DAIRY

1	large onion, thinly sliced
3	tablespoons oil
1	medium eggplant, peeled and cut into ½-inch cubes
¼	cup diced green bell pepper
1	(11-ounce) can tomato mushroom sauce
1	teaspoon salt
2	large tomatoes, peeled and cubed
1	pound low-fat cottage cheese
1½	cups matzoh farfel

- Preheat oven to 350 degrees.
- Sauté onion in oil in a skillet. Add eggplant, bell pepper, tomato mushroom sauce and salt. Cook 15 minutes or until eggplant is tender. Stir in tomatoes.
- Arrange alternate layers of vegetable mixture, cottage cheese and farfel in a greased 2-quart baking dish, beginning and ending with vegetable mixture.
- Bake, uncovered, for 20 minutes.
- 6 servings

Popovers for Passover

PAREVE

¾	cup oil
1½	cups cold water
1½	cups matzoh meal
2	teaspoons sugar
1½	teaspoons salt
6	eggs

- Preheat oven to 400 degrees.
- Combine oil and water in a saucepan and bring to a boil.
- In a bowl, mix matzoh meal, sugar and salt. Add hot water mixture to dry ingredients and mix well. Beat in eggs, one at a time. Pour batter into well greased muffin tins.
- Bake 15 minutes. Reduce oven temperature to 375 degrees and bake 40 minutes longer.
- 12 popovers

Dairy Passover Lasagna

DAIRY

2	eggs		Milk
1	pound cottage cheese	2	(10½-ounce) cans tomato
1	clove garlic, minced, or		sauce
	⅛ teaspoon garlic powder	8	ounces mozzarella cheese,
	Salt and pepper to taste		shredded
3-4	whole sheets matzoh		

- Preheat oven to 350 degrees.
- Beat eggs in a medium mixing bowl. Add cottage cheese, garlic and salt and pepper and mix well.
- Wet matzoh with milk until moistened but not soggy. Pour a little tomato sauce into an 8x8-inch baking pan, tilting pan to distribute evenly. Layer matzoh, cottage cheese mixture, tomato sauce and mozzarella cheese, repeating layers twice and ending with mozzarella cheese.
- Bake 45 to 60 minutes. Let stand at room temperature 5 to 10 minutes before serving.
- 6 servings

Matzoh Meal Pancakes

PAREVE

½	cup matzoh meal	3	eggs, separated
½	cup boiling water	½	teaspoon salt

- Scald matzoh meal with boiling water. Beat egg yolks and add to matzoh mixture with salt.
- Beat egg whites until stiff. Fold egg whites into matzoh meal mixture. Drop by spoonfuls onto a well greased griddle.
- Fry until brown on both sides. Serve with sugar, jam or syrup.

My father usually just walked through the kitchen or sat down at the table. During Passover though, he actually made these delicious pancakes like his mom had made for him. We put lots of jam on them so they were really sweet.

Farmer Cheese Latkes for Chanukah or Passover

DAIRY

4	eggs	¼	teaspoon salt
8	ounces farmer cheese	½	cup matzoh meal or flour
3	tablespoons sugar	½	cup vegetable oil for frying
1	teaspoon vanilla		
3	tablespoons vegetable oil		

- Beat eggs in a large bowl. Add cheese, sugar, vanilla, oil and salt and blend well. Stir in matzoh meal until smooth.
- Heat vegetable oil in a skillet. Drop batter by large spoonfuls into oil. Fry 3 to 5 minutes on each side or until golden.

Serve with sugar, cinnamon sugar, maple syrup,
sour cream, yogurt or fruit. For variety, add raisins,
dried cranberries, fresh blueberries, etc. to batter.

Chocolate Macaroons

DAIRY

2	(1-ounce) squares unsweetened chocolate, melted	3	cups shredded coconut
½	(14-ounce) can sweetened condensed milk	2	teaspoons vanilla

- Preheat oven to 250 degrees.
- Blend together melted chocolate and milk in a bowl. Add coconut and vanilla and mix. Drop by teaspoonfuls onto a greased or parchment paper-lined baking sheet.
- Bake 30 minutes or until golden brown.

FORGOTTEN COOKIES
PAREVE

2	egg whites	1	cup semisweet chocolate chips
⅔	cup sugar		
¼	teaspoon salt	1	cup chopped nuts (optional)
¼	teaspoon vanilla, or ½ teaspoon almond extract		

- Preheat oven to 400 degrees.
- Beat egg whites until stiff. Continue beating and gradually add sugar, salt and vanilla. Beat until stiff peaks form.
- Fold in chocolate chips and nuts. Drop by spoonfuls onto a wax paper-lined baking sheet.
- Place baking sheet in oven and immediately turn off heat. Leave cookies in oven for 2 hours or longer.
- 3 dozen cookies

Add a drop of food coloring to mixture to
create a different look for special occasions.

PASSOVER APPLE FRITTERS
PAREVE

1	cup matzoh meal	½	cup water
3	eggs	3	tart apples, peeled and very thinly sliced
2	tablespoons oil, plus extra for frying		Cinnamon sugar
½	teaspoon salt		

- Beat together matzoh meal, eggs, 2 tablespoons oil, salt and water. Add apples.
- Drop batter by spoonfuls into hot oil. Fry until golden brown; drain. Sprinkle with cinnamon sugar.

MANDEL BREAD
PAREVE

Pareve

2	cups sugar	½	teaspoon salt
2	sticks margarine, softened	1	(6-ounce) package semisweet chocolate chips
6	eggs		
2¾	cups cake meal	1	cup chopped nuts (optional)
¾	tablespoon potato starch		

Topping

1	teaspoon cinnamon	2	tablespoons sugar

- Preheat oven to 350 degrees.
- Cream sugar and margarine. Beat in eggs, one at a time.
- Sift together cake meal, potato starch and salt. Fold dry ingredients into creamed mixture. Add chocolate chips and nuts and mix well.
- Form dough into 2 loaves, or 4 small loaves and place on a lightly greased or parchment paper-lined baking sheet. Sprinkle top with a mixture of cinnamon and sugar.
- Bake 30 minutes. Slice while still warm.

Melt extra chocolate chips to use as a topping instead of cinnamon sugar.
Drizzle on mandel bread once baked and cooled.
Or, prepare half of recipe with cinnamon sugar topping and
half with chocolate topping. Freezes well.

CHOCOLATE CHIP COOKIES
PAREVE

1	stick margarine, softened	½	cup plus 3 tablespoons cake meal
6	tablespoons brown sugar		
6	tablespoons granulated sugar	9	ounces semisweet chocolate chips
1	egg		

- Preheat oven to 350 degrees.
- Beat margarine, both sugars and egg together. Stir in cake meal and mix well. Stir in chocolate chips. Drop dough by teaspoonfuls onto lightly greased or parchment paper-lined baking sheets; do not flatten dough.
- Bake about 8 minutes. Cool.

Recipe doubles easily and freezes well.
Alternative "mix-ins" may be substituted for the chocolate chips.

MACAROONS
DAIRY

2⅔	cups sweetened coconut flakes	1	teaspoon vanilla
⅔	cup sweetened condensed milk		

- Preheat oven to 350 degrees.
- Combine all ingredients in a bowl. Drop mixture by teaspoonfuls onto a greased baking sheet.
- Bake 10 to 12 minutes. Remove from baking sheet while still warm and place on wax paper. Store in an airtight container.

For an added treat, dip the bottoms in melted chocolate,
then refrigerate until hardened.
These are always a big hit - most never make it to the dessert table.
Recipe can be doubled.

Passover Jelly Cookies
DAIRY OR PAREVE

2	sticks butter or margarine, softened	2	cups cake meal
1	cup sugar	1	teaspoon lemon extract
2	eggs		Jelly or jam, any flavor

- Cream butter and sugar in a bowl. Add eggs, cake meal and lemon extract. Refrigerate dough overnight.
- Preheat oven to 350 degrees.
- Form dough into small balls and place on a parchment paper-lined baking sheet. Make an indentation with your thumb in each ball and fill with jelly.
- Bake 15 to 20 minutes, watching carefully.

Cookies freeze well.

Pine Nut Cookies
DAIRY OR PAREVE

½	cup cake meal	½	cup sugar
½	cup potato starch	1	egg yolk
¾	cup (heaping) pine nuts	1	teaspoon vanilla
1	stick butter or margarine, softened		

- Preheat oven to 300 degrees.
- Sift together cake meal and potato starch; set aside.
- Roast pine nuts until light in color and set aside to cool.
- Cream butter and sugar until creamy. Beat in egg yolk, vanilla and dry ingredients and blend thoroughly. Fold in ½ cup pine nuts and blend well.
- Form dough into small rounds on a baking sheet that has been greased and dusted with cake meal. Flatten slightly and press 3 to 4 of remaining pine nuts onto top of each cookie.
- Bake 20 to 25 minutes or until pale golden; do not overbake. Cool on baking sheet for a minute or so. While still warm, carefully remove with a spatula to a cake rack or board to cool completely. Handle with care — cookies are delicate.

Cookies may be frozen.

Matzoh "Roca"
DAIRY

½ pound matzoh	1 (12-ounce) package semisweet chocolate chips
2 sticks butter	
1 cup brown sugar	½ cup sliced almonds, lightly toasted

- Preheat oven to 450 degrees.
- Arrange matzoh in a single layer in aluminum foil- or parchment paper-lined baking sheets.
- Melt butter with sugar in a 2-quart saucepan over medium heat, stirring often, for 5 minutes to dissolve sugar. Pour mixture over matzoh, covering all surfaces well with a pastry brush or spoon.
- Bake 4 minutes or until caramel begins to bubble.
- While baking, melt chocolate over a double boiler or in a microwave and stir until smooth, being careful not to overheat or burn.
- Remove matzoh from oven after 4 minutes and sprinkle with almonds. Drizzle melted chocolate over top, covering all areas. Cool. Break matzoh into desired pieces and store in an airtight container.

Grandpa Gerry's Favorite Mock Oatmeal Cookies
PAREVE

2 cups matzoh meal	⅔ cup vegetable oil
2 cups matzoh farfel	1 cup chopped nuts or chocolate chips, or a mixture of both
1½ cups sugar	
1 teaspoon cinnamon	
½ teaspoon salt	1 cup raisins
4 eggs, or 3 eggs plus ⅓ cup orange juice	

- Preheat oven to 350 degrees.
- Combine matzoh meal, matzoh farfel, sugar, cinnamon and salt. Beat in eggs and vegetable oil. Gently stir in nuts and raisins. Drop dough by teaspoonfuls onto greased baking sheets.
- Bake 30 minutes or until lightly browned.
- About 3 dozen cookies

Passover Brownies
PAREVE

2	eggs	¼	teaspoon salt
1	cup sugar	5½	tablespoons cocoa powder
½	cup oil	½	cup nuts (optional)
½	cup cake meal		

- Preheat oven to 350 degrees.
- Beat together eggs and sugar until light and fluffy. Add oil. Gradually mix in cake meal, salt and cocoa. Add nuts. Pour batter into a greased 9x9-inch baking pan.
- Bake 20 minutes and test for doneness. Bake 5 to 10 minutes longer if needed. Cool and cut into squares.

Flourless Chocolate Cake
DAIRY

1	pound bittersweet chocolate, chopped into small pieces	¾	cup plus 1 tablespoon granulated sugar Confectioners' sugar for dusting
2	sticks unsalted butter		
9	eggs, separated	2	cups heavy cream, whipped

- Preheat oven to 350 degrees.
- Melt chocolate and butter in the top of a double boiler.
- In a separate bowl, whisk egg yolks with granulated sugar until a light yellow color. Whisk in a little melted chocolate mixture to temper the eggs, then whisk in remaining chocolate mixture.
- Beat egg whites until stiff peaks form. Fold in chocolate mixture. Pour chocolate batter into a greased 9-inch springform pan.
- Bake 20 to 25 minutes or until the cake is set, the top starts to crack and a toothpick inserted in the cake comes out with moist crumbs clinging to it. Let stand 10 minutes before removing from pan.
- Dust with confectioners' sugar. Serve with whipped cream.

Passover Apple Cake
PAREVE

Filling

6	McIntosh or 4 Granny Smith apples, peeled and sliced	¾	cup sugar
		2	teaspoons cinnamon
			Juice of 1 lemon

Batter

6	eggs	2	cups cake meal
2	cups sugar	2	teaspoons potato starch
1	cup oil		

- Preheat oven to 350 degrees.
- Combine all filling ingredients and let stand 5 minutes.
- Meanwhile, prepare batter. Beat eggs with sugar, oil, cake meal and potato starch.
- Pour half of batter into a lightly greased 9x13-inch baking pan. Add apple filling and spread remainder of batter over filling.
- Bake 45 minutes or until a cake tester comes out dry.

Delicious for breakfast and easy to prepare. Freezes well.

Passover Nut Cake
PAREVE

9	eggs, separated	3	tablespoons potato starch
1½	teaspoons lemon juice	½	cup chopped walnuts
1½	cups sugar		Pinch of salt
¾	cup sifted cake meal		

- Preheat oven to 325 degrees.
- Beat egg whites in a large bowl until stiff; set aside.
- In a separate bowl, beat egg yolks with lemon juice and sugar. Combine cake meal, potato starch, walnuts and salt. Fold yolk mixture alternately with dry ingredients into egg whites. Pour batter into an ungreased tube pan.
- Bake 45 to 50 minutes. Invert pan 1 hour or until cool before removing cake from pan.

Passover Cheesecake with Brownie Crust

DAIRY

Crust

1	(12-ounce) package Passover brownie mix	1	tablespoon potato starch
¼	cup cake meal	4	tablespoons butter or margarine, melted

Filling

1	cup sugar	3	eggs
2	tablespoons potato starch	1	tablespoon lemon juice
¼	teaspoon cinnamon	1	teaspoon lemon zest
½	cup sour cream		
3	(8-ounce) packages cream cheese, softened		

- Preheat oven to 350 degrees.
- To make crust, combine brownie mix, cake meal and potato starch in a medium bowl. Add butter and mix thoroughly. Press mixture into the bottom and 1-inch up the sides of a greased 9-inch springform pan.
- For filling, combine sugar, potato starch and cinnamon in a large bowl. Add sour cream and cream cheese and beat until fluffy. Add eggs, one at a time, stirring well before each addition. Mix in lemon juice and zest and blend thoroughly. Pour filling into crust.
- Bake 1 hour. Turn off oven and leave cake inside oven with door closed for 30 minutes longer. To serve, loosen crust from sides of pan with a knife.

Passover Blueberry Muffins
PAREVE

1	stick margarine, softened	¼	cup potato starch
¾	cup sugar	½	cup chopped pecans (optional)
3	eggs		
½	teaspoon vanilla	1	cup frozen blueberries
¼	teaspoon salt		Cinnamon sugar for topping
½	cup cake meal		

- Preheat oven to 350 degrees.
- Cream margarine and sugar in a bowl. Mix in eggs, one at a time. Add vanilla, salt, cake meal and potato starch and mix well. Fold in pecans and blueberries. Pour batter into paper-lined muffin tins. Sprinkle with cinnamon sugar.
- Bake 35 to 40 minutes.
- 12 muffins

Passover Jelly Roll
PAREVE

5	eggs, separated	¼	cup potato starch
8	tablespoons sugar, divided	6	tablespoons thick preserves

- Preheat oven to 400 degrees.
- Grease an 11x17-inch jelly roll pan and line with wax paper, then grease wax paper.
- Beat egg yolks. Add 5 tablespoons sugar and beat until light and thick. Add potato starch and mix well.
- In a separate bowl, beat egg whites until stiff. Fold whites into batter. Pour batter into prepared pan.
- Bake 12 minutes.
- Sprinkle remaining 3 tablespoons sugar onto a large piece of wax paper. Invert hot cake onto sugar and remove pan and wax paper. Roll up cake and cool. Unroll and spread preserves over cake. Reroll cake tightly and chill.

GRANDMA GUSSIE'S SPONGE CAKE
PAREVE OR DAIRY (IF USING WHIPPED CREAM)

½	cup cake meal	1-2	tablespoons lemon juice
½	cup potato starch	1	teaspoon orange zest
8	egg yolks	1	teaspoon lemon zest
1	cup sugar	8	egg whites, chilled
⅓	cup honey	¼	teaspoon salt
¼	cup orange juice		

- Preheat oven to 350 degrees.
- Mix cake meal and potato starch; set aside.
- In a separate mixing bowl, beat egg yolks until lemon colored. Gradually add sugar and beat until thick and lemon colored. Beat in honey and fruit juices and zests. Mix in cake meal mixture.
- Beat egg whites with salt until stiff, then gently fold into batter. Pour batter into an ungreased tube pan.
- Bake 50 to 60 minutes or until a cake tester comes out clean. Invert tube pan as soon as it is removed from oven and allow to cool.

Serve with whipped cream and fresh strawberry slices,
or serve on a platter surrounded by chocolate-dipped strawberries.

FROZEN FRUIT DESSERT
PAREVE

2	containers frozen pareve whipping cream, slightly thawed	2	bags frozen no-sugar-added berries, slightly thawed

- Whip cream with berries with an electric mixer on high speed until thick and well blended. Pour mixture into a mold or an oblong loaf pan. Freeze.

CHOCOLATE MOUSSE TORTE

DAIRY OR PAREVE

1	teaspoon butter or margarine	¼	cup boiling water
1	tablespoon matzoh meal	8	eggs, separated
8	ounces semisweet chocolate	⅔	cup sugar
1	tablespoon instant coffee	1	teaspoon vanilla
		⅛	teaspoon salt

Optional Topping

1½	cups heavy cream or nondairy whipping cream	Semisweet chocolate chips or chocolate curls for garnish
⅓	cup sugar	

- Preheat oven to 350 degrees.

- Grease a 9-inch glass pie plate with butter and dust with matzoh meal; set aside.

- Place chocolate in a glass bowl. Dissolve coffee in boiling water and pour over chocolate. Melt chocolate in microwave, stirring occasionally until smooth. Cool slightly.

- In a small bowl, beat egg yolks with an electric mixer on high speed for 5 minutes or until pale lemon color and thickened. Gradually add sugar and beat 5 minutes longer. Add vanilla and melted chocolate mixture and beat slowly, scraping sides of bowl with a rubber spatula, until blended. Remove from mixer.

- In a large bowl, beat egg whites with salt until stiff but not dry. Gradually, in 2 to 3 additions, fold half of whites into chocolate, then fold chocolate into remaining whites, folding until no white shows.

- Handling as little as possible, gently remove and set aside 4 cups of mousse; cover and refrigerate. Turn remainder of mousse into prepared pie plate and very gently spread to even; mixture will barely reach the top.

- Bake 25 minutes. Turn off oven and leave mousse in oven 5 minutes longer. Remove and cool on a rack. Mousse will rise during baking and settle as it cools.

- When cooled, spoon reserved mousse into center of baked mousse shell, mounding higher in center. Refrigerate 3 hours.

- For optional topping, whip cream with sugar until thick. Spread over mousse and refrigerate until ready to serve. Garnish with semisweet chocolate chips or chocolate curls.

Pineapple Orange Cake with Pineapple Sauce

PAREVE

Batter

¼ cup frozen pineapple juice concentrate, thawed

¼ cup frozen orange juice concentrate, thawed

1 egg white

1 cup potato starch

¾ cup sugar

1 cup crushed pineapple
Zest of 1 orange
(about 2 tablespoons)

Sauce

2 cups pineapple juice

¼ cup orange juice

1 tablespoon potato starch

2 tablespoons sweet Passover wine

- Preheat oven to 325 degrees.
- Combine juice concentrates in a small bowl.
- In a large bowl, beat egg white with an electric mixer until glossy soft peaks form. With mixer on low speed, blend in potato starch and sugar.
- With a spoon, blend in juice concentrates, crushed pineapple and orange zest. Spoon batter evenly into an ungreased 10-inch tube pan.
- Bake 50 minutes or until cake springs back when touched and is lightly brown. Remove from oven and invert pan onto a cooling rack until thoroughly cooled. Loosen sides and center of pan with a knife and unmold onto a cake platter.
- Combine all sauce ingredients in a saucepan over medium heat. Cook and stir until mixture thickens slightly. Serve cake with sauce on the side.
- 8-10 servings, 2 cups sauce

LEMON HEAVENLY PIE
DAIRY

Meringue Shell

¾ cup sugar

¼ teaspoon cream of tartar

3 egg whites

Lemon Filling

4 egg yolks

½ cup sugar

3 tablespoons lemon juice

1 tablespoon lemon zest

⅛ teaspoon salt

½ pint heavy cream, plus extra for decoration

- Preheat oven to 275 degrees.
- Sift together sugar and cream of tartar. Beat egg whites until stiff but not dry. Gradually add sugar mixture, continuing to beat until very stiff and glossy. Spread two-thirds of meringue in the bottom of a greased pie plate. Drop remaining meringue in mounds around the inside edge of pie plate.
- Bake 1 hour; cool.
- For filling, lightly beat egg yolks. Stir in sugar, lemon juice and zest and salt. Cook in the top of a double boiler until very thick. Remove from heat and cool.
- Whip ½ pint cream and gently fold into cooled filling. Fill meringue shell with lemon filling. Refrigerate 24 hours before serving. Whip additional cream and use to decorate top of pie.

TINY PASSOVER FRUIT CAKES
PAREVE

3 eggs, or 1 egg plus 2 whites

1 cup dates, finely diced

1 cup golden raisins

1½ cups chopped pecans

- Preheat oven to 325 degrees.
- Beat eggs well in a medium mixing bowl. Add dates, raisins and pecans. Spoon mixture into greased mini muffin tins.
- Bake 20 minutes or until cooked through and golden brown. Cakes will keep at room temperature for several days.

CHOCOLATE CHIP CAKE
DAIRY

10	eggs, separated	2	teaspoons cocoa powder
1⅓	cups sugar, divided	1	heaping teaspoon instant coffee
½	cup orange juice		
1	teaspoon orange zest	1	cup mini chocolate chips
½	cup cake meal	1½	cups finely chopped walnuts
¼	cup potato starch		

- Preheat oven to 325 degrees.
- Beat egg yolks in a bowl. Add 1 cup sugar, orange juice and zest.
- Sift together cake meal, potato starch, cocoa powder and instant coffee. Add dry ingredients to yolk mixture.
- Beat egg whites. Beat in remaining ⅓ cup sugar. Fold yolk mixture into egg whites. Fold in chocolate chips and walnuts. Pour batter into a tube pan.
- Bake 1 hour. Invert pan to cool.

RITA'S HOT FRUIT COMPOTE
PAREVE

1	(16-ounce) can sliced pineapple, drained	1	(10-ounce) package dried pitted prunes
1	(16-ounce) can sliced pears, drained	2	apples, peeled and sliced
1	(16-ounce) can sliced peaches, drained	2	tablespoons honey
1	(10-ounce) package dried apricots	1	(16-ounce) can whole cranberries
		½	cup Passover wine
			Cinnamon to taste

- Preheat oven to 350 degrees.
- Line a large casserole dish with pineapple slices. Layer pears, peaches, apricots, prunes and apples in order listed over pineapple.
- In a small saucepan, bring honey and cranberries to a slow boil. Pour mixture over fruit layers. Cover with wine and sprinkle with cinnamon.
- Bake, covered, for 1 hour.

PASSOVER HAZELNUT TORTE
DAIRY OR PAREVE

Batter

8	eggs, separated		1	whole egg
1	cup sugar		1	teaspoon lemon juice
1	teaspoon vanilla			
1	cup finely ground hazelnuts, plus extra for decoration			

Glaze

2	ounces semisweet chocolate, broken into small pieces		3	tablespoons brandy
			3	tablespoons butter or pareve margarine

- Preheat oven to 350 degrees.
- Beat egg whites until stiff but not dry; set aside.
- In a separate bowl, beat egg yolks with sugar for 5 minutes or until thick and lemon color. Add vanilla, 1 cup hazelnuts, whole egg and lemon juice and beat until well mixed. Carefully fold in egg whites. Pour batter into a greased 9-inch springform pan.
- Bake 45 minutes or until browned. Turn off oven and let torte cool in oven for about 45 minutes. Cake will rise at first and then fall in the center, making a well for the glaze. Place torte on a rack to cool completely.
- For glaze, melt chocolate with brandy in the top of a double boiler. Beat in butter, 1 tablespoon at a time. Cool glaze slightly but it should still be of a pouring consistency. Pour glaze over torte and smooth over the sides. Decorate with extra hazelnuts. Refrigerate 1 hour before serving.

CHOCOLATE CREAM PASSOVER TORTE
DAIRY

Batter

⅓ cup blanched slivered almonds	2 tablespoons butter or margarine, softened
⅓ cup plus 1 tablespoon cocoa powder, divided	1 teaspoon vanilla
¼ cup boiling water	6 eggs, separated
	⅔ cup granulated sugar, divided

Cocoa Whipped Cream

1½ cups heavy cream, chilled	3 tablespoons cocoa
⅓ cup sugar	¾ teaspoon vanilla

- Preheat oven to 350 degrees.
- Spread almonds in a thin layer in a shallow baking pan. Bake 8 to 10 minutes or until light golden brown, stirring occasionally. Cool completely. Grind toasted almonds in a food processor until fine.
- Line the bottom of a 15 ½x10 ½x1-inch jelly roll pan with parchment paper or foil, extending paper or foil slightly over the sides, then grease paper or foil.
- Stir together ⅓ cup cocoa and boiling water in a small bowl until mixture is smooth. Stir in butter and vanilla; cool.
- Combine egg yolks and ½ cup sugar in a large bowl. Beat with an electric mixer on medium speed for 5 minutes or until light and fluffy. Add chocolate mixture and almonds and beat until well blended.
- In a separate large bowl, beat egg whites until foamy. Gradually add remaining sugar and beat until stiff peaks form. Fold one-fourth of egg whites into chocolate mixture. Add remaining whites and fold well. Pour batter into prepared pan.
- Bake 18 to 20 minutes or until cake springs back when touched lightly in the center. Dust cake with remaining 1 tablespoon cocoa and cover with a clean, dry towel. Cool completely in pan on a wire rack.

- Meanwhile, combine all cocoa whipped cream ingredients in a chilled large bowl. Beat with chilled beaters of an electric mixer until stiff. Reserve 1¼ to 1½ cups whipped cream to frost sides of cake.

- To assemble, cut cake into 4 equal pieces. Remove paper or foil. Place 1 piece on a serving plate and spread top with some of remaining whipped cream. Repeat layering with remaining cake pieces and whipped cream, ending with cream. Spread reserved whipped cream around sides of cake. Garnish as desired and refrigerate until serving time. Cover and refrigerate leftovers.

- 12 servings, 3 cups whipped cream

PASSOVER FROZEN MOUSSE CAKE

DAIRY

½	cup sugar, divided	1	cup heavy cream, whipped
1	teaspoon vanilla		
1	(8-ounce) package cream cheese, softened	¾	cup chopped pecans Shaved chocolate for garnish
2	eggs, divided		
6	ounces semisweet chocolate, melted		

- Cream ¼ cup sugar and vanilla with cream cheese until well blended. Beat egg yolks and stir into creamed mixture along with melted chocolate.

- Beat egg whites until soft peaks form while gradually adding remaining ¼ cup sugar. Fold whites into chocolate mixture. Fold in whipped cream and pecans. Spoon batter into a 9-inch springform pan lined with plastic wrap. Tap pan on counter to release any trapped air bubbles. Shave chocolate over top and cover with plastic wrap. Freeze well.

- When ready to serve, remove from freezer and peel plastic from cake. Place on a serving platter and serve within 10 minutes. Refreeze leftovers.

Mousse can be spooned into individual ramekins.

Mousse can also be made with a cookie crust made with 1½ cups crushed chocolate Passover cookies mixed with 5 tablespoons melted butter or margarine. Press the crust mixture into the bottom of the pan and bake at 325 degrees for 10 minutes. Cool before adding mousse. A non-Passover version can be made with chocolate wafer or sandwich cookies.

PASSOVER CHOCOLATE ROLL

DAIRY

Batter

8	eggs	¾	cup sugar, divided
8	ounces dark chocolate		Cocoa powder
¼	cup very strong brewed coffee		

Whipped Cream Filling

1	pint heavy cream	1	teaspoon vanilla
¼	cup confectioners' sugar		

- Preheat oven to 350 degrees.
- Separate eggs, being careful not to get any yolk in the whites. Set whites aside and allow to come to room temperature.
- Melt chocolate with coffee and stir until smooth; cool slightly. Beat egg yolks with ½ cup sugar until fluffy and pale yellow. Add cooled chocolate.
- In a separate bowl with clean beaters, beat egg whites until soft peaks form. Add remaining ¼ cup sugar and beat until stiff. Very carefully, so as to not deflate the whites, fold whites into chocolate batter until fully mixed. Pour batter into a well-greased sheet pan with sides that are lined with greased wax paper.
- Bake 15 to 20 minutes or until firm. Cool about 10 minutes on a wire rack. Dampen a cotton dish towel and place directly over roll to cool completely.
- Meanwhile, prepare whipped cream filling. Beat heavy cream in a chilled bowl with chilled beaters until soft peaks form. Beat in confectioners' sugar and vanilla.
- To roll, sprinkle cake with cocoa powder and cover with plastic wrap. Invert pan to turn cake out onto plastic wrap. Remove wax paper from the cake. Spread whipped cream filling over the roll. Tightly roll up cake.

The cake may have some cracks in it, which can be hidden with a dusting of confectioners' sugar or chocolate sauce.

Egg whites mount the best when at room temperature and if beaten in a copper bowl.

I serve the chocolate sauce on the side so the cake does not become soggy.

CHOCOLATE FUDGE SAUCE
DAIRY

4	ounces unsweetened chocolate
3	tablespoons butter
⅔	cup very hot water
1⅔	cups sugar
6	tablespoons corn syrup

- Melt chocolate and butter together in a saucepan. Whisk in hot water. Add sugar and corn syrup and mix until smooth and mixture starts to boil. Gently boil for 8 minutes.
- Serve with anything you want! Ice cream, cakes, cookies, pies, etc.

RUTH GOODMAN'S
NEW YEAR'S HONEY CAKE
DAIRY OR PAREVE

3	cups sifted all-purpose flour	½	cup chopped nuts
			Zest of 1 orange
1	tablespoon cinnamon	½	cup shortening
1	tablespoon baking powder	1	cup sugar
¼	cup raisins	3	eggs
½	cup chocolate chips (optional)	¾	cup honey
		1	cup very strong brewed coffee

- Preheat oven to 350 degrees.
- Sift together flour, cinnamon and baking powder in a bowl. Mix in raisins, chocolate chips, nuts and orange zest; set aside.
- In a separate large mixing bowl, cream shortening and sugar until light and fluffy. Beat in eggs, one at a time, alternating with honey. Blend thoroughly. Add dry ingredients alternately with coffee, beginning and ending with dry ingredients. Turn batter into a greased and lightly floured 10-inch tube pan.
- Bake 1 hour or until a cake tester comes out clean.

Honey Cake
PAREVE

2	cups sifted all-purpose flour
1	teaspoon baking soda
1	teaspoon baking powder
1	teaspoon top-grade cocoa powder
1	teaspoon cinnamon
2	eggs
1	cup sugar
½	cup plus 1 tablespoon oil
1	cup raw honey
1	cup strong brewed coffee, room temperature
½	cup finely chopped walnuts

- Preheat oven to 375 degrees.
- Sift flour. Measure and sift again with baking soda, baking powder, cocoa and cinnamon.
- In a separate bowl, mix eggs, sugar, oil and honey with an electric mixer. Add dry ingredients gradually and mix until smooth. Slowly blend in coffee. Stir in walnuts. Divide batter evenly between 2 foil loaf pans greased on bottom and sides.
- Bake, side by side in center of oven, for 45 minutes. Reduce temperature to 350 degrees and bake 5 to 10 minutes longer or until top springs back when touched and cake begins to pull away from the sides of the pan. If top of cake begins to burn while baking, lay a piece of foil loosely over the pan.

Honey Cake - sweetness for a sweet year - a Rosh Hashanah tradition.

BAKED APPLES WITH APRICOTS AND DATES
PAREVE

½	cup chopped dried dates
½	cup chopped dried apricots
3	tablespoons honey
1	tablespoon pomegranate molasses or maple syrup
¾	cup sweet white wine or apple cider
1	teaspoon cinnamon
⅛	teaspoon ground cloves (optional)
⅛	teaspoon ground nutmeg
6	large, firm apples

- Preheat oven to 325 degrees.
- Combine dates, apricots, honey, pomegranate molasses, ½ cup wine, cinnamon, cloves and nutmeg.
- Core apples, stuff with fruit filling and place in a baking dish. Pour remaining ¼ cup wine over apples. Bake, basting often, for 45 minutes or until soft. Serve with some of syrup from pan.

WHITE AND SWEET POTATO LATKES
PAREVE

3	cups peeled and shredded white potatoes	½	cup flour
5	cups peeled and shredded sweet potatoes	1	teaspoon salt
1½	cups chopped onion	½	teaspoon black pepper
		3	eggs, lightly beaten
			Vegetable oil for frying

- Combine all ingredients except frying oil and mix well.
- Heat oil until hot. Spoon batter into hot oil and cook until golden on each side. Drain latkes on double layers of paper bags. (Paper bags sop up the oil better than anything.)

POTATO PANCAKES
DAIRY OR PAREVE

2	pounds potatoes, grated into a bowl of cold water	3	tablespoons flour
1	medium onion, finely chopped	1½	teaspoons salt
2	eggs	½	teaspoon baking powder
		½	teaspoon black pepper
			Vegetable oil for frying

- Soak potatoes in cold water for 10 minutes; drain and squeeze dry with a kitchen towel.
- Combine potatoes with onion, eggs, flour, salt, baking powder and black pepper in a large bowl and mix thoroughly.
- Pour vegetable oil into a large skillet to ⅛-inch in depth and place over medium heat. For each pancake, pour ½ cup batter into skillet and flatten slightly. Cook about 8 minutes or until crispy and brown, turning once. Repeat, adding more oil as needed, until batter is gone.
- Serve with sour cream and applesauce.
- 12 servings

Grandma Rosie's Plum Jam with Walnuts and Bay Leaves

PAREVE

6 pounds Italian prune plums, pitted and cut into eighths	½ cup sugar per 1 cup fruit 9-12 bay leaves ¾ cup chopped walnuts

- Mix plums with sugar in a large saucepan and let stand 15 minutes. Place over heat and cook 30 minutes, stirring if white foam forms.
- Add bay leaves and walnuts and cook 30 minutes longer or until plum skins are shriveled.
- Pour jam into sterile jars. Cover to seal and refrigerate. Jam will keep for months in the refrigerator.

My grandmother made plum jam to welcome the Jewish New Year; and it has become a wonderful family tradition. This jam makes a lovely gift for a sweet new year.

Hermit Cookies

PAREVE

1 (12-ounce) package honey cake mix	1 egg
1 tablespoon instant coffee	1 cup chopped nuts
2 tablespoons peanut oil	1 cup raisins

- Preheat oven to 350 degrees.
- Combine cake mix and coffee. In a measuring cup, combine oil and egg and add enough water to measure ½ cup. Add egg mixture to cake mix and beat well. Mix in nuts and raisins.
- Chill batter in refrigerator at least 1 hour. Drop by teaspoonfuls onto a greased baking sheet.
- Bake about 15 minutes.
- About 4 dozen

"On Yom Kippur, Jews fast to 'afflict the soul to atone for the sins of the past year.' According to the Talmud, eating the day before Yom Kippur is a mitzvah equal to the mitzvah of fasting on Yom Kippur. Your pre-fast meal is called Seudah Mafseket."

Hamantashen I

DAIRY

2	sticks butter, softened	2	cups flour
1	(8-ounce) package cream cheese, softened		Prune butter or jam of choice for filling

- Preheat oven to 350 degrees.
- Cream butter and cream cheese together until completely blended. Beat in flour a little at a time until blended.
- Divide dough into 4 parts. Press each part into a circle on a sheet of plastic wrap. Wrap well and refrigerate at least 1 hour. The dough is delicate and will be hard to work with if left out for too long, so work with only one section of dough at a time, leaving other sections refrigerated until needed.
- Sprinkle dough with a small amount of flour and roll out to $\frac{1}{16}$- to $\frac{1}{4}$-inch thick. Cut dough into 2-inch circles. Wet rim of dough circles with a finger dipped in water. Place 1 teaspoon of filling in center of each circle and pinch into tri-corner shaped cookies. Place cookies on a baking sheet.
- Bake 15 minutes or until cookies begin to turn golden, being careful that bottoms of cookies do not burn.

Hamantashen

1. Prepare dough of your choice.

2. On a floured board roll out dough to ⅛-inch thick. Cut a 3-inch circle with a glass or biscuit cutter.

3. Place ⅔ teaspoon filling in the center of the circle.

4. Shape into a triangle — lift up the right and left sides while leaving the bottom down. Bring both sides to meet at the center of the filling.

5. Bring the top flap down to meet the sides and pinch together.

HAMANTASHEN II
PAREVE

Filling

½   cup raisins
8   ounces pitted prunes
½   cup chopped nuts
     (optional)

Juice and zest of 1 lemon
½   cup sugar

Dough

2½   cups sifted all-purpose
     flour
2   teaspoons baking powder
¼   teaspoon salt
3   eggs, divided

½   cup sugar
½   cup oil
1   teaspoon vanilla
     Juice and zest of ½ orange

- Preheat oven to 350 degrees.
- For filling, soak raisins in warm water; drain. Mix raisins with prunes, nuts, lemon juice and zest and sugar.
- For dough, sift together flour, baking powder and salt in a bowl.
- In a separate mixing bowl, beat 2 eggs with sugar, oil, vanilla and orange juice and zest. Mix in dry ingredients. Knead dough until smooth. Roll out dough to ¼-inch thick on a floured surface. Cut dough with a round cookie cutter or glass tumbler.
- Place a spoonful of filling in the center of each circle. Draw up sides of circle to form a triangle, pinching edges together.
- Beat remaining egg and brush over top of each pastry.
- Bake 30 minutes.

Optional filling ideas include canned prunes, canned poppy seed filling, canned apricot, chocolate chips, chocolate hazelnut spread and peanut butter and jelly.

FRITTER BATTER

A great recipe for the tradition of Chanukah.

DAIRY

6	eggs	2	teaspoons baking powder
9	ounces milk	2	teaspoons salt
1	pound flour		Vegetable oil for frying
¼	cup sugar		

- Use an electric mixer to beat together all ingredients except oil until well combined.
- Fill a skillet halfway with oil and heat until hot. Note: Dip banana, apple slices or vegetable of choice and desired size in fritter batter. Drop fritters into hot oil and fry until golden.

SUFGANIYOT

DAIRY OR PAREVE

1	scant tablespoon (1 package) dry yeast	2	eggs, separated
4	tablespoons sugar, divided	2	tablespoons butter or margarine, softened
¾	cup lukewarm milk or water		Apricot or strawberry preserves
2½	cups all-purpose flour Pinch of salt		Vegetable oil for deep-frying
1	teaspoon ground cinnamon		Sugar for topping

- Mix yeast, 2 tablespoons sugar and lukewarm liquid. Let stand until mixture bubbles.
- Sift flour into a bowl. Mix in remaining 2 tablespoons sugar, salt, cinnamon, egg yolks and yeast mixture.
- Knead the dough until it forms a ball. Add butter and knead until butter is well absorbed. Cover with a towel and let rise overnight in the refrigerator.
- Roll out dough to ⅛-inch thickness. Cut out 24 rounds using a 2-inch diameter cutter. Place ½ teaspoon preserves in center of 12 rounds. Top with other 12 rounds. Brush edges with egg whites and press down to seal; crimping with the thumb and second finger works well. Let rise for about 30 minutes.
- Heat 2-inches of oil to about 375 degrees. Drop doughnuts into hot oil, working in batches of 4 to 5 at a time. Turn to brown on both sides. Drain on paper towels. Roll doughnuts in sugar.
- 12 doughnuts

Use butter and milk if serving at a milk meal, use water and margarine for a meat meal.